Joey Green's Gardening MAGIC

MORE THAN 1,120 INGENIOUS GARDENING SOLUTIONS USING BRAND-NAME PRODUCTS

BY **JOEYGREEN** AUTHOR OF *MAGIC BRANDS* AND *AMAZING KITCHEN CURES*

RODALE

Printed in the United States of America. Rodale Inc. makes every effort to use
acid-free ∞ , recycled paper ♻ .

Cover and interior design by Tara Long
Cover photograph by Mitch Mandel/Rodale Images
Interior illustrations by Jason Schneider

"The Moldy Moldy Man" by John Lennon (on page 179) © 1964, renewed 1992 Yoko Ono.
Used by permission. All rights reserved.

Library of Congress Cataloging-in-Publication Data

Green, Joey.
   Joey Green's gardening magic : more than 1,120 ingenious gardening
solutions using brand-name products / by Joey Green.
      p.   cm.
   Includes bibliographical references (p.   ) and index.
   ISBN 1–57954–854–7 hardcover
   ISBN 1–57954–855–5 paperback
   1. Gardening—Miscellanea.   2. Organic gardening—Miscellanea.
3. Brand name products—United States.   I. Title.
SB453.G79 2003
635'.0484—dc21   2003011327

Distributed to the book trade by St. Martin's Press

     6 8 10 9 7   hardcover
4 6 8 10 9 7 5 3   paperback

FOR MORE OF OUR PRODUCTS

www.RODALESTORE.com
(800) 848-4735

RODALE

WE INSPIRE AND ENABLE PEOPLE TO IMPROVE
THEIR LIVES AND THE WORLD AROUND THEM

To Jeremy Solomon,
for believing in me

ALSO BY JOEY GREEN

Hellbent on Insanity

The Unofficial Gilligan's Island Handbook

The Get Smart Handbook

The Partridge Family Album

Polish Your Furniture with Panty Hose

Hi Bob!

Selling Out

Paint Your House with Powdered Milk

Wash Your Hair with Whipped Cream

The Bubble Wrap Book

Joey Green's Encyclopedia

The Zen of Oz

The Warning Label Book

Monica Speaks

You Know You've Reached Middle Age If . . .

The Official Slinky Book

The Mad Scientist Handbook

Clean Your Clothes with Cheez Whiz

The Road to Success Is Paved with Failure

Clean It! Fix It! Eat It!

Joey Green's Magic Brands

Jesus and Moses: The Parallel Sayings

The Mad Scientist Handbook 2

Senior Moments

Joey Green's Amazing Kitchen Cures

Jesus and Muhammad: The Parallel Sayings

Contents

But First, a Word from Our Sponsor xiii

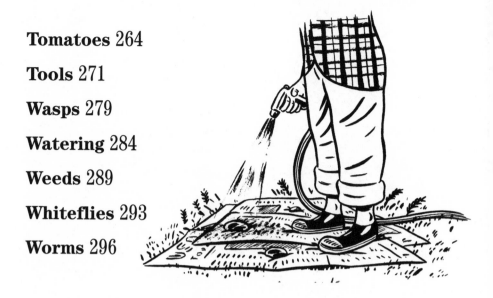

But First, a Word from Our Sponsor

In the 2002 hit comedy movie *My Big Fat Greek Wedding*, the immigrant father of the bride proudly embraces American culture by obsessively using Windex as a cure-all for every problem he encounters—psoriasis, poison ivy, baldness, warts, acne. Americans clearly love the idea of using brand-name products in ways the manufacturers never intended them to be used—especially when the offbeat tips really work. While Windex will not grow hair on your head, the window cleaner can actually be used to prevent a rash and itching from contact with poison ivy. The ammonia and soaps in Windex with Ammonia-D help remove some of the urushiol, the oil in poison ivy that rapidly penetrates the skin and combines with skin proteins to trigger an allergic reaction.

We Americans are an amazingly resourceful people. When confronted with an everyday problem, we get inventive, innovative, and downright ingenious. And no one gets more creative at solving problems than home gardeners. With imaginations as fertile as your soil, you craft tools from Clorox Bleach jugs, cook up compost with Coca-Cola, kill weeds with Heinz Vinegar, and trap insects with Wilson Tennis Balls. You are an American treasure. And so I decided to write a book for you, a book filled with quirky yet practical ways to save time and money using brand-name products you already have in your kitchen, bathroom, laundry room, and garage to help you grow tomatoes, combat cutworms, and water your rhubarb and rutabagas more efficiently.

I holed myself away in the library and sifted through hundreds of gardening books. I contacted manufacturers to obtain their secret files, talked with dozens of gardeners, and searched through the hundreds of e-mails I receive through my Web site, www.wackyuses.com, where upstanding citizens share their clever uses for brand-name products with me.

I unearthed some startling information. Tabasco Pepper Sauce controls aphids. Maxwell House Coffee fertilizes lawns. Turtle Wax prevents gardening tools from rusting. Budweiser kills slugs. Dannon Yogurt grows moss. Jif Peanut Butter lubricates a lawn mower. Smirnoff Vodka kills poison ivy. Carnation NonFat Dry Milk adds calcium to tomato plants. But I had to know more. Okay, so 7-Up can be used to prolong the life of cut flowers, but what exactly does the name 7-Up mean? A Dustbuster can be used to combat whiteflies, but who invented the Dustbuster, and why? And just what is Cream of Wheat?

My journey into the backyard of American ingenuity yielded some important lessons. For instance, if you have a green thumb, you might want to see a doctor. You can't cure it with Windex.

Ants

- **Albers Grits.** Sprinkle a small mound of Albers Grits around the base of an anthill. Each ant will carry away one grit and eat it. After the ant drinks some water, the grit will expand, causing the ant's stomach to burst.

- **Arm & Hammer Baking Soda.** Dust the ant-infested areas around your plants with Arm & Hammer Baking Soda. The ants eventually disappear because baking soda is poisonous to them.

- **Campbell's Tomato Soup.** Prevent ants from climbing up the legs of an outdoor table when camping. Fill four clean, empty Campbell's Tomato Soup cans halfway with water and set a table leg in each can. The ants will not be able to climb up the table.

- **Con-Tact Paper.** Fold a long piece of Con-Tact Paper in half, with the sticky side out, and wrap the paper around the bases of fruit trees to prevent ants from being able to climb up the trees and reach the fruit.

• **Crayola Chalk.** Draw a thick line of Crayola Chalk across the patio floor, sidewalk, or wherever ants tend to march. Ants will not cross a chalk line.

• **Cream of Wheat.** Pouring Cream of Wheat on an anthill kills the ants. Each ant eats a tiny grain of wheat, which expands in its stomach, causing death by bloating.

• **Dr. Bronner's Peppermint Soap.** Mix one tablespoon Dr. Bronner's Peppermint Soap with two cups water in a sixteen-ounce trigger-spray bottle and spray on plants to both kill and repel ants. The biodegradable soap kills ants on contact, and the peppermint drives away future ants.

• **Gold Medal Flour.** Make an impenetrable line with Gold Medal Flour wherever ants are giving you trouble. Ants will not cross through flour.

• **Grandma's Molasses, Domino Sugar,** and **Fleischmann's Yeast.** In a small bowl, mix one-third cup Grandma's Molasses, six tablespoons Domino Sugar, and six tablespoons Fleischmann's Active Dry Yeast into a smooth paste. Coat strips of cardboard with the mixture or pour it in bottle caps or small jar lids, or fill a small plastic container with a jar lid and punch holes in the container for the ants to enter. Place in and around ant-infested areas. Be sure to keep out of reach of pets and small children.

• **Heinz White Vinegar.** Pour Heinz White Vinegar directly on an anthill or fill a trigger-spray bottle with equal parts vinegar and water and spray affected plants. The acetic acid in vinegar kills ants.

• **Johnson's Baby Powder.** Sprinkle Johnson's Baby Powder wherever ants are marching. Ants will not walk through baby powder.

• **L'eggs Sheer Energy Panty Hose.** To keep fire ants out of your garden, cut off a foot from a pair of clean, used L'eggs Sheer Energy Panty Hose and fill the foot with diatomaceous earth. Wearing a dust mask and goggles, shake the earth-filled panty hose sachet around your garden to create a dust barrier around it. Diatomaceous earth, made from the fossilized remains of diatoms (algae with silicified skeletons), destroys insects' outer skeletons, causing the pests to die from dehydration.

• **Maxwell House Coffee.** Maxwell House Coffee grounds sprinkled in plant beds fertilize the soil with nutrients and simultaneously deter ants. Sprinkling dry Maxwell House Coffee grounds on a fire ant nest kills the ants. They eat the grounds and seem to implode.

• **McCormick Black Pepper.** Sprinkle McCormick Black Pepper wherever ants are giving you problems. Pepper repels ants.

• **McCormick Chili Powder.** Sprinkling McCormick Chili Powder around garden beds helps stop ant invasions. The ants can't stand the potent powder.

• **McCormick Cream of Tartar.** Sprinkle McCormick Cream of Tartar around entrances to ant nests and into cracks and crevices. Cream of tartar, derived from the crude tartar sediment deposited on the insides of casks during wine-making, kills ants when they ingest it.

• **McCormick Ground Cinnamon.** Sprinkle McCormick Ground Cinnamon wherever you want to keep the ants away. Ants will not cross a line of cinnamon—and it happens to smell nice, too.

• **Minute Rice.** Sprinkle uncooked Minute Rice around the base of an anthill or wherever ants are a problem. The ants take the rice back to their nest for the colony to devour. When the ants eat it, the rice swells in their stomachs, killing them.

• **Morton Salt.** To get rid of ants without ant traps laced with pesticide, sprinkle the area with Morton Salt. *Poof!* They're gone!

• **Scotch Packaging Tape.** Wrap strips of Scotch Packaging Tape inside out around the bases of fruit trees to prevent ants from being able to climb up the trees and reach the fruit.

• **20 Mule Team Borax, Domino Sugar,** and **Johnson & Johnson Cotton Balls.** Mix one cup 20 Mule Team Borax, two-thirds cup Domino Sugar, and one cup water. Dip Johnson & Johnson Cotton Balls in the solution and place the cotton balls around ant mounds or trails. The ants ingest the sweet mixture and die.

• **Vaseline Petroleum Jelly.** To prevent ants from climbing up the pole to a birdhouse, rub a small dab of Vaseline Petroleum Jelly around the bottom of the pole.

STRANGE FACTS

• Ants lay a scent trail of pheromones to lead other ants from the nest to a food source. Ants release other pheromones with a distinctive smell to warn nestmates of danger.

• Leaf-cutter ants bring pieces of leaves back to their nests to fertilize gardens of fungi.

• Carefully pouring three gallons of boiling water on a fire ant mound kills the colony—easily, safely, and effectively.

• Ants use their antennae for hearing, smelling, touching, and tasting.

• Ant nestmates share their food through mouth-to-mouth regurgitation.

• Ants have lived on earth for more than 100 million years, according to dated fossils preserved in amber.

• All worker ants—the vast majority of any ant colony—are female, not male.

• A queen ant lives anywhere from ten to twenty years, laying thousands of eggs during her lifetime. Worker ants live from less than one year to more than five years. Male ants live less than a few months.

• Ants can lift between ten and fifty times their weight.

- The heart of an ant is a long tube that stretches from the brain to the end of the ant's body.

- Male and queen ants have wings but use them only once—during the mating flight, after which the males die and the queens tear off their own wings.

- Ants eat more than half the termites hatched each year in the tropics.

- In the 1954 science fiction movie *Them!* nuclear tests in the desert generate gigantic mutant ants that menace cities in the American Southwest. The Cold War film stars James Whitmore, Edmund Gwenn, James Arness, Joan Weldon, and Fess Parker.

- Fear of ants is called *myrmecophobia*.

- *The Atom Ant Show*, created by Hanna-Barbera and broadcast on NBC from 1965 to 1967, featured the cartoon adventures of superhero Atom Ant, an animated ant who could fly, lift ten times his weight, and communicate with his superiors via his antennae.

- Rock singer Adam Ant, born Stuart Leslie Goddard, changed his name to Adam after the biblical story of the Garden of Eden and named his band the Ants, choosing an insect name along the lines of the Beatles.

- The black bulldog ant, indigenous to Australia and Tasmania, can kill a human being.

- In the 1998 animated movie *Antz*, Woody Allen provides the voice of Z, a neurotic worker ant who attempts to assert his individuality and find his true self within the confines of an oppressively conformist ant colony.

What's Cooking with Cream of Wheat

During the depression of 1893, the Diamond Milling Company of Grand Forks, North Dakota, experienced a severe slump in business due to falling prices and low demand for its flour. To reverse the company's fortunes, head miller Tom Amidon, a Scottish immigrant who discovered that unused wheat middlings could be made into a tasty porridge for his family, convinced the company owners to try to market the wheat middlings with their New York broker.

Amidon made the first cardboard packages for the cereal, hand-lettered with the name Cream of Wheat (a name volunteered by another worker whose identity has been lost to history). He decorated the boxes with the image of a black chef with a saucepan over his shoulder—an old printing plate found by Emery Mapes, one of the company owners.

The Diamond Milling Company shipped ten cases of Cream of Wheat unannounced to its New York broker along with its regular boxcar-load of flour. "Forget the flour," read the resulting telegram from New York. "Send us a car of Cream of Wheat."

The company ceased production of flour to focus only on Cream of Wheat but still could not keep up with the high demand. In 1897, the Diamond Milling Company moved to a larger plant in Minneapolis.

• In 1925, the original Cream of Wheat chef was updated by the more realistic version still seen on the box to this day. According to legend, Mapes paid a handsome waiter working in Kohlsaat's Restaurant in Chicago five dollars to pose for a photograph to be used as the Cream of Wheat symbol. Unfortunately, no one recalls the name of the waiter.

• Mick Liebfried, who worked at the Minneapolis Cream of Wheat factory for thirty-six years, has one of the most extensive private Cream of Wheat collections in the world with more than three thousand different pieces, including boxes of Cream of Wheat, bowls, cups, tins, stand-up store posters, and store advertising.

• Today, many people consider the black chef depicted on every box of Cream of Wheat—with a smile on his face and a piping hot bowl of Cream of Wheat in his hands—to be a racist portrayal of a subservient African-American man. Advertisements for Cream of Wheat frequently showed the black chef holding an inviting bowl of steaming Cream of Wheat while benevolently watching over white children at play. Kraft Foods, however, points out that the Cream of Wheat chef is indeed a chef (not a servant) and the beloved symbol represents quality and goodness.

• In 1990, *Time* magazine reported that *Good Morning America*'s Joan Lunden "goes down as easy in the morning as mom's Cream of Wheat."

Aphids

- **Carnation NonFat Dry Milk.** Mix Carnation NonFat Dry Milk with water according to the instructions on the box, fill a trigger-spray bottle with the solution, and mist the infected plants with the solution. The aphids get stuck in the milky residue as it dries on the plant leaves.

- **Country Time Lemonade.** Mix four teaspoons Country Time Lemonade powdered drink mix and two cups water in a sixteen-ounce trigger-spray bottle. Spray the mixture on plant leaves being attacked by aphids. The limonoids in the mixture kill the pests.

- **Domino Sugar.** Spraying a solution of one part sugar with ten parts water onto aphid-susceptible plants attracts beneficial insects that feed on aphids.

- **Dr. Bronner's Peppermint Soap.** Mix one tablespoon Dr. Bronner's Peppermint Soap with two cups water in a sixteen-ounce trigger-spray bottle and spray on plants to repel aphids. The mint drives them away.

- **Ivory Dishwashing Liquid.** Mix one-half ounce Ivory Dishwashing Liquid and two cups water in a sixteen-ounce trigger-spray bottle. Spray on both sides of infested plant leaves, let sit for one hour, then spray clean with water.

- **ReaLemon.** Mix four teaspoons ReaLemon lemon juice and two cups water in a sixteen-ounce trigger-spray bottle. Spray the mixture on plant leaves being attacked by aphids. The limonoids in the lemon oil in the mixture kill the pests.

- **Reynolds Wrap.** Place sheets of Reynolds Wrap on the ground between rows of plants and secure in place with rocks. In the sunlight, the glittering foil keeps away insects like thrips and aphids. Check the tomato plants daily to make sure the aluminum foil is not reflecting too much light back onto the plant, burning it.

- **Smirnoff Vodka.** To keep aphids off houseplants, wash the aphids off the plants with tap water, then mix one-half cup Smirnoff Vodka and 1.5 cups water in a sixteen-ounce trigger-spray bottle and spray on plant leaves in the cool of the day. Do not use alcohol on delicate plants such as African violets. (Before treating the entire plant, test this alcohol formula on one of the plant's leaves and wait one day to make certain it doesn't burn the leaf.)

- **Star Olive Oil** and **Ivory Dishwashing Liquid.** Mix one cup Star Olive Oil, three drops Ivory Dishwashing Liquid, and two cups water in a sixteen-ounce trigger-spray bottle. Spray the plants with the solution, then spray the plants with water. (Do not use this solution on cabbage, cauliflower, or squash, otherwise you risk giving those plants leaf burn.)

- **Tabasco Pepper Sauce, McCormick Garlic Powder,** and **Ivory Dishwashing Liquid.** To repel aphids, mix two teaspoons Tabasco Pepper Sauce, two teaspoons McCormick Garlic Powder, one teaspoon Ivory Dishwashing Liquid, and two cups water. Fill a sixteen-ounce trigger-spray bottle and coat the leaves of the plant with the spicy solution.

• **Tang.** Mix four teaspoons Tang drink mix and two cups water in a sixteen-ounce trigger-spray bottle. Spray the mixture on plant leaves being attacked by aphids. The limonoids in the mixture kill the pests.

• **Wesson Corn Oil** and **Ivory Dishwashing Liquid.** Oils sprayed as an emulsion in water can be an effective control against aphids. Mix one ounce Wesson Corn Oil, three drops Ivory Dishwashing Liquid, and two cups water in a sixteen-ounce trigger-spray bottle.

• **Wilson Tennis Balls** and **Vaseline Petroleum Jelly.** To kill aphids, use an electric drill with a one-eighth-inch bit to drill a hole in a Wilson Tennis Ball, screw an eyehook into the hole, give the ball a thick coat of Vaseline Petroleum Jelly, and hang it over the afflicted plant. Aphids, lured to the color yellow, get stuck in the gooey petroleum jelly and die. (See Ziploc Storage Bags below.)

• **Ziploc Storage Bags.** To make the process of killing aphids less messy (see Wilson Tennis Balls above), place a Ziploc Storage Bag around each yellow ball and coat the plastic bags (instead of the balls) with the Vaseline Petroleum Jelly. This way, when the bags get coated with bugs you can simply replace the bags.

STRANGE FACTS

• The aphid has a tube for a mouth. The insect uses this tube to pierce the stems of plants and suck out the juices.

• Predators usually gobble up aphids, unless, of course, the sprays used on plants in the hopes of killing aphids also repel the beneficial insects.

• Aphids excrete a sweet fluid called *honeydew*, a favorite food of the ant. Ants are known to protect colonies of aphids so they can feast on an endless supply of honeydew. The ants will also move the aphids from one plant to another to help sustain the colony.

• Aphids reproduce through a process called *parthenogenesis*. Males and females mate in the fall, causing the females to lay fertilized eggs that hatch in the spring. Only female aphids hatch. The female aphids give birth to living female aphids hatched from unfertilized eggs in their bodies. This fatherless process continues for several generations, until the fall, when aphids develop into males and females, restarting the cycle.

• In ancient Greece, King Aphidas ruled Tegea and was the father of Aleus, who built a Temple of Athena in Tegea (sixteen miles southeast of Tripolis in Arcadia, Peloponnese, Greece).

• Nicknamed "plant lice," aphids can be green, black, pink, or yellow.

• Aphid is the name of a heat-seeking missile (carried by MiG jet fighter planes) that homes in on an enemy jet's fiery exhaust.

Azaleas

• **Budweiser.** Mix one part Budweiser beer to two parts water and pour this mixture on your azaleas for an excellent plant food.

• **Clorox.** Sterilize your pruning tools in a mixture of three-quarters cup Clorox Bleach in a gallon of water after each use to avoid spreading fungal diseases of azaleas. Dip your pruning equipment into the disinfectant solution between cuts or at least between plants. When finished, soak the pruning shears in the solution for one hour, then rinse clean and dry.

• **Coca-Cola.** Watering azaleas with Classic Coke increases the acidity in the soil, which azaleas love, and boosts plant performance. The sugar in the Coke feeds microorganisms in the soil, increasing the organic matter.

• **Epsom Salt.** To increase the acidity of the soil, add one pound of Epsom Salt per three hundred square feet.

• **Heinz White Vinegar.** To grow beautiful azaleas, occasionally water plants with a mixture of two tablespoons Heinz White

Vinegar to one quart water. Azaleas love acid soil and grow best in soils with a pH below 6.5.

- **L'eggs Sheer Energy Panty Hose.** Using a pair of scissors, cut off the toe from the foot of a pair of used, clean L'eggs Sheer Energy Panty Hose, then cut one-inch strips from the leg, creating circular loops of panty hose. Use the loops to gently tie stems, vines, and thin plant trunks to stakes with a figure-eight loop.

- **Lipton Tea.** Watering azaleas with cold, strongly brewed Lipton Tea increases nitrogen content in the soil for healthy leaf growth and adds acidity, which azaleas love. You can also split open used tea bags and sprinkle the leaves on the soil.

- **Listerine.** To avoid spreading fungal diseases of azaleas, sterilize your pruning tools by cleaning them with Listerine after each use. Mix one cup Listerine per gallon of water in a bucket and dip your pruning equipment into the antiseptic solution between cuts or at least between plants. When finished, soak the pruning shears in the solution for one hour, then rinse clean and dry.

- **Maxwell House Coffee.** Fertilize azaleas with Maxwell House Coffee grounds by working used grounds around the base of these acid-loving plants once a month.

- **Nestea.** Mix up a quart of unsweetened Nestea instant iced tea according to the directions (without adding sugar or ice) and water azaleas with the tea. Or sprinkle the powdered mix directly on the soil around the plant. Tea enhances both the acidity and nitrogen content of the soil, energizing azaleas.

- **Smirnoff Vodka.** Sterilize your pruning tools by disinfecting them with Smirnoff Vodka after each use to avoid spreading fungal diseases of azaleas. Mix two cups Smirnoff Vodka per gallon of water in a bucket and dip your pruning tools into the alcohol solution between cuts or at least between plants. When finished, soak the pruning shears in the solution for one hour, then rinse clean and dry.

• **S.O.S Steel Wool Soap Pads.** When planting azaleas, line the hole with used S.O.S Steel Wool Soap Pads. Watering slowly breaks down the steel pads (made from iron filaments), producing the essential iron that ericacious plants need to survive and perform. With well established plants, bury used steel wool pads directly in the soil around the plant.

STRANGE FACTS

• Callaway Gardens, a world-famous family resort in Pine Mountain, Georgia, is home to the world's largest azalea garden. The Callaway Brothers Azalea Bowl contains more than five thousand hybrid and native azaleas and encompasses forty acres. The azaleas, planted in masses around the one-acre Mirror Pond, create a spectacular reflection.

• While many gardeners believe azaleas form the genus *Azalea*, botanists classify azaleas in the genus *Rhododendron*.

• Azaleas, when given as a gift, symbolize temperance.

• The word *azalea* is the feminine form of the Greek word *azaléos*, meaning "dry." Azaleas are so named because they grow in dry soil.

• In 1947, South Carolina governor Strom Thurmond, then 44 years old, appointed Jean Crouch, the 21-year-old daughter of an old family friend, to be "Miss South Carolina" to preside over Charleston's Azalea Festival. They were married later that year.

• In the play *Kentucky Cycle*, awarded the 1992 Pulitzer Prize, one character equates Moses' burning bush with a scarlet azalea.

Barbecues

CLEANING

- **Arm & Hammer Baking Soda.** To clean a barbecue grill, make a paste by mixing equal parts Arm & Hammer Baking Soda and water, apply with a wire brush, wipe clean, and dry with a cloth.

- **Easy-Off Oven Cleaner** and **Glad Trash Bags.** Place the grill in a Glad Trash Bag, spray the racks thoroughly with Easy-Off Oven Cleaner, close the bag, and secure with a twist tie. Let set for four hours in the sun. Rinse well with a garden hose.

- **Pam Original Cooking Spray.** To make cleaning a barbecue grill easy, coat the grill with Pam Cooking Spray before barbecuing. After cooking, when the grill is cool to the touch, scrub the grill with a wire brush.

- **Reynolds Wrap.** After barbecuing, place a sheet of Reynolds Wrap on the hot grill and close the lid. The next time you use the barbecue, peel off the foil, crumple it into a ball, and use it to scrub the grill clean, easily removing all the burnt food.

COOKING

- **Coca-Cola** and **Heinz Ketchup**. Make an excellent barbecue sauce by mixing Coca-Cola with Heinz Ketchup. Brush the mixture on chicken or ribs while grilling.

- **Forster Toothpicks**. Identify rare, medium, and well-done steaks on your barbecue grill by using colored Forster Toothpicks to mark steaks on the barbecue.

- **Glad Trash Bags**. When your outdoor grill is cool, cover it with a Glad Trash Bag to protect it from the elements.

- **Maxwell House Coffee**. A clean, empty Maxwell House Coffee can makes an excellent disposable pot to be used on the grill to cook bratwurst in beer.

- **Maxwell House Coffee**. Give store-bought barbecue sauce a Cajun bite by adding a tablespoon of dissolved Maxwell House Instant Coffee to the sauce.

- **Morton Salt**. After barbecuing, sprinkle Morton Salt over the smoldering charcoal to prevent the embers from flaring up into a roaring fire again.

IGNITING

- **Conair Pro Style 1600 Hair Dryer**. Light a charcoal fire by using a Conair Pro Style 1600 hair dryer to fan the charcoal briquettes in a barbecue grill.

- **Maxwell House Coffee**. Using a can opener, remove the top and bottom of an empty Maxwell House Coffee can. Use tin snips to cut a few tabs around the bottom rim of the coffee can. Stand the can in the center of your barbecue grill, place one sheet of crumpled newspaper inside, fill the rest of the can with charcoal briquettes, add lighter fluid, and light the newspaper through the holes you snipped in the bottom. When the coals glow, carefully remove the hot can with tongs and set in a safe place.

- **Tidy Cats.** Prevent grease fires in barbecue grills by covering the bottom of the grill with a one-inch layer of unused Tidy Cats cat box filler (clay variety).

INSECTS

- **Aunt Jemima Original Syrup.** Lure insects away from a barbecue by coating a few small pieces of cardboard with Aunt Jemima Original Syrup and placing them around the perimeter of the yard. Stinging insects, such as wasps, bees, and yellow jackets, will be attracted to the syrup instead of your guests.

- **Budweiser.** Place open cans of Budweiser beer around the perimeter of the yard to attract bees and yellow jackets away from a barbecue and your guests.

- **Heinz Apple Cider Vinegar.** Fill a large bowl with Heinz Apple Cider Vinegar and set near the table of food to attract flies, mosquitoes, and moths. By the end of the barbecue, you'll have a bowl full of floating winged insects. (For more ways to repel and kill insects, see pages 1, 180, and 279.)

STRANGE FACTS

- More than three out of four households in the United States own barbecue grills. Those who own grills use them an average of five times a month, and nearly half barbecue year-round.

- According to legend, President Lyndon Johnson asked French chef Rene Verdon, hired by Jacqueline Kennedy, if he could cook Texan. Verdon purportedly replied, "I don't cook fried chicken, corn bread, or barbecue." Verdon soon quit his White House post to open a restaurant in San Francisco.

- When Brazilian companies mine iron ore from the Amazon rainforest, they chop down the surrounding forests and burn the trees to make charcoal to power the smelters that convert the ore into pig iron. Pig-iron production consumed nearly two-thirds of the forests in the state of Minas Gerais in southeastern Brazil.

• The largest one-day barbecue in the world was held at the Iowa State Fairgrounds in Des Moines, Iowa, on June 21, 1988, with 35,072 people in attendance. The crowd achieved the world record for the greatest amount of meat consumed at a one-day barbecue, devouring 20,130 pounds of pork in five hours.

• The word *barbecue* is frequently abbreviated as "BBQ," although this abbreviation does not appear in *Webster's Ninth New Collegiate Dictionary*.

• In Australia, a barbecue is referred to as a "barbie."

Beans

• **Bounty.** To soften the hard outer coats of bean seeds to pre-pare them for planting, place the seeds between two damp sheets of Bounty Paper Towel overnight.

• **Forster Clothes Pins.** Secure bean plants to a trellis by simply clipping the plants in place with Forster Clothes Pins.

• **Glad Trash Bags.** To get bean seedlings off to a good start in cold soil at least two weeks before your early target date, slice open the sides of black Glad Trash Bags to make long sheets and place the black plastic on the garden bed as mulch. Secure the plastic in place with stones, and then plant the pre-sprouted seeds in holes in the black plastic at the proper planting inter-vals. The radiant heat created by the plastic warms the soil an additional 3 degrees Fahrenheit. The plastic sheets can be rolled up at the end of the season and reused the next year. Be certain to water beneath the impermeable plastic sheet with a drip line or soaker hose.

- **Ivory Dishwashing Liquid.** To kill stink bugs on bean plants, shake the plants over trays filled with a mixture of one teaspoon Ivory Dishwashing Liquid to one quart water.

- **L'eggs Sheer Energy Panty Hose.** Using a pair of scissors, cut off the toe from the foot of a pair of used, clean L'eggs Sheer Energy Panty Hose, then cut one-inch strips from the leg, creating circular loops of panty hose. Use the loops to gently tie bean vines to a stake or trellis with a figure-eight loop.

- **Oral-B Mint Waxed Floss.** To make a trellis for bean plants, string Oral-B Mint Waxed Floss between two stakes, along galvanized eye screws spaced up the side of a wall, or around nails hammered around a door.

- **Oral-B Mint Waxed Floss, Reynolds Wrap,** and **Scotch Magic Tape.** String Oral-B Mint Waxed Floss across your garden just a few inches above a row of bean plants. (Attach the floss to stakes.) Using a pair of scissors, cut a dozen or more strips of Reynolds Wrap one inch wide by five inches long. Tape the strips of foil along the string of dental floss every few feet. The strips of reflective foil flapping in the breeze will repel birds.

- **Slinky.** Hang several Slinkys in a row from the side of the house or an overhang to give bean plants a trellis to slink their way up.

- **Tabasco Pepper Sauce, McCormick Garlic Powder,** and **Ivory Dishwashing Liquid.** To kill spider mites on bean plants, mix two tablespoons Tabasco Pepper Sauce, two tablespoons McCormick Garlic Powder, three drops Ivory Dishwashing Liquid, and two cups water in a sixteen-ounce trigger-spray bottle and spray on the plants.

- **Ziploc Freezer Bags.** Parboil freshly picked beans in boiling water for two minutes, drain, cool under running cold water, place in small Ziploc Freezer Bags, and freeze. The frozen beans will last up to one year.

STRANGE FACTS

- The screw bean grows pods that look like spirally twisted wire.

- The four most prominent families in ancient Rome—Lentulus, Fabius, Ciceros, and Pisos—named themselves after beans. Lentulus means lentils, Fabius means favas, Ciceros means chickpeas, and Pisos means peas.

- The asparagus bean can grow bean pods up to three feet long.

- The ancient Greeks and Romans used beans to cast their votes in political elections and legal trials.

- In the sixteenth century, peasants in England relied on dried peas to survive a famine.

- In the seventeenth century, people incorrectly believed that eating beans cured baldness.

- President Theodore Roosevelt claimed that the nutritious beans eaten by his Rough Riders were responsible for the United States' victory at the 1898 Battle of San Juan Hill in Cuba.

- In 1911, L.L. Bean, a resident of Freeport, Maine, working out of his basement, invented and tested his Maine Hunting Shoe. The following year, Bean launched his company with a four-page mailer to out-of-state sportsmen, and by 1917, he had opened a store on Freeport's Main Street. Today, L.L. Bean is a multimillion-dollar mail-order company with stores across the United States.

- In 1929, toy salesman Edwin Lowe, driving from Atlanta, Georgia, to Jacksonville, Florida, stopped along the way to look inside a brightly lit carnival tent. He discovered people seated at tables playing a game called Beano. Each player had a pile of beans and a game card hand-stamped with numbers. As the emcee called out a number, the players placed a bean over that number on their card, until someone got five beans in a row. When Lowe tried playing the game at home, one excited player mistakenly called out "Bingo" instead of "Beano," giving Lowe the inspiration for the name of the new game.

• During World War II, the United States Army floated waterproof bags filled with beans from ships to beachheads to feed American troops.

• Accountants are derogatorily called "bean counters."

• Orson Bean, born Dallas Frederick Burrows, was a panelist on the television game show *To Tell the Truth*, made guest appearances on dozens of television shows including *The Twilight Zone* and *Love, American Style*, and appeared in the 1959 movie *Anatomy of a Murder* and the 1999 movie *Being John Malkovich*.

• Author Barbara Kingsolver titled her first novel *The Bean Trees*.

• Soybeans, a mainstay of Asian cuisine, are processed into bean curd, better known as tofu.

• The 1972 movie *The Life and Times of Judge Roy Bean*, based on a true story, stars Paul Newman as an outlaw who establishes his own brand of law and order in the Wild West town of Langtry in Pecos County, Texas. According to legend, Bean named his saloon and town after the woman he adored, Lily Langtry, a British actress he had never met, and kept a pet bear in his courtroom.

• The 1974 comedy movie *Freebie and the Bean* stars James Caan and Alan Arkin as San Francisco police detectives trying to capture a local hijacking boss.

• In 1979, N. McCoy of Hubert, North Carolina, grew the largest recorded lima bean in United States history, measuring fourteen inches long.

• In the 1990s, a craze for small stuffed animals called Beanie Babies swept the United States, with people paying more than three hundred dollars for one of the animals. Despite their name, Beanie Babies are stuffed with polyvinyl chloride pellets, not beans.

• Beano, a dietary supplement that helps prevent flatulence, is a food enzyme derived from a natural source that breaks down the complex sugars in gassy foods, making them more digestible.

Berries

- **Bubble Wrap.** To prevent strawberries from touching the soil, cut a large doughnut shape from a piece of Bubble Wrap and put it around the plant as a collar.

- **Glad Flexible Straws.** Remove stems from strawberries without cutting off the entire top by simply pushing the straight end of a Glad Flexible Straw into the bottom of the strawberry. The entire stem should poke through the top in one piece.

- **Glad Trash Bags.** Fill small Glad Trash Bags with air, tie them shut, and staple to tall stakes throughout the garden. The plastic bags, flapping in the breeze, frighten away birds.

- **Goodyear Tires.** Place an old Goodyear Tire on the ground, fill with potting soil, and plant strawberry plants inside it. The tire will shelter the sprouting plants from the wind, and the dark rubber will absorb heat from the sun and warm the soil.

- **Heinz White Vinegar.** To grow beautiful blueberries or cranberries, occasionally water plants with a mixture of two tablespoons Heinz White Vinegar to one quart water. Blueberry and cranberry plants love acid soil and grow best in soils with a pH below 6.5.

• **Hula Hoop, Bubble Wrap,** and **Scotch Packaging Tape.** Hasten the ripening of strawberries by covering the plant beds with row covers. Make hoop supports by cutting Hula Hoops in half and inserting the legs firmly into the soil. Cover with a canopy made from sheets of Bubble Wrap draped over the hoop supports and secured in place with Scotch Packaging Tape. Do this in early spring and make certain the sheets of Bubble Wrap are high enough not to touch the plants. You can also secure the Bubble Wrap by staking the ends to the ground with wire. At the end of the season, roll up the Bubble Wrap to be used again the following year.

• **L'eggs Sheer Energy Panty Hose.** Cut open several pairs of clean, used L'eggs Sheer Energy Panty Hose and sew them together to make a large piece of netting to protect berry patches from birds.

• **Maxwell House Coffee.** Fertilize blueberries and cranberries by working used Maxwell House Coffee grounds into the soil around the base of these acid-loving plants once a month.

• **McCormick Black Pepper.** To keep rabbits away from strawberries, sprinkle McCormick Black Pepper in your garden around and over the strawberry patch. Rabbits have a keen sense of smell and are repelled by the scent of pepper. When it rains, be sure to re-pepper the garden.

• **Oral-B Mint Waxed Floss, Reynolds Wrap,** and **Scotch Magic Tape.** Run a string of Oral-B Mint Waxed Floss across your berry patch just a few inches above a row of plants. (Attach each end of the floss to a stake.) Using a pair of scissors, cut a dozen or more strips of Reynolds Wrap one inch wide by five inches long. Tape the strips of aluminum foil along the string of dental floss every few feet. The strips of reflective foil flapping in the breeze will repel birds.

- **ReaLemon.** Remove berry stains from your hands by rinsing your hands with ReaLemon lemon juice.

- **Reynolds Wrap** and **Oral-B Mint Waxed Floss.** Cut circles or star shapes from cardboard, wrap the cardboard cutouts in Reynolds Wrap, punch a hole in each shape, and then hang the glittering shapes from berry bushes with a loop of Oral-B Mint Waxed Floss or string them across a row of plants with stakes. The sunlight, reflecting from the silvery shapes, frightens away birds.

- **Wesson Corn Oil.** To kill earwigs on blueberries, fill a jar lid with Wesson Corn Oil and place it in the garden. The earwigs, attracted to the oil, drown in it.

STRANGE FACTS

- The lemon is actually a type of berry called a *hesperidium.*

- The banana, grapefruit, tomato, and watermelon all fit the botanical definition of a berry.

- As a youth, rock 'n' roll legend Chuck Berry was convicted of armed robbery and spent three years in the Algoa Reform School in Missouri. Before he became a dominant force in the evolution of rock 'n' roll, recording the hit songs "Maybellene," "Roll Over Beethoven," and "Johnny B. Goode," Berry worked as a hairdresser and beautician.

- The twigs and foliage of cherry trees are poisonous, and, if eaten, cause death.

- Ripe cranberries bounce.

- Cranberry Jell-O is the only flavor of Jell-O derived from genuine fruit, rather than artificial flavoring.

- In 1983, G. Anderson of Folkestone, Great Britain, grew the largest recorded strawberry in history, weighing 8.17 ounces.

• Strawberries planted on a slope facing south will fruit at least one week earlier than strawberries planted on a slope that faces north.

• Strawberries are not berries. Botanists classify the strawberry as an "aggregate fruit"—a fleshy fruit receptacle covered with dry, single-seeded fruits on its surface. True berries are pulpy, pitted fruits with a fleshy, soft ovary wall—like blueberries, grapes, and cranberries. The strawberry was originally called "strewberry" because the fruit appears strewn among the plant's leaves, but mispronunciation changed the name to "strawberry."

• In an episode of the television comedy *Gilligan's Island*, Thurston Howell the Third exclaims, "Ah, the dreaded Wasubi berry! One succulent drop and your body's covered with hair, your teeth turn into fangs, your hands into claws! My mother-in-law must have had a batch of those!"

• At the end of the Beatles' song "Strawberry Fields Forever," John Lennon mutters the words "cranberry sauce." Some Beatles fans, convinced that the Beatles had placed clues in their songs that Paul McCartney was dead, claimed that the words Lennon mutters are "I buried Paul." In *The Beatles in Their Own Words*, Paul McCartney states: "That's John's humor. John would say something totally out of synch, like 'cranberry sauce.' If you don't realize that John's apt to say 'cranberry sauce' when he feels like it, then you start to hear a funny little word there, and you think 'Aha!'"

Birds

- **Barnum's Animals.** Crumbled-up Barnum's Animal Crackers in a seed table will attract birds to your yard.

- **Campbell's Tomato Soup.** Protect corn from birds by removing the bottom of a clean, empty Campbell's Tomato Soup can with a can opener, poking holes around the outside of the can with a hammer and awl, and then placing the can over an ear of corn.

- **Cheerios.** Attract birds to your yard by filling a bird feeder with Cheerios.

- **Crisco All-Vegetable Shortening.** Keep squirrels away from a bird feeder by greasing the pole with Crisco All-Vegetable Shortening. The squirrels will try to climb up the pole—but will slide right back down, providing you with hours of free entertainment. (For more ways to repel squirrels from a bird-feeder, see page 254.)

- **Domino Sugar.** To attract hummingbirds and orioles, mix one part Domino Sugar to four parts water in a commercial hummingbird feeder or a water bottle made for hamsters or rabbits and then suspend it upside down. Clean out the feeder once a week and refill with a fresh batch of formula.

• **Efferdent.** Clean a hummingbird feeder by filling the bottle with hot water and dropping in one-half Efferdent tablet. Wait five minutes and then rinse clean.

• **Frisbee.** Make a birdbath by punching three equidistant holes along the circumference of a Frisbee. Insert wire through the holes and hang the Frisbee upside down from a tree or post. Fill with water or let the rain do it naturally. Clean the Frisbee and replace the water regularly.

• **Gatorade.** To store birdseed, pour an open box or bag of birdseed into a clean, empty Gatorade bottle and secure the lid to keep the birdseed fresh and free from insects and mice.

• **Glad Trash Bags.** Fill small Glad Trash Bags with air, tie them shut, and staple to tall stakes throughout the garden. The plastic bags, flapping in the breeze, frighten away birds. (For more ways to make a scarecrow, see page 234.)

• **Heinz White Vinegar.** To keep cats away from a birdbath, fill a trigger-spray bottle with Heinz White Vinegar and spray around the base of the birdbath. The smell of vinegar repulses cats and neutralizes the smell of cat urine used to mark their territory.

• **Jif Peanut Butter, Hartz Parakeet Seed,** and **Oral-B Mint Waxed Floss.** Roll a pinecone in Jif Peanut Butter, then roll the sticky pinecone in Hartz Parakeet Seed. Use a piece of Oral-B Mint Waxed Floss to hang the homemade bird feeder from a tree branch to attract birds to your yard.

• **L'eggs Sheer Energy Panty Hose** and **Oral-B Mint Waxed Floss.** To prevent birds from destroying growing fruits and vegetables, cut off the feet from a clean, used pair of L'eggs Sheer Energy Panty Hose, slip a foot over an apple, pear, tomato, eggplant, grape cluster, or broccoli or cabbage head, and seal the open end closed with a piece of Oral-B Mint Waxed Floss. The synthetic fibers keep birds away, and the flexible hose expands as the fruit or vegetable grows. You can also cut a section from the leg of the panty hose, tie one end closed with dental floss, cover the fruit or vegetable, and then secure the open end shut.

• **McCormick Ground (Cayenne) Red Pepper.** Keep squirrels out of your bird feeder by sprinkling the birdseed with McCormick Ground Red Pepper. The birds cannot taste the cayenne pepper, but squirrels can and want nothing to do with it.

• **Pam Cooking Spray.** Prevent barn or cliff swallows from building nests in an undesirable spot by removing any gathered nesting material from the site and spraying the nook or cranny with Pam Cooking Spray. If the birds try to rebuild a nest in the slippery spot, the Pam Cooking Spray causes the new nesting material to simply slide off.

• **Oral-B Mint Waxed Floss, Reynolds Wrap,** and **Scotch Magic Tape.** Run a string of Oral-B Mint Waxed Floss across your garden between two stakes just a few inches above a row of plants. Using a pair of scissors, cut a dozen or more strips of Reynolds Wrap one inch wide by five inches long. Tape the strips of aluminum foil along the string of dental floss every few feet. The strips of reflective foil flapping in the breeze will repel birds.

• **Orville Redenbacher's Gourmet Popping Corn.** Birds love freshly popped popcorn. Just make sure you buy a natural—and not butter-flavored—variety.

• **Quaker Oats.** A bird feeder filled with uncooked Quaker Oats will attract birds to your yard.

• **Reynolds Wrap** and **Oral-B Mint Waxed Floss.** Cut circles or star shapes from cardboard, wrap the cardboard cutouts in Reynolds Wrap, punch holes in the shapes, and then hang them from fruit trees and berry bushes with a loop of Oral-B Mint Waxed Floss. The sunlight, reflecting from the silvery shapes, will frighten away birds.

• **Scotch Packaging Tape.** To prevent sparrows from usurping a birdhouse before purple martins return home, seal off the entrance to the birdhouse by sticking a piece of Scotch Packaging Tape over the hole—until the insect-catching martins return.

• **Slinky.** Birds nesting under your awnings? Stretch out a Slinky and wrap it into a tangled ball, then wedge it into the crevice where birds nest. Or stretch a Slinky across the spot and your troubles are gone.

• **SueBee Honey, Hartz Parakeet Seed, Charmin,** and **Oral-B Mint Waxed Floss.** Make a simple bird feeder by rolling an empty cardboard tube from a roll of Charmin Bath Tissue in SueBee Honey, then rolling the honey-coated tube in the Hartz Parakeet Seed. Use Oral-B Mint Waxed Floss to hang the birdseed-coated tube outdoors.

• **Sun-Maid Raisins.** Attract robins and bluebirds to your yard by filling a seed table with Sun-Maid Raisins.

• **Vaseline Petroleum Jelly.** Prevent ants from climbing into a hummingbird feeder by rubbing Vaseline Petroleum Jelly on the chain or string from which you hang your hummingbird feeder.

STRANGE FACTS

• Lure birds to your garden in the winter with birdhouses and birdbaths (so the birds will eat the destructive insects), but take down the birdhouse and cover birdbaths during the growing season (so birds won't be attracted to eat ripening fruit).

• To stay airborne, birds must fly at an average speed of eleven miles per hour.

• A flock of larks is called an "exaltation."

• Legend holds that swallows faithfully return to the mission of San Juan Capistrano every year on March 19. In reality, the swallows, following a typical pattern of bird migration—spending the winter in South America and winging to California in the spring—do not arrive in San Juan Capistrano in a single flock or on the same day each year. The swallows arrive between the last week in February and the last week in March. They build their mud nests in cliffs or in suitable stone or concrete structures like the mission, founded in 1776 as the first building in town. Today, with many other buildings to choose from, few swallows build their nests in the mission.

• Planting birdseed in your garden yields plants that grow birdseed, attracting birds and freeing you from forever having to refill a birdfeeder.

• The most common bird in the world is the starling.

• The song of the white-breasted wren of Mexico sounds like the opening of Beethoven's Fifth Symphony.

• A woodpecker's tongue is attached to the hyoid, a combination of bone and elastic tissue that loops back around the top of the bird's skull and into its nostrils.

• Fear of birds is called *ornithophobia*.

• Crows can be domesticated as pets and sometimes taught to speak a few words, just like parrots can.

• Baby robins, known as greedy eaters, consume up to fourteen feet of earthworms every day.

• The heart of an active hummingbird beats five hundred times a minute. When that same hummingbird sleeps, its heart slows to less than ten beats a minute.

BIRD POOP

✂ **Colgate Toothpaste.** A dollop of Colgate Regular Flavor Toothpaste and a hard brush cleans bird droppings off any surface.

✂ **Heinz Apple Cider Vinegar.** Fill a trigger-spray bottle with Heinz Apple Cider Vinegar and spray the spot, or apply the vinegar with a rag. Wait a few moments, then wipe off the droppings with ease.

✂ **Reynolds Wrap.** A crumpled-up piece of Reynolds Wrap makes an excellent scrubber for cleaning birdbaths.

- Hummingbirds, able to fly backwards, sideways, and upside down, cannot walk.

- The *birdie*—the golf term for scoring one stroke under par on a hole—probably got its name from the *feathery*—the name for the original golf ball used until 1848, which was made from leather and stuffed with feathers.

- "Wet birds do not fly at night" was a code for the French Resistance during World War II.

- The vervain hummingbird of Jamaica lays the smallest bird egg in the world, weighing less than .0132 ounce.

- Eggs do not crush under the weight of a mother bird as she sits on the nest because when a force is applied to an egg, the curve of the egg distributes the force over a wide area away from the point of contact.

- In Alfred Hitchcock's 1963 movie *The Birds*, based on the short story by Daphne du Maurier, thousands of birds violently attack people in a quaint New England town. The movie stars Rod Taylor, Tippi Hedren, Jessica Tandy, and Suzanne Pleshette. When asked by a reporter how he got the birds to act so well, Hitchcock replied, "They were very well paid, ma'am."

- In the 1977 Mel Brooks comedy movie *High Anxiety*, a spoof on the films of Alfred Hitchcock, birds gather ominously on a jungle gym in a park and poop all over Mel Brooks as he attempts to flee the scene.

- The hummingbird, the only bird capable of hovering in the air, beating its wings up to seventy times a second, provided the inspiration for the helicopter.

- If NASA sent birds into space, they would die. Birds need gravity to swallow.

- Some scientists theorize that birds have a tiny magnetic crystal in their brain, enabling them to migrate by detecting Earth's magnetic field.

Roaring with Barnum's Animals

In the late nineteenth century, Americans imported "Animals" or "Circus Crackers" (animal-shaped cookies) from England. As demand for the animal crackers grew, local American bakeries began making versions of the treats.

In 1898, Adophus Green consolidated several American baking companies into the National Biscuit Company (which eventually became known as Nabisco). The National Biscuit Company quickly began creating easily identifiable packaging for its products, and in 1902, the company gave its "Animal Biscuits" a new name— "Barnum's Animals"—in honor of renowned showman P. T. Barnum (1810–1891), who called his circus "The Greatest Show on Earth." For Christmas, the company redesigned the package as a circus wagon cage with a string handle, so the box could be hung as a Christmas tree ornament. Barnum's Animals, selling for five cents a box, were an instant hit and immediately became a year-round favorite.

• During its first year of business in 1898, Nabisco's sales accounted for 70 percent of the cracker and cookie business in America.

• In 1899, Nabisco created a new light and flaky soda cracker sold in a package specially designed to preserve its crispness under the brand name Uneeda Biscuit, advertised with the Uneeda Biscuit slicker boy. In 1900, Nabisco sold more than 100 million boxes of Uneeda biscuits—roughly six packages for every family in America.

• Nabisco's symbol, an oval topped by a double-barred cross, was used as a pressmark by Venetian printers Nicolas Jensen and Johannes de Colonia as early as 1480. In medieval times, the mark symbolized the triumph of the spiritual world over the material world.

• The box of Barnum's Animals was the first product designed with a string handle. To produce boxes of Barnum's Animals, Nabisco uses eight thousand miles of string every year.

• A box of Barnum's Animals provides 10 percent of the United States Recommended Daily Allowance of calcium.

• Barnum's Animals currently feature a menagerie of seventeen different animal-shaped crackers: bears, bison, camels, cougars, elephants, giraffes, gorillas, hippopotamuses, hyenas, kangaroos, lions, monkeys, rhinoceroses, seals, sheep, tigers, and zebras.

• The average box of Barnum's Animal Crackers contains twenty-two crackers.

• Nabisco sells more than forty million boxes of Barnum's Animal Crackers each year.

• In the 1935 movie *Curly Top*, Shirley Temple sings "Animal Crackers in my Soup," possibly the world's most famous reference to animal crackers.

Bulbs

• **Clorox.** To protect bulbs from moles, gophers, and rodents, cut off the top half from a clean, empty Clorox Bleach jug, punch drain holes in the sides and base of the bottom half of the jug, sink the jug into a flower bed, fill with soil, and plant bulbs inside it.

• **CoverGirl NailSlicks Classic Red.** Make a convenient ruler to measure the depth for planting bulbs by using CoverGirl Nail-Slicks Classic Red nail polish to mark off inches along the edge of your garden trowel. You can also use the nail polish to cali-brate feet on the handle of a rake, shovel, or hoe.

• **Dannon Yogurt.** Protect bulbs from tunneling voles by planting each bulb inside a clean, empty Dannon Yogurt cup punched with drainage holes.

• **L'eggs Sheer Energy Panty Hose.** To store plant bulbs, fill the foot of a pair of L'eggs Sheer Energy Panty Hose and hang it high to keep the contents dry. The synthetic fibers of the panty hose also repel rodents and insects.

• **Liquid Paper.** Use Liquid Paper to mark off inches along the edge of your garden trowel to make a convenient ruler to measure the depth for planting bulbs. You can also use Liquid Paper to calibrate feet on the handle of a rake, shovel, or hoe.

• **Listerine.** Protect gladiolas and freesia bulbs from thrips by soaking them for twelve hours in a mixture of 2.5 tablespoons Listerine in a gallon of water. Remove the bulbs from the Listerine dip and, without rinsing them off, plant them in your garden.

• **McCormick Ground (Cayenne) Red Pepper.** Deter rodents from digging up bulbs by sprinkling McCormick Ground Red Pepper around bulb plantings.

• **Reynolds Wrap.** Forcing crocus and hyacinth bulbs requires darkness. Place these bulbs on a cold windowsill and cover with a cone made from Reynolds Wrap. When the crocus shoots grow two inches or the hyacinth bulbs grow four inches, remove the foil cone.

• **Tabasco Pepper Sauce, McCormick Chili Powder,** and **Ivory Dishwashing Liquid.** To prevent squirrels, chipmunks, or mice from digging up bulbs, mix three teaspoons Tabasco Pepper Sauce, one teaspoon McCormick Chili Powder, one-half teaspoon Ivory Dishwashing Liquid, and two cups water in a sixteen-ounce trigger-spray bottle. Spray the solution into the soil around freshly planted bulbs.

STRANGE FACTS

• The pointy tip of a bulb is the top of the bulb, from which the central bud sprouts. Roots grow from the bottom of the bulb.

• When the stems, leaves, and flowers of a bulb plant die, the bulb stays alive underground, living off food stored in its layers of fleshy scales. In the next growing season, the bulb sends out a new shoot, again producing a stem, leaves, and flowers.

• In the seventeenth century, "Tulipmania" swept Europe as owning rare breeds of tulips became a status symbol. The middle class, realizing how much money the upper classes spent on tulip bulbs, began breeding the bulbs, which were sold by weight—usually while still in the ground. Traders earned as much as 44,000 dollars a month. In 1637, the same year that three Rembrandt tulip bulbs sold for 25,000 dollars, the tulip market crashed.

- In William Thackeray's 1855 novel *The Rose and the Ring*, Angelica cries out, "My bold, my beautiful, my Bulbo!"

- In Italian, the word for bulb is *bulbo*.

- The bulbs of the hyacinth, if eaten, cause death.

- On their 1986 album *Made in USA*, the rock band Sonic Youth performs the song "The Dynamics of Bulbing."

Uncovering Liquid Paper

In 1951, twenty-seven-year-old divorcée Bette Nesmith worked as an executive secretary at Texas Bank & Trust in San Antonio, Texas. Nesmith, having worked her way up from the typing pool, ran into a problem with her new IBM electric typewriter. When she tried to fix her mistakes with a pencil eraser, the ink from the carbon-film ribbon in the new machine smudged the paper, creating a bigger mess. Inspired by the holiday window painters who brushed over smudges and flaws in their work, Nesmith decided to paint over her mistakes with a bottle of white tempera paint and a watercolor brush.

Nesmith's simple yet ingenious idea caught on with other secretaries at work, and by 1956, Nesmith was mixing up batches of "Mistake Out," combining paint and other chemicals in her kitchen blender and bottling the product in her garage. When demand skyrocketed, she renamed the product "Liquid Paper" and applied for a patent and a trademark.

In 1962, Bette Nesmith married Robert Graham, and by 1975, when the couple divorced, her company was making twenty-five million bottles of Liquid Paper a year, distributed to thirty-one countries. In 1979, Bette Nesmith Graham sold her company to Gillette for 47.5 million dollars.

- Bette Nesmith Graham's son, Michael Nesmith, starred in the television series *The Monkees* with Davy Jones, Peter Tork, and Micky Dolenz. After the Monkees broke up, Nesmith, through lavish spending and poor tax planning, lost most of the million dollars he made with the group. When his mother died in 1980, he inherited approximately 25 million dollars from her Liquid Paper fortune. To this day he earns a royalty on every bottle of Liquid Paper sold.

- Bette Nesmith attempted to persuade IBM to market Liquid Paper, but the multinational corporate giant was not interested.

- In 1958, after General Electric Company ordered four hundred bottles of Liquid Paper in three colors, Bette Nesmith put the name of her company on her employer's letterhead. She was immediately fired from Texas Bank & Trust.

Cabbage

• **Gold Medal Flour** and **L'eggs Sheer Energy Panty Hose.** To protect green cabbage varieties from cabbageworms, cut off a leg from a clean, used pair of L'eggs Sheer Energy Panty Hose, fill it with three cups Gold Medal All-Purpose Flour (not self-rising), and tie a knot in the end. In the early morning, when dew is still on the plants, shake the flour-filled panty hose sachet to dust Gold Medal All-Purpose Flour over the moist leaves of broccoli, Brussels sprouts, cauliflower, and cabbage. The caterpillars eat the flour, which expands in their digestive system, and die. After two days, use a hose with a fine spray to wash the flour off the plant leaves.

• **Hula Hoops, Bubble Wrap,** and **Scotch Packaging Tape.** Building row covers can stop flea beetles that spread viruses from infecting your cabbage patch. Make hoop supports by cutting Hula Hoops in half and inserting the legs firmly into the soil. Cover with a canopy made from sheets of Bubble Wrap and secure to the hoops with Scotch Packaging Tape, making sure the sheets of Bubble Wrap are high enough not to touch the plants. You can also secure the Bubble Wrap by staking the ends to the ground with wire. At the end of the season, roll up the Bubble Wrap to be used again the following year. (Be sure to monitor the temperatures inside this minigreenhouse to make certain you do not burn out your plants, or substitute sheer curtains for the Bubble Wrap.)

• **L'eggs Sheer Energy Panty Hose and Oral-B Mint Waxed Floss.** To prevent cabbageworms, birds, rodents, raccoons, and squirrels from destroying growing cabbage, cut off the feet from clean, used pairs of L'eggs Sheer Energy Panty Hose, then slip a foot over each head of cabbage and seal the open end closed with a piece of Oral-B Mint Waxed Floss. The synthetic fibers keep birds away, and the flexible hose expands as the cabbage grows. You can also cut a section from the leg of the panty hose, tie one end closed with dental floss, cover the cabbage head, and then secure the open end shut.

• **McCormick Ground (Cayenne) Red Pepper and Ivory Dishwashing Liquid.** To keep cabbageworms, cabbage loopers, and diamond-back moth larvae at bay, dissolve one tablespoon McCormick Ground Red Pepper and six drops Ivory Dishwashing Liquid in two quarts water in a bucket. Let the solution sit overnight, then fill a trigger-spray bottle with it and mist cabbage plants once a week. The pepper spray repels moths, preventing the pests from laying eggs on the cabbage leaves.

• **Q-Tips Cotton Swabs.** To fight cabbageworms, use a wet Q-Tips Cotton Swab to wipe their yellowish oval eggs from the undersides of cabbage leaves.

• **Saran Wrap.** Preserve picked cabbage heads for up to three months by wrapping the heads in Saran Wrap and storing in your refrigerator at a temperature near freezing.

STRANGE FACTS

• The word *cabbage* is slang for money, *cabbagehead* is slang for idiot, and *cabbaging* means stealing or pilfering.

• In his 1532 novel *Gargantua and Pantagruel*, French satirist François Rabelais wrote, "Happy are those who plant cabbages."

• In his 1894 novel *Pudd'nhead Wilson*, Mark Twain wrote: "Cauliflower is nothing but cabbage with a college education."

• Baseball legend Babe Ruth wore a cabbage leaf under his baseball cap to keep cool during games, changing the moist leaf every two innings.

• In 1989, B. Lavery of Llanharry, Great Britain, grew the largest recorded cabbage in history, weighing 124 pounds.

• In 1996, Mattel introduced the Cabbage Patch Snacktime doll, a Cabbage Patch doll with a motorized jaw that enabled it to mimic eating plastic cookies and other foods. When parents reported that the doll also ate children's hair and fingers, Mattel—facing an investigation by the Consumer Product Safety Commission—put warning labels on the dolls and admitted that it had failed to test the doll for possible hair entanglement. Finally, Mattel recalled the dolls and offered each consumer a forty dollar refund.

Cats and Dogs

- **Arm & Hammer Baking Soda.** To prevent dogs from urinating on your lawn and causing yellow burn spots, dissolve one cup Arm & Hammer Baking Soda in one gallon water in a watering can and saturate the urine spots every three days. The baking soda deodorizes the area, preventing the offending dog from recognizing the spot, and simultaneously neutralizes the acidity of the urine, enabling the grass to regain its color.

- **Bounce.** Repel cats by hanging fresh sheets of Bounce Classic from your fence posts, shrubs, or trees. The fragrance (oleander, a natural repellent) keeps cats away. Misting the Bounce Classic sheets with water every so often revives the scent.

- **Gold Medal Flour, French's Mustard,** and **McCormick Ground (Cayenne) Red Pepper.** To repel cats, dissolve two tablespoons Gold Medal Flour, two tablespoons French's Mustard, one tablespoon McCormick Ground Red Pepper, and two cups water in a sixteen-ounce trigger-spray bottle. Shake well and spray around flowerbeds, vegetable gardens, or the perimeter of your yard.

- **Heinz White Vinegar.** To repel cats, fill a trigger-spray bottle with Heinz White Vinegar and spray around the border of your garden and birdbath. The smell of vinegar repulses cats and neutralizes the smell of cat urine used to mark their territory.

- **Maxwell House Coffee.** Fertilizing houseplants and plants around your garden with used Maxwell House Coffee grounds repels cats and prevents them from digging up the soil.

- **McCormick Black Pepper.** Keep dogs and cats out of your garbage cans by sprinkling McCormick Black Pepper around the trash bins. Both these animals have a keen sense of smell. They catch a whiff of the pepper and take off for someone else's garbage cans.

- **Tabasco Pepper Sauce** and **McCormick Ground (Cayenne) Red Pepper.** To prevent dogs from digging up your compost pile, mix four tablespoons Tabasco Pepper Sauce and four table-spoons McCormick Ground Red Pepper in one quart water. After you've turned your compost, sprinkle the solution over the pile.

- **Tabasco Pepper Sauce, McCormick Chili Powder,** and **Ivory Dish-washing Liquid.** Mix three teaspoons Tabasco Pepper Sauce, one teaspoon McCormick Chili Powder, one-half teaspoon Ivory Dishwashing Liquid, and two cups water in a sixteen-ounce trigger-spray bottle. Spray the solution around the perimeter of the yard to repel cats and dogs.

- **Tabasco Pepper Sauce, McCormick Garlic Powder,** and **Wesson Corn Oil.** Mix four tablespoons Tabasco Pepper Sauce, four ta-blespoons McCormick Garlic Powder, and one-half teaspoon Wesson Corn Oil in one quart of water. Fill a trigger-spray bottle with the solution and spray the perimeter of your yard to repel cats and dogs.

STRANGE FACTS

- Every United States president since Warren G. Harding has had a dog while in the White House—with the exception of

Calvin Coolidge, who had two pet raccoons named Rebecca and Horace.

• Novelist Ernest Hemingway's house in Key West, Florida, is home to more than sixty cats, all descendants of the author's original cats.

• Cats can hear ultrasound.

• The most popular dog name is Brandy. The most popular cat name is Kitty.

• During his presidency, Lyndon Baines Johnson's entire First Family had the initials LBJ. His wife was Lady Bird Johnson, his daughters were Linda Bird Johnson and Lucy Baines Johnson, and his dog was named Little Beagle Johnson.

• Fear of cats is called *ailurophobia*.

• Paul McCartney wrote the Beatles song "Martha My Dear" about his sheepdog Martha.

Clothing

BOOTS AND SHOES

- **Alberto VO5 Conditioning Hairdressing.** Protect leather shoes and boots from water and mud by rubbing Alberto VO5 Conditioning Hairdressing into the leather.

- **Aqua Net Hair Spray.** Coat your sneakers with Aqua Net Hair Spray to prevent the canvas and leather from absorbing dirt and mud. After gardening, you'll be able to easily wipe off the dirt with a damp rag.

- **Conair Pro Style 1600 Hair Dryer.** To dry wet boots or sneakers, insert the nozzle of a Conair Pro Style 1600 hair dryer into the boot or sneaker and use on a low warm setting for five minutes.

- **Glad Trash Bags.** Make impromptu boots by simply slipping a Glad Trash Bag over each shoe and securing in place with masking tape.

- **Scotchgard.** Make shoes and boots waterproof by spraying them with a coat of Scotchgard.

• *USA Today.* Dry wet shoes or boots by stuffing them with crumpled pages of *USA Today.* Let dry overnight (away from a heat source). The newsprint absorbs moisture while simultaneously deodorizing the footwear.

• **Ziploc Storage Bags.** Protect shoes when working in the mud by wearing a gallon-size Ziploc Storage Bag over each shoe.

EYEGLASSES

• **Colgate Toothpaste.** To defog eyeglasses, rub a dab of Colgate Toothpaste over both sides of the lenses, then wipe clean. The glycerin in the toothpaste prevents the eyeglasses from fogging up.

• **Secret Deodorant.** To prevent eyeglasses from slipping down your nose, rub a dab of Secret Deodorant on the bridge of your nose.

HATS

• **Stayfree Maxi Pads.** To prevent perspiration stains on the inside of a hat's headband, stick a self-adhesive Stayfree Maxi Pad inside the hat along the headband where your forehead rests. When the maxi pad gets full of sweat, replace it with a fresh one.

KNEE PADS

• **Bubble Wrap** and **Scotch Packaging Tape.** Make knee pads for working in the garden by simply rolling up two foot-long sheets of Bubble Wrap. Use Scotch Packaging Tape to adhere the air-cushioning material to the front of each knee.

• **L'eggs Sheer Energy Panty Hose.** Cut off the legs from a pair of clean, used L'eggs Sheer Energy Panty Hose, stuff them with foam rubber, old sponges, rags, or Bubble Wrap, and tie the ends to create handy kneeling pads.

• **Scotch-Brite Heavy Duty Scrub Sponge.** Sew pockets onto the knees of an old pair of pants and slip Scotch-Brite Heavy Duty Scrub Sponges inside to make excellent knee pads.

- **Stayfree Maxi Pads.** Peel the adhesive strip from the back of two Stayfree Maxi Pads and stick the pads to your knees.

RAINCOAT

- **Glad Trash Bags.** Improvise a raincoat by cutting slits in a Glad Trash Bag for your head and arms.

Growing Pains

CLEANING DIRTY CLOTHES

✗ **Arm & Hammer Baking Soda.** Sprinkle grease stains with Arm & Hammer Baking Soda and scrub gently with a wet scrub brush. The baking soda lifts the grease.

✗ **Cascade** and **Oral-B Toothbrush.** Wet the fabric and sprinkle Cascade dishwashing powder on the dirt or grease stain. Scrub gently with a clean, old Oral-B Toothbrush, rinse, and run through the regular wash cycle.

✗ **Cheez Whiz.** To clean grease from clothes, rub a dollop of Cheez Whiz into the stain and run through a regular wash cycle with detergent. The enzymes in Cheez Whiz help loosen grease stains.

✗ **Clairol Herbal Essences Shampoo.** Clean ring-around-the-collar by rubbing Clairol Herbal Essences Shampoo into the sebum oil stain and then laundering as usual.

✗ **Coca-Cola.** Saturate a grease-stained garment with a can of Coke, then toss the garment in your regular wash with your regular detergent. The phosphoric acid in Coca-Cola helps loosen grease stains.

✗ **Comet** and **Oral-B Toothbrush.** Wet the stain with water, sprinkle Comet over the area, and scrub lightly with a clean, old Oral-B Toothbrush to form a paste. Let set overnight, then rinse out with water.

✗ **Dawn.** Pour Dawn Dishwashing Liquid over a grease stain, rub the fabric together, then toss in your regular wash. Dawn cuts through grease.

✗ **Domino Sugar.** To clean grass stains from clothes, dissolve one part Domino Sugar in two parts water, heat the mixture in the microwave oven for one minute, then pour over the stains. Let the clothes sit for one hour before washing them in your washing machine.

✗ **Formula 409.** Pretreat stains with Formula 409, then toss the garment in your regular wash.

✗ **Gunk Brake Cleaner.** Spray grease stains on clothes with Gunk Brake Cleaner, then launder the garment as usual.

✗ **Heinz White Vinegar.** Clean perspiration stains from clothes by saturating the spots with Heinz White Vinegar and then tossing the garment in your regular wash.

✗ **Heinz White Vinegar.** Deodorize smelly clothes by adding one cup Heinz White Vinegar to your washer while the machine is filling with water. If the perspiration smells really pungent, let the laundry soak for an hour before starting the wash cycle.

✗ **Karo Corn Syrup.** Clean grass stains from clothes by rubbing Karo Corn Syrup into the stains and then washing as usual.

✗ **Kingsford's Corn Starch.** Cover grease stains with Kingsford's Corn Starch, wait twelve hours, brush off, then launder as usual.

✗ **Lestoil.** Rubbing Lestoil into stains and laundering as usual works better than most stain removers.

✗ **McCormick Cream of Tartar.** To clean ring-around-the-collar, wet the collar with warm water, rub in McCormick Cream of Tartar, then launder as usual.

✗ **Mr. Clean.** Clean a grass stain from a garment by saturating the stain with Mr. Clean, letting sit for ten minutes, then tossing the garment in your regular wash.

✗ **Murphy Oil Soap.** Rub Murphy Oil Soap into grass or grease stains on clothes, then wash the garment in your regular wash load.

✗ **Pine-Sol.** To clean grass or grease stains from clothes, saturate the stains with Pine-Sol, let sit for ten minutes, then launder as usual.

✗ **Smirnoff Vodka.** Remove a grass stain by rubbing the stain with a clean cloth soaked in Smirnoff Vodka, then rinsing thoroughly.

SHINING SHOES

✗ **ChapStick.** Shine shoes by rubbing ChapStick over the leather and buffing with a dry, clean cloth.

✗ **Coppertone.** A few drops of Coppertone sunscreen rubbed into leather shoes gives them a clean glow (and prevents your shoes from getting sunburned).

✗ **Endust.** Spray Endust on shoes and shine with a cloth.

✗ **Huggies Baby Wipes.** To clean mud stains from shoes, simply wipe the shoes with a Huggies Baby Wipe.

✗ **L'eggs Sheer Energy Panty Hose.** Soldiers swear by panty hose as the best way to shine shoes and boots for inspections. Simply use a pair of clean, used L'eggs Sheer Energy Panty Hose to buff the shoes or boots. The nylon is a mild abrasive.

✗ **Lubriderm.** Rub a dab of Lubriderm on each shoe and buff thoroughly.

✗ **Mop and Glo.** For shining shoes, Mop and Glo makes an excellent polish.

✗ **Mr. Coffee Filter.** Ball up a lint-free Mr. Coffee Filter to buff shoes.

✗ **S.O.S Steel Wool Soap Pads.** Use a wet S.O.S Steel Wool Soap Pad to gently clean dirty sneakers.

✗ **Spam.** Rub a block of Spam over leather shoes or boots and then buff. The animal oils in Spam polish leather.

✗ **Spray 'n Wash.** A few squirts of Spray 'n Wash helps clean grease from leather shoes.

✗ **Tampax Tampons.** Many soldiers in the United States military buff their shoes and boots with Tampax Tampons to achieve an impressive shine for inspections.

✗ **Turtle Wax.** Dab Turtle Wax on shoes and buff with a clean, soft cloth.

✗ **Vaseline Petroleum Jelly.** Rub Vaseline Petroleum Jelly over leather shoes and wipe off the excess with a clean cloth.

✗ **Windex.** Clean dirt from shoes by spraying it with a fine mist of Windex and buffing with a clean cloth.

STRANGE FACTS

• Dungaree cloth was developed in Dungri, India, a suburb of Bombay, as early as the seventeenth century. Denim, also developed in the seventeenth century, originated in Nimes, France. Called *serge de Nimes* in Europe, the name of the fabric was pronounced *denim* in the United States. In the 1860s, a Jewish tailor named Levi Strauss, who had been making overalls from canvas for miners in California's gold rush, switched to denim, dying the fabric indigo blue to hide stains, making the sturdy pants even more popular.

• Panama hats originated in the town of Jipijapa, Ecuador, where locals wove the hats from the leaves of the *Carludovica palmata* tree. Few Panamanians wear Panama hats. The hats received their name during the 1800s, when Panama became a hub for shipping the hats from Ecuador to other countries.

• In L. Frank Baum's classic children's book *The Wonderful Wizard of Oz*, Dorothy wears silver shoes. Hollywood screenwriter Noel Langley changed them to ruby slippers in the script for MGM's classic 1939 movie *The Wizard of Oz*.

• Moths do not eat clothes. Female moths of six species of the family *Tineidae* lay huge numbers of eggs on woolen and silk fabrics, and on furs. The caterpillars that hatch feed on these materials, damaging clothes, carpets, and upholstery. The adult moths do not eat these materials.

• Laws in the African country of Malawi prohibit women from wearing trousers or skirts that do not cover the knees.

• Guards at the Amalienborg Palace, home to Denmark's royal family, wear pots filled with flowers as a part of their elaborate headgear.

Compost

- **Bubble Wrap**. Cover your compost bin by draping a large sheet of Bubble Wrap over the sides of the pile. The Bubble Wrap cover can protect a sufficiently moist compost bin from rain or keep moisture in the compost bin when the sun is out.

- **Coca-Cola**. Boost a compost bin with Coca-Cola. Pouring flat Coca-Cola into the compost pile helps jump-start the microorganisms. The Real Thing increases the acidity and the sugar feeds the microorganisms, increasing the organic matter in the compost.

- **Goodyear Tires** and *USA Today*. Fill the inside of the rims of five or six old Goodyear Tires with shredded pages of *USA Today*. Stack the tires on top of each other on the ground and fill them with layers of shredded newspaper, kitchen scraps, and a few red wiggler starter worms. Add indoor and outdoor organic matter to this worm-powered compost bin. The rubber tires insulate the worms from harsh winter weather, and as the rubber heats up, the worms make their way higher inside the tires.

- **Lipton Tea.** Pour strongly brewed Lipton Tea into the compost heap. The liquid speeds up the decomposition process, and the tea attracts acid-producing bacteria, creating an acid-rich compost.

- **Maxwell House Coffee.** Pour that pot of leftover Maxwell House Coffee into the compost heap, rather than pouring it down the drain. The liquid expedites the decomposition process, and the coffee attracts acid-producing bacteria, generating an acid-rich compost.

- **Maxwell House Coffee.** Clean, empty Maxwell House Coffee cans make excellent canisters for collecting compost ingredients in the kitchen.

- **McCormick Black Pepper.** Before you add layers of kitchen waste to your compost bin, sprinkle the foods with McCormick Black Pepper. The pungent aroma and taste of the pepper helps repel animals from your compost pile.

- **Nestea.** Mix up a quart of unsweetened Nestea instant iced tea according to the directions (without adding sugar or ice) and pour the liquid into the compost pile. The tea not only speeds up the decomposition process but also attracts acid-producing bacteria, giving you an acid-enriched compost.

- **Tabasco Pepper Sauce** and **McCormick Ground (Cayenne) Red Pepper.** To prevent dogs from digging into your compost pile, mix four tablespoons Tabasco Pepper Sauce and four tablespoons McCormick Ground Red Pepper in one quart water. After you've turned your compost, sprinkle the solution over the pile.

- **USA Today.** Add shredded pages of USA Today to your compost pile to help the worms and microorganisms fortify your compost with nitrogen, potassium, and phosphorus.

- **Ziploc Freezer Bags.** Store kitchen scraps intended for the compost bin in a Ziploc Freezer Bag and keep it in the freezer until you have time to add the scraps to your compost pile.

STRANGE FACTS

• Compost, a mixture of decomposed and partially decomposed organic material used to amend soil and fertilize plants, can be easily made by covering a layer of fallen leaves, grass clippings, and kitchen scraps (uncooked vegetables and fruits, peelings and cores, eggshells, coffee grounds, tea bags, newspaper, and paper towels) with a thin layer of soil. Add additional layers of organic material as it becomes available. Keep the pile moist, turn it occasionally with a shovel or pitchfork, and wait roughly three to six months for the microorganisms in the soil to decompose the organic materials into nutrient-enriched compost.

• In 1989, *Time* magazine reported that fallen leaves and lawn clippings, which can easily be composted into natural fertilizer, constituted 18 percent of all municipal solid waste.

• The Los Angeles Sanitation Department collects leaves, grass cuttings, and tree trimmings from its citizens through regular trash pickup and then offers free compost made from the yard waste to anyone who wants it.

• Never add barbecue ashes, dog or cat feces, or magazines to a compost pile. Barbecue ashes may contain sulfur oxides, dog or cat manure may contain disease organisms, and magazines may contain harmful inks.

• On April 22, 1990, hundreds of thousands of people gathered in Central Park in New York City to demonstrate in favor of Earth Day. The participants left behind 154.3 tons of litter.

• The Middleborough Botanic Centre in England uses old shredded banknotes as compost.

Corn

- **Bounty.** De-silk an ear of corn easily and effortlessly by shucking the ear and then wiping it in a single stroke from top to bottom with a dampened sheet of Bounty Paper Towel.

- **Campbell's Tomato Soup.** Protect corn from birds and squirrels by removing the bottom of a clean, empty Campbell's Tomato Soup can with a can opener, poking holes around the outside of the can with a hammer and awl, and then placing the can over an ear of corn.

- **Carnation NonFat Dry Milk.** To flavor corn on the cob without using sugar or salt, simply sprinkle a little Carnation NonFat Dry Milk into the pot of water when boiling the ears of corn. The powdered milk enhances the taste of the corn.

- **Glad Trash Bags.** To get an earlier start on your corn crop, sprout the corn seedlings early indoors, slice open the sides of black Glad Trash Bags to make long sheets, and place the black plastic on the garden bed as mulch. Secure the plastic in place with stones and then plant the seedlings in holes in the black plastic at the proper planting intervals. The radiant heat created by the plastic warms the soil an additional 3 degrees Fahrenheit. The plastic sheets can be rolled up at the end of the season and reused the next year. Be certain to water beneath the impermeable plastic sheet with a drip line or soaker hose.

• **Irish Spring Soap** and **L'eggs Sheer Energy Panty Hose.** To prevent deer from eating corn, cut off the legs from pairs of clean, old L'eggs Sheer Energy Panty Hose, slip a bar of Irish Spring Soap into each foot, and hang the legs from stakes around your corn patch. The deer are repelled by the smell of deodorant soap.

• **Johnson's Baby Oil.** To prevent earworms from attacking a corn crop, fill an eyedropper with Johnson's Baby Oil and apply the mineral oil to the base of the ear a few days after the silk first emerges. Repeat every few days.

• **L'eggs Sheer Energy Panty Hose.** Using a pair of scissors, cut off the toe from the foot of a pair of used, clean L'eggs Sheer Energy Panty Hose, then cut one-inch strips from the leg, creating circular loops of panty hose. Use the loops to gently tie stems, vines, and thin plant trunks to stakes with a figure-eight loop.

• **L'eggs Sheer Energy Panty Hose** and **Oral-B Mint Waxed Floss.** To prevent squirrels or raccoons from stealing growing corn, cut off the feet from clean, used pairs of L'eggs Sheer Energy Panty Hose, slip one foot over each pollinated ear of corn, and seal the open end closed with a piece of Oral-B Mint Waxed Floss. The synthetic fibers keep squirrels and raccoons away, and the flexible hose expands as the corn grows. You can also cut a section from the leg of the panty hose, tie one end closed with dental floss, cover the ear of corn, and then secure the open end shut.

• **Oral-B Mint Waxed Floss, Reynolds Wrap,** and **Scotch Magic Tape.** Run a string of Oral-B Mint Waxed Floss between two stakes across your cornfield just a few inches above a row of young corn plants. Using a pair of scissors, cut a dozen or more strips of Reynolds Wrap one inch wide by five inches long. Tape the strips of aluminum foil along the string of dental floss every few feet. The strips of reflective foil flapping in the breeze will repel birds.

• **Reynolds Wrap** and **Oral-B Mint Waxed Floss.** Cut circles or star shapes from cardboard, wrap the cardboard cutouts in Reynolds Wrap, punch a hole in each cutout, and then hang the glittering shapes from cornstalks with a loop of Oral-B Mint Waxed Floss. The sunlight, reflecting from the silvery shapes, will frighten birds away.

• *USA Today.* To repel raccoons from cornfields, place crumpled-up pages of *USA Today* between rows of ripening corn. Raccoons hate walking over rustling newspaper.

• **Ziploc Freezer Bags.** Place a portable radio inside a gallon-size Ziploc Freezer Bag, turn the radio on, and seal the bag shut. The noise from a radio, particularly one tuned to a rock 'n' roll station, chases away raccoons and deer.

• **Ziploc Freezer Bags.** To enjoy sweet corn year-round, pick corn at the height of the summer season, husk the ears, clean off the silk, and blanch the ears in a pot of boiling water for seven minutes. Cool the ears in a sink of cold water, then pack in Ziploc Freezer Bags and store in the freezer.

STRANGE FACTS

• Botanists believe that corn originated in North America. Native Americans grew corn from as far north as present-day Canada to the southern tip of South America. Christopher Columbus brought corn to Europe, and the Native Americans taught early European settlers how to grow corn.

• Native Americans called corn *maize*, which translates to mean "our life."

• Early American colonists frequently used corn as money.

- On February 20, 1943, a volcano began forming from a crack in the earth in a farmer's cornfield in Paricutín, Mexico (near the southwestern city of Uruapan). Within six days, the volcanic material formed a cinder cone over five-hundred feet high. Two months later, the cone reached one thousand feet. The lava destroyed the villages of Paricutín and San Juan Paragaricútiru. Today the volcano, which ceased activity in 1952, stands 1,345 feet high.

- In 1970, a blight wiped out 15 percent of the corn crop in the United States because modern hybrids of corn, while having greater sugar content, lacked natural resistance to disease.

- In 1983, D. Radda of Washington, Iowa, grew the tallest recorded cornstalk in United States history, measuring thirty-one feet high.

- In the 1984 movie *Children of the Corn*, based on the novel by Stephen King, children in a Midwestern farming town start killing the adults in cornfields.

- In 1989, during the United States invasion in Panama, Pentagon spokespeople announced finding fifty kilograms of cocaine in General Manuel Antonio Noriega's refrigerator. The Pentagon later admitted that the white powder was actually fifty kilograms of cornmeal intended for making tamales.

- Corn is pollinated by the wind, which blows pollen from the plant's tassels to the silks on the plant's ears.

- Each individual cornstalk produces between one and two ears of corn.

- In the 1989 movie *Field of Dreams*, based on the novel *Shoeless Joe*, by W. P. Kinsella, Kevin Costner stars as an Iowa farmer who hears a voice telling him to build a baseball diamond in the middle of his cornfield.

Cut Flowers

- **Alka-Seltzer.** Prolong the life of cut flowers in a vase by dropping in two Alka-Seltzer tablets per quart of water.

- **Aqua Net Hair Spray.** Preserve floral arrangements by spraying Aqua Net Hair Spray on baby's breath, broom grass, and cattails to help preserve blossoms and keep them from dropping off.

- **Arm & Hammer Baking Soda.** Cut flowers last longer if you add one teaspoon Arm & Hammer Baking Soda per quart of water in the vase.

- **Bayer Aspirin.** Prolong the life of cut flowers in a vase by dropping in two Bayer Aspirin tablets per quart of water.

- **Bounty.** To revitalize wilted flowers, add a few ice cubes to the vase and cover the flowers with a sheet of Bounty Paper Towel dampened with cold water.

- **Clorox.** Adding one-quarter teaspoon Clorox Bleach per quart of water in a vase of cut flowers prolongs the life of the flowers by killing the harmful bacteria in the water.

- **Crayola Crayons.** To seal cut flowers, carefully melt a green Crayola Crayon and dip the end of the stem of a cut flower into the hot wax. The green wax seals the stem and keeps the flower looking fresh longer.

- **Domino Sugar** and **Heinz White Vinegar.** Extend the life of cut flowers by dissolving three tablespoons Domino Sugar and two tablespoons Heinz White Vinegar per quart of warm water in a vase, making sure the stems are covered by three to four inches of the prepared water. The vinegar inhibits bacterial growth while the sugar feeds the plants.

- **Gatorade.** Make a vase by removing the label from a clean, empty Gatorade bottle, fill one-quarter of the way with marbles (to weight down the bottle), fill halfway with water, and add flowers.

- **Glad Flexible Straws.** Elongate flower stems that have been cut too short for a vase by inserting each stem into a Glad Flexible Straw cut to the desired length.

- **Hydrogen Peroxide.** To sustain the life of cut flowers in a vase, add a capful of hydrogen peroxide every time you change the water. Hydrogen Peroxide kills stem-clogging bacteria that cause the flowers to wilt prematurely.

- **Johnson & Johnson Cotton Balls.** To prolong the life of freshly cut amaryllis, daffodils, and delphiniums, condition the flowers by cutting off two inches from the ends of the stems and placing the flowers in a bucket of cold water in a cool spot away from direct sunlight for a few hours. Then turn the flowers upside down, fill each hollow stem with water, plug with a Johnson & Johnson Cotton Ball, and put the stems in a water-filled vase.

- **Kingsford Charcoal Briquets.** Place an untreated Kingsford Charcoal Briquet in the bottom of an opaque vase before adding cut flowers and water. The briquet prevents mold and acts as a deodorizer.

• **Listerine.** Adding one-half teaspoon Listerine (original or Cool Mint) per quart of water in a vase extends the life of cut flowers. The antiseptic inhibits the growth of harmful bacteria.

• **McCormick Food Coloring.** Tint cut flowers by mixing food coloring in warm water and placing the flower stems in the

Growing Pains

DIRTY VASES

✗ **Alka-Seltzer.** To remove grime from the bottom of a glass vase, fill with water and drop in two Alka-Seltzer tablets. Let sit for ten minutes, then rinse clean.

✗ **Cascade.** Place one teaspoon Cascade dishwashing powder in a dirty glass vase, fill with water, and let sit overnight. The next morning, rinse clean.

✗ **Clorox.** Deodorize a filthy vase by washing with diluted Clorox Bleach (three-quarters cup bleach per gallon of water), then rinse.

✗ **Conair Pro Style 1600 Hair Dryer.** Prevent water spots on a crystal vase after cleaning by using a Conair Pro Style 1600 hair dryer to blow warm air into the vase.

✗ **Crayola Crayons.** Mend a leaking ceramic vase by carefully holding a lit match under the pointed end of a Crayola Crayon that matches the color of the vase. Let the melted wax drip into the crack. After the wax cools, scrape away the excess.

✗ **Efferdent.** To clean grime from the bottom of a glass vase, fill the vase with water, drop in two Efferdent tablets, wait ten minutes, then rinse. The denture cleanser gently bubbles away the grime in all the nooks and crannies without a brush, leaving the vase sparkling.

✗ **Heinz White Vinegar.** Remove hard water stains from inside a crystal vase by filling the vase with Heinz White Vinegar. Let sit for thirty minutes, then rinse clean. The acetic acid in vinegar dissolves lime deposits.

✗ **Uncle Ben's Converted Brand Rice.** Pour one tablespoon uncooked Uncle Ben's Converted Brand Rice and a cup of warm water into a dirty vase. Cup your hand over the opening, shake vigorously, then rinse.

solution overnight. The stems will absorb the colors by morning, revealing intriguing designs on the petals in different colors.

• **Morton Salt.** Prolong the life of freshly cut flowers by adding a pinch of Morton Salt to the vase's water. Salt slows the growth of harmful bacteria.

• **Mrs. Stewart's Liquid Bluing.** Color freshly cut carnations by placing them in a vase of water tinted with a high content of Mrs. Stewart's Liquid Bluing. Osmosis quickly carries the blue color into the tips of the petals.

• **Oral-B Mint Waxed Floss.** To prevent the stems of primroses from bending over in a vase, use a piece of Oral-B Mint Waxed Floss to gently tie the stems together just beneath the flowers.

• **Pampers.** Using a pair of scissors, carefully cut open a Pampers disposable diaper. Pour the superabsorbent polymer flakes from the diaper into a vase and add water. The polymer flakes absorb three hundred times their weight in water, giving the vase a decorative look. Then add the flowers to the vase.

• **Scotch Magic Tape.** Keep flowers standing upright in a vase by crisscrossing pieces of Scotch Magic Tape across the mouth of the vase.

• **7-Up.** Filling a vase of cut flowers with one part 7-Up to two parts water makes the flowers last longer and look healthier. The high sugar content in the Uncola nourishes the plants.

• **Smirnoff Vodka.** Prolong the life of cut tulips by adding a few drops of Smirnoff Vodka to the vase water. The alcohol kills harmful bacteria.

• *USA Today.* To transport freshly cut flowers in a car, wrap the bouquet in a damp section of *USA Today* and place in the trunk or in a dark space to shelter the flowers from the heat of the sun's rays.

STRANGE FACTS

- In Greek mythology, the gods bestowed upon a young man named Narcissus beauty and youth that would never fade, provided he never looked upon his own reflection. When the wood nymph Echo fell helplessly in love with the self-absorbed Narcissus, he showed her no interest. Consumed by love, Echo slowly disappeared until nothing was left but her voice.

The Lowdown on 7-Up

In 1920, Charles L. Grigg, banking on his thirty years of experience in advertising and merchandising, founded the Howdy Corporation in St. Louis, Missouri, and created the successful Howdy Orange drink. Determined to create a new lemon-flavored soft drink for national distribution, Grigg spent more than two years testing eleven different formulas, finally introducing "Bib-Label Lithiated Lemon-Lime Soda" two weeks before the stock market crash of October 1929.

Grigg's pricey caramel-colored lemon-lime soda, marketed as a soft drink that "takes the 'ouch' out of grouch," sold amazingly well during the Depression—possibly because it contained lithium, a strong drug now prescribed to treat manic-depression. Grigg soon changed the soda's cumbersome name to 7-Up, referring to the soda's original seven-ounce bottle and the bubbles rising from the soda's original heavy carbonation, which was later reduced.

In 1936, Grigg changed the name of the Howdy Corporation to the Seven Up Company. The label on the bottle listed lithium as an ingredient until the mid-1940s. By the end of the decade, 7-Up had become the third–best-selling soft drink in the world.

In 1978, Philip Morris acquired the Seven Up Company. In 1986, an investment company bought the Seven Up Company and merged it with the Dr Pepper Company. In 1995, Cadbury Schweppes bought Dr Pepper/Seven Up Inc.

- The earliest advertisement for 7-Up featured a winged 7-Up logo and described the soft drink as "seven natural flavors blended into a savory, flavory drink with a real wallop."

- In 1967, the Seven Up Company began advertising 7-Up as "The Uncola," sending 7-Up sales skyrocketing.

- The 1971 movie *The Seven-Ups*, starring Roy Scheider, was a disappointing sequel to the 1972 Academy Award-winning movie *The French Connection*.

Determined to get revenge, the goddess Nemesis led Narcissus to a shimmering lake, where, transfixed by his own reflection, he died of hunger and thirst. The gods rescued Narcissus from oblivion by causing a flower to spring up where he had lain. To this day, in the language of flowers, the narcissus symbolizes vanity and egoism.

• Since the early seventeenth century, Dutch tulip hybridizers have attempted to breed a pure black tulip, but none have succeeded.

• The slogan "Say it with flowers," used by the Society of American Florists, was coined by Patrick O'Keefe in the December 15, 1917, issue of *Florists' Exchange*.

• In the 1937 Marx Brothers' movie *A Day at the Races*, Groucho Marx, starring as Dr. Hugo Z. Hackenbush, says, "Have the florist send some roses to Mrs. Upjohn and write 'Emily, I love you' on the back of the bill."

• The Kingston Trio recorded the 1962 hit song "Where Have All the Flowers Gone?" written by folk singer Pete Seeger. Seeger had been inspired by three lines from a Ukrainian folk song that he read in the novel *And Quiet Flows the Don* by Mikhail Sholokhov. The lines were:

Where are the flowers? The girls have plucked them.
Where are the girls? They've all taken husbands.
Where are the men? They're all in the army.

• Actor Cliff Robertson optioned the rights to a short story by Daniel Keyes entitled "Flowers for Algernon" and recruited Stirling Silliphant to write the screenplay. The resulting 1968 movie, *Charly*, won Robertson an Academy Award for Best Actor.

• On their 1971 album *Sticky Fingers*, the Rolling Stones recorded the song "Dead Flowers." In the lyrics, a lovelorn man tells the woman who broke his heart to send him dead flowers every morning and to "Say it with dead flowers" at his wedding. In bittersweet irony, he promises to put roses on her grave.

Cuttings

• **Clorox.** Before cutting plants or flowers, sanitize pruning shears or knives in a mixture of three-quarters cup Clorox Bleach per gallon of water in a bucket. Soak the tools in the solution to disinfect them and prevent the spread of diseases to your cuttings.

• **Hydrogen Peroxide.** To prevent cuttings from getting infected with fungal spores, add a few drops of hydrogen peroxide to a sixteen-ounce trigger-spray bottle filled with water and mist the cuttings with the solution.

• **Reynolds Wrap.** Some plant cuttings will root in a glass of water. Place Reynolds Wrap across the top of a glass jar filled with water. Poke holes in the foil and insert the cuttings securely in place. The foil also prevents the water from evaporating too quickly. Maintain the water level and change the water if it turns green. When roots appear, plant the cuttings in moistened potting mix.

• **Saran Wrap.** To make a simple greenhouse to propagate your plant cuttings, fill a pan with at least three inches of soil and insert the cuttings. With a pair of pliers, clip off the hook from three wire clothes hangers and bend the wires to form hoops. Insert a hoop into the soil at each end of the pan and insert the third hoop in the middle. Cover the tray and hoops with a piece of Saran Wrap. Use a pin to make pinholes in the Saran Wrap for ventilation. The plastic will fog up with humidity, but if large water droplets form, remove the Saran Wrap temporarily to prevent the cuttings from getting moldy.

• **Ziploc Storage Bag** and **Glad Flexible Straws.** To make a simple greenhouse to propagate plant cuttings in a small terra-cotta pot, fill the pot with potting soil and insert the cuttings. Insert two or three Glad Flexible Straws into the soil. Cover the support straws with a Ziploc Storage Bag and secure the bag to the top of the pot with a rubber band. Use a pin to make air holes in the plastic bag for ventilation. The plastic will fog up with humidity, but if the plastic starts dripping water, remove it temporarily to prevent the cuttings from getting moldy.

STRANGE FACTS

• Simply cutting off a part of a plant and rooting it in soil propagates the original plant, creating what is essentially a clone of the original plant.

• In 1789, Thomas Jefferson, having lived in Paris during the French Revolution, returned to the United States with grapevine cuttings to replant at Monticello, his Virginia estate. None of the cuttings took root.

• With some plants, just cutting off a leaf, cutting the veins, laying the leaf flat on soil, and watering it will cause new leaves to sprout from the cut veins.

• Smaller cuttings root faster and more successfully than larger cuttings.

• A small hardwood branch from any plant, if planted topside up in the soil and watered, will eventually form calluses on the lower end, from which roots will sprout.

• Covering cuttings with a plastic bag creates a greenhouse filled with humidity to prevent the new plant from losing water through its leaves.

• Cuttings grow into new plants through a process called regeneration, much the same way a lizard, having lost its tail, grows a new one. In the case of plants, however, the tail can also grow into a new lizard.

Cutworms

- **Bounty.** To prevent cutworms from feeding on plant stems, use empty cardboard tubes from rolls of Bounty Paper Towels. Cut the tubes into two-inch sections, slide the sections over young plants, and push them one inch into the soil.

- **Campbell's Tomato Soup.** Protect young garden plants from cutworms by removing the top and bottom from a clean, empty Campbell's Tomato Soup can and pushing the can into the earth around the plant.

- **Dixie Cups.** Remove the bottom of a paper Dixie Cup and push the cup into the soil around a seedling to create a protective collar.

- **Forster Toothpicks.** Inserting a toothpick in the soil about one-quarter inch away from the stem of each seedling prevents cutworms from completely encircling the plant's stem to sever it.

- **Glad Flexible Straws.** Protect seedlings from cutworms by cutting Glad Flexible Straws into 1.5-inch pieces, slitting each piece lengthwise, and then slipping a section around each stem after transplanting. The straws will prevent cutworms from destroying the plants, and as the plants grow, the cut straws will gently expand to accommodate them.

• **Ivory Dishwashing Liquid.** To determine whether rapidly growing bare patches in your lawn are being caused by cutworms, mix one tablespoon Ivory Dishwashing Liquid and one gallon water in a bucket and drench one square yard with the soapy solution. If cutworms rise to the surface, you've identified the problem.

• **Mr. Coffee Filters.** To plant pepper seedlings, first dip a Mr. Coffee Filter in water and wrap it around each plant stem. The paper wrapping keeps the plant moist and deters cutworms.

• **Reynolds Cut-Rite Wax Paper.** Protect a seedling from cutworms by wrapping the stem loosely with a double-folded four-inch piece of Reynolds Cut-Rite Wax Paper, with two inches of the wax paper pushed into the soil.

• **Reynolds Wrap.** Before planting eggplant, pepper, or tomato seedlings, wrap each stem loosely with a four-inch tube of Reynolds Wrap, giving the seedling room to grow. Plant the seedling with two inches of the foil in the soil. The foil tube will protect the plant from cutworms.

• **Vaseline Petroleum Jelly.** If you've sunk a barrier (such as a can, drinking straw, or aluminum foil) into the soil around a plant to deter cutworms, coat the barrier with Vaseline Petroleum Jelly to prevent the worms from climbing over it.

STRANGE FACTS

• Cutworms are named for the fact that these hairless larvae of night-flying moths encircle their bodies around the stems of young plants and cut them off near ground level.

• During the daytime, cutworms hide in the ground, curled up like a piece of rolled licorice.

• Cutworms can destroy entire beds of young garden vegetables overnight.

• On Christmas, southern Africans eat plump, fuzzy caterpillars of the emperor moth (*Gonimbrasia belina*), fried in oil.

• In her 1937 poem "Tombstones in the Starlight," Dorothy Parker wrote:

> He'd have the best, and that was none too good;
> No barrier could hold, before his terms.
> He lies below, correct in cypress wood,
> And entertains the most exclusive worms.

• In 1993, China's Women's Running Team broke three world records at the Chinese National Games in Beijing. The coach credited their success to a diet fortified with dried worms.

• Cuban dictator Fidel Castro vilifies Cubans who fled the revolution as *gusanos*—Spanish for "worms."

Deer

• **Bounce.** Repel deer by hanging fresh sheets of Bounce Classic from your fence posts, shrubs, or trees. The fragrance (oleander, a natural repellent) keeps deer away. Misting the Bounce Classic sheets with water every so often revives the scent.

• **Bubble Wrap.** Since deer will not walk on Bubble Wrap, lay sheets of Bubble Wrap—held in place with stones—on the ground around the perimeter of your garden.

• **Dial** and **Oral-B Mint Waxed Floss.** To repel deer, push a nail through a bar of Dial Soap, tie a loop of Oral-B Mint Waxed Floss through the hole, and hang this antibacterial deodorant soap from fruit trees and fence posts and around crops. Deer mistake the smell of deodorant soap for humans and flee. Should your neighbors ask why you have bars of soap dangling from a tree, you can always confound them further by insisting they grew there.

• **Glad Trash Bags.** Staple small Glad Trash Bags to tomato stakes. The plastic bags, flapping in the breeze, frighten deer away.

• **Irish Spring Soap** and **L'eggs Sheer Energy Panty Hose**. Cut off the leg from a pair of clean, old L'eggs Sheer Energy Panty Hose, slip a bar of Irish Spring Soap into the foot, and hang it from fruit trees, fence posts, and around crops to prevent deer from eating plants. The deer are repelled by the smell of deodorant soap (although some people argue that the deer are actually turned off by the sight of panty hose hanging from a tree).

• **Jif Peanut Butter** and **Reynolds Wrap**. If you have an electrified fence, drape a folded piece of Reynolds Wrap spread with Jif Peanut Butter over a single wire. Deer are attracted to the peanut butter, but when they get zapped by the electricity conducted through the foil, they'll quickly learn to seek food elsewhere.

• **McCormick Peppermint Oil, Johnson & Johnson Cotton Balls,** and **L'eggs Sheer Energy Panty Hose**. Saturate a few cotton balls with McCormick Peppermint Oil, place inside the foot of a pair of clean, used L'eggs Sheer Energy Panty Hose, and hang from a fence post, tree branch, or bush. The smell of mint repels deer.

• **Slinky**. To prevent deer from destroying your garden, drape a few metal Slinkys around the perimeter of the garden by simply stretching them across two fence posts or draping them over tree branches. That trademark "Slinkity" sound and the shiny reflection of the metal frightens away deer. You can also hang Slinky Juniors from sturdy trees and bushes, which simultaneously adds a unique decorative touch that is sure to make you the envy of all your neighbors.

• **Ziploc Freezer Bag**. Place a portable radio inside a gallon-size Ziploc Freezer Bag, turn the radio on, and seal the bag shut. The noise from the radio, particularly one tuned to an all-night talk show, chases away deer (and sometimes pesky neighbors, as well).

STRANGE FACTS

• Members of the deer family are the only animals in the world with bones on their heads. Unlike horns, which are hard layers of skin, antlers are pure bone.

• The deer family includes moose, caribou, elk, and reindeer.

• Thanks to the song "Do-Re-Mi" from the Academy-Award winning 1965 movie musical *The Sound of Music*, most Americans know that a doe is a female deer. However, a female caribou, elk, or moose is called a cow.

• The pudu, the smallest deer in the world, grows up to one foot tall and weighs less than twenty pounds. Pudu are indigenous to western South America.

• Deer run on tiptoe. Each foot is composed of two center toes, protected by a cloven hoof.

• Most deer have front teeth only on their lower jaw. Instead of upper front teeth, deer have a thick pad of skin.

• Soho, a section of London that was originally part of King Henry VIII's hunting grounds, got its name because hunters spying a deer yelled "Tally-Ho!" but finding a smaller prey shouted "So-Ho!"

Diseases

• **Arm & Hammer Baking Soda** and **Wesson Corn Oil.** To protect against powdery mildew and black spot, mix one teaspoon Arm & Hammer Baking Soda and five drops Wesson Corn Oil in one quart water. Fill a trigger-spray bottle or sprayer with the solution and spray directly on roses, houseplants, and cucurbit crops. Apply once a week for approximately two months. Reapply after rain. (Before treating the entire plant, test this oily formula on one of the plant's leaves and wait one day to make certain it doesn't burn the leaf.). (For more ways to combat fungus, see page 95.)

• **Carnation NonFat Dry Milk.** Prevent blight, blossom-end rot, and other common tomato diseases by sprinkling a handful of Carnation NonFat Dry Milk in the hole before planting tomato transplants. After planting, sprinkle two more tablespoons powdered milk on top of the soil. Repeat this topdressing every few weeks. Carnation NonFat Dry Milk adds calcium to the soil.

• **Cascade.** To avoid spreading diseases when transplanting seedlings or plants into pots, clean pots and flats thoroughly by soaking them for ten minutes in a bathtub filled with warm water and one tablespoon Cascade dishwashing powder, then scrubbing the pots in the solution with a stiff brush. Rinse clean and let dry thoroughly in the sun.

• **Clorox.** Sterilize your pruning tools after use with a mixture of three-quarters cup Clorox Bleach in one gallon water to avoid spreading fungal diseases or blight. Dip your pruning equipment into the disinfectant solution between cuts or at least between plants. When finished, soak the pruning shears in the solution for one hour, then rinse clean and dry.

• **Crayola Chalk.** To prevent diseases caused by calcium deficiency, use a mortar and pestle to grind up a box of Crayola Chalk and then sprinkle the chalk dust (calcium carbonate) over the soil around the plant.

• **Epsom Salt.** Mix one tablespoon Epsom Salt in one gallon water and spray the mixture on your plants to aid in disease resistance. Epsom Salt is magnesium sulfate, which lowers the pH of the soil and provides magnesium.

• **Geritol.** Revive an ailing plant by giving the plant two tablespoons Geritol twice a week for three months. New leaves should begin to grow within the first month.

• **Glad Trash Bags.** To get rid of the fungi causing rust spots on the leaves of geraniums, place the geranium plant inside a Glad Trash Bag, and set outside in the full sunlight for a few hours. The temperature inside the bag will quickly reach 90 degrees Fahrenheit, killing the fungi.

• **Grandma's Molasses.** Fight fungal diseases by dissolving one cup Grandma's Molasses in one gallon warm water in a bucket. Fill a trigger-spray bottle, small pressure sprayer, or pump sprayer with the solution and spray infected plants. The plants quickly absorb the molasses, which contains sugar to feed the plants and sulfur to kill the fungi.

• **Heinz White Vinegar.** To prevent potato tubers from being disfigured by common scab, keep the soil slightly acid by watering the plants with a mixture of two tablespoons Heinz White Vinegar per quart of water.

• **Hula Hoops, Bubble Wrap,** and **Scotch Packaging Tape.** Building row covers can stop insects that spread diseases from infecting your crops. Make hoop supports by cutting Hula Hoops in half and inserting the legs firmly into the soil. Cover with a canopy made from sheets of Bubble Wrap and secure to the hoops with Scotch Packaging Tape, making sure the sheets of Bubble Wrap are high enough not to touch the plants. You can also secure the Bubble Wrap by staking the ends to the ground with wire. At the end of the season, roll up the Bubble Wrap to be used again the following year. (Be sure to monitor the temperatures inside this minigreenhouse to make certain you do not burn out your plants, or substitute sheer curtains for the Bubble Wrap.)

• **Hydrogen Peroxide.** To prevent damping-off from killing seedlings, soak the affected area with a mixture of equal parts hydrogen peroxide and water.

• **Hydrogen Peroxide.** To kill anthracnose (a plant disease evidenced by little sunken black spots), fill a sixteen-ounce trigger-spray bottle with one ounce Hydrogen Peroxide and two cups water, and mist the plants once a week with the solution.

• **Hydrogen Peroxide.** Prevent late blight on tomato plants by filling a trigger-spray bottle with Hydrogen Peroxide and misting the plants every evening from late August until early September.

• **Ivory Dishwashing Liquid** and **Arm & Hammer Baking Soda.** To fight foliar infections, mix one tablespoon Ivory Dishwashing Liquid, one tablespoon Arm & Hammer Baking Soda, and one gallon water. Fill a trigger-spray bottle with the mixture and spray infected plants thoroughly.

• **Jell-O.** Fight off fungal diseases by adding one teaspoon powdered Jell-O (any flavor) to the soil of diseased houseplants and covering with a light coat of soil. The gelatin helps the plants retain water, the nitrogen in Jell-O enhances plant growth, and the sugar feeds the microbes in the soil, producing more nutrients for the plant.

• **Listerine.** To avoid spreading fungal diseases, sterilize your pruning tools with Listerine after each use. Mix one cup Listerine per gallon of water in a bucket and dip your pruning equipment into the antiseptic solution between cuts or at least between plants. When finished, soak the pruning shears in the solution for one hour, then rinse clean and dry.

• **Lysol.** To prevent viruses from tainting the blades of your pruning shears and spreading diseases to your plants, spray the tool with Lysol, then rinse well and dry. The disinfectant kills germs on contact.

• **McCormick Ground Cinnamon.** Fight mold, mildew, and mushrooms around peonies by lightly dusting McCormick Ground Cinnamon around each plant. Cinnamon contains a natural fungicide—ortho-methoxycinnamaldehyde—that prevents the growth of fungi. (For more ways to combat mildew, see page 177.)

• **Pine-Sol.** To prevent the spread of fire blight bacteria on apple and crabapple trees, after pruning the diseased trees, clean your pruning tools with full-strength Pine-Sol cleanser, then rinse well and dry. The pine oil kills the bacteria.

• **Purell.** Disinfect pruning tools by coating the blades with Purell Instant Hand Sanitizer. The ethyl alcohol in Purell kills bacteria and fungi.

• **Reynolds Wrap.** Deter viruses and fungal diseases on squash or tomato plants by spreading sheets of Reynolds Wrap as mulch on the soil bed surrounding the plants. The glimmer from the aluminum foil repels aphids and thrips, which carry viruses. Check the plants daily to make sure the aluminum foil is not reflecting too much light back onto the plant, burning it.

• **Reynolds Wrap.** Prevent soilborne diseases by sterilizing your homemade potting mix. Place the potting mix in an oven tray, cover with a piece of Reynolds Wrap, and bake for one hour at 250 degrees Fahrenheit with plenty of ventilation.

• **Smirnoff Vodka.** Sterilize your pruning tools with a mixture of two cups Smirnoff Vodka per gallon of water after each use to avoid spreading fungal diseases. Dip your pruning tools into the alcohol solution between cuts or at least between plants. When finished, soak the pruning shears in the solution for one hour, then rinse clean and dry.

• **Star Olive Oil** and **Dr. Bronner's Peppermint Soap.** Prevent fungal diseases from attacking shiny-leaved fruit trees, vegetables, and flowers by mixing one teaspoon Star Olive Oil, one teaspoon Dr. Bronner's Peppermint Soap, and one gallon water in a bucket. Fill a trigger-spray bottle, small pressure sprayer, or pump sprayer with the solution and spray a fine mist on plants early every morning for a week, then once a week, then once a month. Do not use this oil spray when the temperature goes below 32 degrees or above 85 degrees Fahrenheit. (Before treating the entire plant, test this oil formula on one of the plant's leaves and wait one day to make certain it doesn't burn the leaf.)

• **Tabasco Pepper Sauce, McCormick Garlic Powder,** and **Ivory Dishwashing Liquid.** Mix one-half teaspoon Tabasco Pepper Sauce, one-half teaspoon McCormick Garlic Powder, one drop Ivory Dishwashing Liquid, and two cups water in a sixteen-ounce trigger-spray bottle. Lightly mist any plants evidencing early symptoms of fungal disease (leaves with white powder, curling, or unusual patterns).

• **Ziploc Storage Bags.** Use Ziploc Storage Bags to protect grapes from disease. When the grapes are the size of peas, use a hole puncher to punch a dozen holes in a gallon-size Ziploc Storage Bag, place the bag over the cluster of grapes, and zip the bag closed up to the stem.

STRANGE FACTS

• Most plant diseases are caused by bacteria, fungi, or viruses. Bacteria, single-celled microorganisms unable to produce their own food, attack green plants to obtain nutrients, causing bacterial diseases. Fungi, multicellular organisms that obtain their food parasitically from green plants and reproduce by releasing spores into the air or water, cause fungal diseases in plants. Microscopic viruses invade and reproduce in plant tissue, causing abnormal growth, discoloration, or foliage variegation.

• Plant diseases can be spread by an infected shovel, gloves, or gardening shoes. Washing tools, gloves, and shoes with warm, soapy water kills the diseases.

• Before spraying plants to ward off a disease, add a drop of liquid soap or vegetable oil to the spray solution. Soap or oil breaks the surface tension and helps the liquid stick to plant leaves.

• In the 1971 science fiction movie *The Andromeda Strain*, scientists race to isolate a deadly virus brought to earth from outer space.

• Ergot—a fungus that infects barley, rye, and wheat—produces chemicals that, when eaten in bread made from the infected grains, can cause ergotism, an illness whose symptoms include cramps, spasms, and a form of gangrene.

• Cigarette smoke can spread the plant disease tobacco mosaic. Smokers should not smoke in the garden or near plants and should wash their hands before handling plants.

Eggplants

• **Glad Trash Bags.** Protect young eggplant plants from flea beetles by slicing open the sides of black Glad Trash Bags to make long sheets and placing the black plastic on plant beds as mulch. Secure the plastic in place with stones, and cut slits into the plastic to accommodate transplants. The radiant heat created by the plastic warms the soil an additional 3 degrees Fahrenheit. You can roll up the plastic sheets and reuse them the following year. Be certain to water beneath the impermeable plastic sheet with a drip line or soaker hose.

• **Goodyear Tires.** To protect eggplants in your garden, lay Goodyear Tires on the ground and plant eggplants inside them. The tires will shelter the sprouting plants from the wind, and the dark rubber will absorb heat from the sun and warm the soil.

• **Hula Hoops, Bubble Wrap**, and **Scotch Packaging Tape.** Building row covers can stop flea beetles that spread viruses from infecting your eggplants. Make hoop supports by cutting Hula Hoops in half and inserting the legs firmly into the soil. Cover with a canopy made from sheets of Bubble Wrap and secure to the hoops with Scotch Packaging Tape, making sure the sheets of Bubble Wrap are high enough not to touch the plants. You can also secure the Bubble Wrap by staking the ends to the ground with wire. At the end of the season, roll up the Bubble Wrap to be used again the following year. (Be sure to monitor the temperatures inside this minigreenhouse to make certain you do not burn out your plants, or substitute sheer curtains for the Bubble Wrap.)

• **L'eggs Sheer Energy Panty Hose** and **Oral-B Mint Waxed Floss.** To prevent insects, birds, squirrels, or raccoons from destroying growing eggplants, cut off the feet from a clean, used pair of L'eggs Sheer Energy Panty Hose, slip a foot over the eggplant, and seal the open end closed with a piece of Oral-B Mint Waxed Floss. The synthetic fibers keep pests away, and the flexible hose expands as the eggplant grows. You can also cut a section from a leg of the panty hose, tie one end closed with dental floss, cover the eggplant, and then secure the open end shut.

• **Reynolds Wrap.** After planting eggplant seedlings, wrap each stem loosely with a four-inch tube of Reynolds Wrap, giving the seedling room to grow. Push the bottom two inches of the foil into the soil. The foil tube will protect the eggplant from cutworms.

STRANGE FACTS

• Eggplants, named after the fact that the vegetable is shaped like a purple egg, were once thought to be poisonous and can grow almost to the size of a football.

• In the United Kingdom, eggplants are called aubergines. The French word *aubergine* comes from the Catalan word *albergínia*, derived from the Arabic word *al-badhinjan*.

• For Asian cuisine, the small Chinese eggplant is usually cooked with tofu.

• 'Neon' is a variety of eggplant with a hot pink hue.

• 'Ghostbuster' is a variety of eggplant that bears oval fruit with white skin.

The Spin on Hula Hoops

Children in ancient Egypt played with hoops made from dried grapevines and other plants by rolling and throwing them or twirling them around their waists and limbs. Over time, these hoops became wood or metal.

In 1957, an Australian visiting California told Richard Knerr and Arthur "Spud" Melin, founders of the Wham-O Company, that Australian children twirled bamboo hoops around their waists in gym class. Knerr and Melin, envisioning the popularity of such a toy in America, created a hollow plastic prototype and tested it on local schoolchildren, winning enthusiastic approval.

The following year, Wham-O began marketing the Hula Hoop, named after the Hawaiian dance its users seemed to imitate by gyrating their hips to keep the hoop rotating around their waists. Wham-O sold twenty-five million brightly colored plastic hoops within two months, creating a national craze.

• In ancient Greece, physicians recommended hoop twirling to adults to lose weight.

• In the fourteenth century, English doctors denounced hoop twirling as a cause of sprains, dislocated backs, and heart attacks.

• South American cultures made hoops from sugarcane plants.

• The hula was originally a religious dance performed by Hawaiians to promote fertility.

• Wham-O, unable to patent an ancient toy, reinvented the hoop for the modern world by using Marlex, a lightweight plastic invented by Phillips Petroleum.

• On the television series *Batman*, Vincent Price played Egghead, the smartest villain in the world (with an egg-shaped head), whose vocabulary included such exclamatories as "eggstraordinary," "eggceptional," and "eggciting."

• 'Ichiban' is a variety of eggplant that bears thin, foot-long fruit with deep purple skin.

• The 'Slim Jim' variety of eggplant grows clusters of lavender fruit the size of peanuts.

• In 1984, J. & J. Charles of Summerville, South Carolina, grew the largest recorded eggplant in United States history, weighing 5 pounds, 5.4 ounces.

• The 'Easter Egg' variety of eggplant bears ivory-colored fruit about two inches long that looks exactly like a chicken's eggs.

Fertilizer

• **Aunt Jemima Original Syrup.** Revive an ailing plant by adding two tablespoons Aunt Jemima Original Syrup at the root of the plant once a month.

• **Budweiser.** Dilute one part Budweiser beer to two parts water and pour this mixture into the soil around azaleas, shrubs, and ornamental grasses to enrich the soil.

• **Budweiser, Epsom Salt, Ivory Dishwashing Liquid,** and **Listerine.** Mix one cup Budweiser, one cup Epsom Salt, one cup Ivory Dishwashing Liquid, and one cup Listerine in a one-quart jar. Spray this on up to 2,500 square feet of lawn with a hose-attached sprayer in May and again in late June.

• **Clorox.** Create a handy fertilizer scooper by capping an empty, clean Clorox Bleach jug and cutting it diagonally across the bottom.

• **Epsom Salt.** For every foot of a plant's height, sprinkle one teaspoon Epsom Salt evenly around the plant's base for better blossoms and deeper greening. Adding Epsom Salt to any plant food will also enrich the color of any flowering plants and aid in disease resistance. Or mix one tablespoon Epsom Salt in one gallon water and spray the mixture on the plant. Epsom Salt is magnesium sulfate, which lowers the pH of the soil and provides magnesium.

• **Gatorade.** Watering plants with Gatorade adds potassium to the soil and the sugar feeds microorganisms, adding nitrogen.

• **Geritol.** Revive an ailing plant by giving the plant two tablespoons Geritol twice a week for three months. New leaves should begin to grow within the first month.

• **Grandma's Molasses** and **L'eggs Sheer Energy Panty Hose.** Fill one-quarter of a five-gallon bucket with compost, fill the bucket with water, and add one tablespoon Grandma's Molasses. Let stand for two to four days. Strain this solution through a clean, used pair of L'eggs Sheer Energy Panty Hose. Dilute the solution with water until it's the color of iced tea, then apply to plants.

• **Jell-O.** To give plants additional nitrogen, mix an envelope of powdered Jell-O into one cup of boiling water, stir until the gelatin powder dissolves, mix with three cups cold water, then apply around the base of the plant.

• **Jell-O.** Boost liquid fertilizer by adding one teaspoon powdered Jell-O (any flavor) to one gallon liquid fertilizer or compost tea. Mix well and use immediately (to avoid coagulation) by pouring directly on the soil.

• **Kellogg's Frosted Mini-Wheats.** Add leftover crumbs from cereal boxes such as Kellogg's Frosted Mini-Wheats to your garden soil or planter mix. The sugar feeds microorganisms, adding nitrogen to the soil, and the cereal adds potassium and other nutrients.

• **L'eggs Sheer Energy Panty Hose.** Cut apart the legs from a pair of used, clean L'eggs Sheer Energy Panty Hose. Place the first leg inside the second leg, then fill with finished compost, tie a knot in the open end, and place in a barrel of water. Let compost tea steep for one week, then apply the liquid to your plants.

• **L'eggs Sheer Energy Panty Hose.** Strain fertilizer mixtures through a clean, used pair of L'eggs Sheer Energy Panty Hose to remove debris and avoid clogging your sprayer.

- **Lipton Tea Bags.** Put Lipton Tea Bags (new or used) on the soil around plants in garden beds and planters. Cover the tea bags with mulch. Every time you water the plants, the nutrients from the decomposing tea leaves work their way into the soil.

- **Maxwell House Coffee.** Maxwell House Coffee grounds are full of nutrients that plants love. Instead of throwing out the used coffee grounds after you make a pot of coffee, give them to your houseplants and plants in the garden. Just work the grounds into the soil. It may keep them up all night, but you can always use the decaf. If you're really ambitious, you can also use Maxwell House Coffee grounds to fertilize your entire lawn.

- **Maxwell House Coffee.** To spread granular fertilizer, punch holes in the bottom of an empty can of Maxwell House Coffee with a hammer and a punch, fill with fertilizer, cover with the plastic lid, and shake the can as you walk through your garden.

- **Nestea.** Mix up a quart of unsweetened Nestea instant iced tea according to the directions (without adding sugar or ice) and fertilize plants with the solution. Or simply sprinkle the powdered mix directly on the soil. As the tea decomposes, the nutrients work their way into the soil.

- **Star Olive Oil.** Add two tablespoons Star Olive Oil to the bases of ferns or palm plants once a month.

- **Tide.** Cut off the top of an empty, clean liquid Tide bottle just above the handle to make a heavy-duty scooper for fertilizer.

- *USA Today.* Help the earthworms living in the soil create natural fertilizer by giving them a food they love. Place six to eight sheets of *USA Today* on the soil and cover with a layer of mulch.

STRANGE FACTS

- People used fertilizers for thousands of years before they understood how fertilizers work. They observed that plants thrived when scattered with animal droppings, wood ashes, and certain minerals.

• Long before the advent of synthetic fertilizers, gardeners collected ashes from their fireplaces and worked them into the soil a few weeks before planting. Hardwood ash contains roughly 40 percent potash, a plant nutrient.

• Gardeners in New England plowed seaweed into the soil so the high salt content would kill weeds and speed up decomposition.

• Peruvians imported guano as fertilizer. The bird and bat excrement contains 10 percent nitrogen and 10 percent phosphorus. When Carlsbad Caverns was discovered in New Mexico, 100,000 tons of bat guano was mined from the caves (and shipped to Peru).

• In the late nineteenth century, gardeners would fill a one-hundred-pound burlap sack with cow, horse, and chicken manure, then let it soak in a sixty-gallon steel drum of water for four to six weeks. They used the resulting "manure tea" as liquid fertilizer for plants.

• Melting snow actually helps fertilize plants by supplying nitrogen compounds and minerals acquired as the snow fell through the atmosphere.

• An old Chinese proverb states: "The best fertilizer in the garden may be the gardener's own shadow." In other words, daily attention to plants is better than artificial additives.

• The United States manufactures more fertilizer than any other country in the world, producing more than 5.5 billion dollars' worth of fertilizer every year.

• Green plants require large amounts of nine chemical elements to photosynthesize the food they need. The elements most frequently deficient in the soil are nitrogen, phosphorus, and potassium.

• In the fall of 1999, when engineers at a sanitation plant in Los Angeles cycled the power off and on to conduct a Y2K readiness test, a valve defaulted to its open position, causing millions of gallons of raw sewage to spill into Balboa Park in Encino.

• Clairol introduced its Mist Stick curling iron in Germany only to discover that in German the word *mist* is slang for manure.

Flowers

- **Bubble Wrap.** Help prevent potted perennials from freezing in the winter by lining the inside of the planter with Bubble Wrap before planting. To allow for drainage, do not line the bottom of the planter.

- **Epsom Salt.** For every foot of a plant's height, sprinkle one teaspoon Epsom Salt evenly around the plant's base for better blossoms and deeper greening. Adding Epsom Salt to plant food will also enrich the color of flowering plants and aid in disease-resistance. Or mix one tablespoon Epsom Salt in one gallon water and spray the mixture on the plant. Epsom Salt is magnesium sulfate, which lowers the pH of the soil and provides magnesium.

- **Forster Clothes Pins.** When cutting flowers or pruning, use a Forster Clothes Pin as a clamp to hold the stems of thorny plants to avoid pricking your fingers.

- **Glad Trash Bags.** To get rid of the fungi causing rust spots on the leaves of geraniums, place the geranium plant inside a Glad Trash Bag, and set outside in the full sunlight for a few hours. The temperature inside the bag will quickly reach 90 degrees Fahrenheit, killing the fungi.

- **Gold Medal Flour, French's Mustard**, and **McCormick Ground (Cayenne) Red Pepper.** To keep cats away from flowerbeds, dissolve two tablespoons Gold Medal Flour, two tablespoons French's Mustard, one tablespoon McCormick Ground Red Pepper, and two cups water in a sixteen-ounce trigger-spray bottle. Shake well and spray around flowerbeds.

- **Heinz White Vinegar.** To prevent cats from getting into your flowerbeds, fill a trigger-spray bottle with Heinz White Vinegar and spray around the border of the garden. The smell of vinegar repulses cats and neutralizes the smell of cat urine used to mark their territory.

- **Heinz White Vinegar.** To grow beautiful azaleas, camellias, cardinal flowers, gardenias, heather, and rhododendrons, occasionally water these acid-loving plants with a mixture of two tablespoons Heinz White Vinegar to one quart water.

- **Kodak 35mm Film.** Take photographs of your flowerbeds every two weeks to make a visual record of when each type of flower in your garden blooms. Using the photographs, you can better plan future plantings. Be sure to label your photographs with the dates and types of flowers.

- **L'eggs Sheer Energy Panty Hose.** Using a pair of scissors, cut off the toe from the foot of a pair of used, clean L'eggs Sheer Energy Panty Hose, then cut one-inch strips from the leg, creating circular loops of panty hose. Use the loops to gently tie stems, vines, and thin plant trunks to stakes with a figure-eight loop.

- **Lipton Tea Bags.** Place Lipton Tea Bags (new or used) on the soil around plants in flowerbeds. Cover the tea bags with mulch. Every time you water the plants, the nutrients from the decomposing tea leaves work their way into the soil.

- **Maxwell House Coffee.** Fertilize azaleas, camellias, cardinal flowers, gardenias, heather, and rhododendrons with Maxwell House Coffee grounds by working used grounds around the bases of these acid-loving plants once a month.

- **McCormick Ground Cinnamon.** Fight mold, mildew, and mushrooms around peonies by lightly dusting McCormick Ground Cinnamon around each plant. Cinnamon contains a natural fungicide—ortho-methoxycinnamaldehyde—that prevents the growth of fungi. (For more ways to combat mildew, see page 177.)

• **Nestea.** Mix up a quart of unsweetened Nestea instant iced tea according to the directions (without adding sugar or ice) and fertilize your flowerbeds with the solution. Or simply sprinkle the powdered mix directly on the soil. As the tea decomposes, the nutrients work their way into the soil.

• **S.O.S Steel Wool Soap Pads.** Grow African violets with larger, more colorful blossoms by planting a few used S.O.S Steel Wool Soap Pads in the potting mix around the plant to give the violets more iron. Water slowly breaks down the steel pads (made from iron filaments), giving the violets the essential iron they need to flourish.

• **Tabasco Pepper Sauce, McCormick Chili Powder,** and **Ivory Dishwashing Liquid.** To prevent squirrels or chipmunks from devouring tulips or rhododendron buds in the spring, mix three teaspoons Tabasco Pepper Sauce, one teaspoon McCormick Chili Powder, one-half teaspoon Ivory Dishwashing Liquid, and two cups water in a sixteen-ounce trigger-spray bottle. Spray the solution into the soil around the tulip or rhododendron beds.

• *USA Today.* To protect the roots of orchids (*Bletilla striata* and *Pleione*) during the winter, place sheets of *USA Today* over the beds and cover with four inches of soil.

• **Ziploc Freezer Bags** and **Tupperware.** Store bareroot perennials by filling Ziploc Freezer Bags with soil and placing one bareroot perennial in each bag. Water each bag and store the bags open (to prevent mold) in an open Tupperware box. Be sure to label each bag with an indelible marker.

STRANGE FACTS

• An annual lives for one season, growing rapidly and blooming with color for the duration of its short lifetime. A perennial lives for years but only blooms for short periods during the year. A biennial blooms in its second year, sets seed, and dies.

• In Greek mythology, Zephyr, the West Wind, killed Hyacinth, the son of the king of Sparta. Apollo, the sun god, bereaved by the death of his friend, gave Hyacinth immortality by turning him into the flower that bears his name to this very day.

• Fear of flowers is called *anthophobia*.

• In Greek mythology, the young and noble shepherd boy Crocus fell deeply in love with the nymph Smilax. The gods granted the couple immortality by turning Crocus into a flower and Smilax into an evergreen—the yew.

• In 1828, Joel Roberts Poinsett, the first United States Ambassador to Mexico, brought a Mexican plant with small yellow flowers surrounded by larger red and green leaves (*Euphorbia pulcherrima*) to the United States. The plant, called "flower of

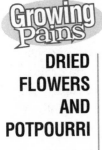

DRIED FLOWERS AND POTPOURRI

✗ **Forster Clothes Pins** and **Oral-B Mint Waxed Floss.** To dry flowers, bundle the flowers together loosely with Oral-B Mint Waxed Floss, then clip the bundled flowers to an indoor clothesline with Forster Clothes Pins.

✗ **Mr. Coffee Filters.** To press flowers dry, place a Mr. Coffee Filter flat on an eight-inch square of thin fiberboard, lay a flat flower or a bud on the filter, lay a second coffee filter flat on top of the flower, and then place a second fiberboard square on top. Secure the boards closed by placing them in a flower press and tightening the screws on all four corners. Let set for one week, then frame the pressed flower.

✗ **Morton Salt.** To make moist potpourri for filling sachets, place a layer of appropriate flowers in the bottom of a glass bowl. Cover the flowers with coarse Morton Salt. Place a second layer of flowers on top of the salt, and cover with more salt. Repeat until you have used all your flowers. Cover the top layer of salt with a flat dish and place a weight on top of it. Set the bowl in a dry place undisturbed for approximately three weeks or until the salt thickens into the consistency of cake. Add essential oils and fixative (if desired) and mix with a wooden spoon. Cover the bowl and store in a cool dark place for six months to age the potpourri.

✗ **Reynolds Cut-Rite Wax Paper.** Preserve autumn leaves by placing the leaves between two sheets of the blessed night" (because it resembled the Star of Bethlehem), was renamed in honor of Poinsett and quickly became a popular decoration for Christmas. If eaten, the leaves and stems of the poinsettia can cause abdominal cramps.

• In 1850, French novelist Alexandre Dumas, author of *The Count of Monte Cristo*, *The Three Musketeers*, and *The Man in the Iron Mask*, published his novel *The Black Tulip*, a romantic tale that created popular fervor for the fictional black tulip.

• In Lewis Carroll's 1872 children's book *Through the Looking Glass*, when Alice asks why she has never heard flowers talk in other gardens, the Tiger-lily replies, "In most gardens they make the beds too soft—so that the flowers are always asleep."

Reynolds Cut-Rite Wax Paper, then placing the wax paper between two sheets of brown paper and pressing with a warm iron to seal. Trim the paper around the leaves.

✗ **20 Mule Team Borax, Albers Corn Meal,** and **Tupperware.** To preserve flowers, mix together one part 20 Mule Team Borax and two parts Albers Corn Meal. Fill the bottom inch of an empty airtight Tupperware canister with the mixture. Place the flowers on the mixture, then gently cover the flowers with more mixture, being careful not to crush the flowers or distort the petals. Flowers with a lot of overlapping petals, such as roses and carnations, are best treated by sprinkling the mixture directly into the blossoms before placing them into the box. Seal the canister and store at room temperature in a dry place for seven to ten days. When the flowers are dried, pour off the mixture and dust the flowers with a soft artist's brush. Borax removes the moisture from blossoms and leaves, preventing wilting.

✗ **Ziploc Storage Bags.** To make potpourri, collect dried roses, juniper sprigs, tiny pinecones, strips of orange rind, bay leaves, cinnamon sticks, whole cloves, and allspice berries. Mix a few drops of rose, cinnamon, and balsam oils with orrisroot (available at your local crafts store). Add all ingredients and seal in a Ziploc Storage Bag for a few weeks to mellow, turning the bag occasionally.

• "Poppies! Poppies will make them sleep!" chants the Wicked Witch of the West in the 1939 movie classic *The Wizard of Oz*, as she casts a spell over a field of flowers. In the book, *The Wonderful Wizard of Oz*, written by L. Frank Baum in 1900, thousands of field mice pull the Cowardly Lion out of the Deadly Poppy Field. In the movie, Glinda—the Good Witch of the North—saves Dorothy, Toto, and the Lion by smothering the deadly scent of the poppies with snow.

• Former Beatle George Harrison dedicated his 1980 book *I, Me, Mine* to "gardeners everywhere." In the book, he wrote, "I'm a gardener. I plant flowers and watch them grow. I don't go out to clubs and partying. I stay at home and watch the river flow." The booklet to his 2002 posthumous album *Brainwashed* includes a photograph of his garden of topiaries.

• In 1992, Gennifer Flowers, a former Nevada lounge singer, told *The Star*, a supermarket tabloid, that she had a twelve-year affair with President Bill Clinton while he was governor of Arkansas. When Clinton denied the accusations, Flowers held a news conference to play audio tapes of intimate telephone conversations between them that she claimed to have secretly recorded.

• The flowers of the 'Envy' zinnia bloom with nearly iridescent yellow-green petals.

• The flowers of *Cosmos atrosanguineus* exude the scent of cocoa.

• In Jamaica and other islands in the West Indies, the sap from the petals of hibiscus flowers is used as shoe polish.

• Hydrangeas grow blue flowers in acid soil and pink flowers in alkaline soil. (White varieties of hydrangeas remain white in both types of soil.)

• The seeds, flowers, and foliage of oleander are toxic if eaten.

• The *Grammatophyllum speciosum*, an orchid native to Malaysia, grows up to twenty-five feet tall.

• The flowers of the orchid *Paphiopedilum sanderianum* have petals that reportedly grow up to three feet long in the wild.

- On Mount Japfu in Nagaland, India, the scarlet rhododendron grows up to sixty-five feet tall.

- Carnations, daylilies, marigolds, nasturtiums, pansies, roses, and violets are all edible flowers.

Partying with Tupperware

In 1936, after twenty-nine-year-old Massachusetts tree surgeon and landscaper Earl Silas Tupper went bankrupt, he found a job at Viscoloid, DuPont's plastics division in Leominster, Massachusetts. After one year, Tupper took his newly acquired design, research, development, and manufacturing experience and founded his own plastics company. The Earl S. Tupper Company, at first a subcontractor for DuPont, began making gas masks and other equipment for American troops during World War II. After the war, Tupper invented a method to transform polyethylene slag (a black, smelly by-product of the crude oil refinement process) into a clean, clear, and translucent plastic that was pliant, solid, and grease-free—a vast improvement over the brittle, slimy, and putrid plastics of the day. Tupper also developed an airtight and watertight seal for containers made of his improved plastic, creating Tupperware—the plastic storage container that still bears his name.

By 1946, Tupper was marketing a wide range of brightly colored Tupperware, but sales were disappointing. In 1948, Tupper learned that two Stanley Home Products salespeople were selling large quantities of his Tupperware. Stanley salespeople, he discovered, introduced their products to homemakers assembled at an in-home sales party. Recalling his own success as a door-to-door salesman as a youth, Tupper teamed up with several Stanley distributors to market Tupperware exclusively through Tupperware Parties. By 1954, sales exceeded 25 million dollars. Nine thousand dealers nationwide were arranging Tupperware parties in the homes of housewives who agreed to host the events in exchange for free Tupperware gifts. Tupperware Parties had become a national phenomenon, firmly establishing Tupperware as an American icon.

- As a boy, Earl Tupper sold poultry and produce door-to-door.
- The lid and bowl of Tupperware containers lock together with the signature Tupperware "burp."
- The October 1947 issue of *House Beautiful* called Tupperware "Fine Art for 39 Cents."
- In 1958, Earl Tupper sold Tupperware Home Parties, Inc., to Rexall Drugs for sixteen million dollars. Tupper became a citizen of Costa Rica, where he died in 1983.
- In a 1998 radio address, President Bill Clinton called gun shows "Tupperware parties for criminals."

Fruit Trees

- **Con-Tact Paper.** Fold a long piece of Con-Tact Paper in half, with the sticky side out, and wrap it around the bases of fruit trees to prevent ants from being able to climb up the trees and reach the fruit.

- **Heinz Apple Cider Vinegar.** To cure fire blight on apple trees, mix equal parts Heinz Apple Cider Vinegar and water in a trigger-spray bottle and mist affected leaves with the acidic solution. Blight is acid-intolerant.

- **Heinz Apple Cider Vinegar** and **Grandma's Molasses.** To prevent coddling moths from destroying ripening apple trees, mix one quart Heinz Apple Cider Vinegar and four ounces Grandma's Molasses in a blender, fill clean, empty soda cans with the solution, and then hang the cans from tree branches. The moths, attracted to the sweet solution, drown in it.

- **L'eggs Sheer Energy Panty Hose.** To make a net basket to pick fruits from high branches, use a pair of pliers to cut apart a wire clothes hanger, form a hoop approximately six inches in diameter, and attach the wire loop to the end of a ten-foot-long wooden pole. Cut off an entire leg from a pair of used, clean L'eggs Sheer Energy Panty Hose, stretch the open end of the leg around the hoop, and sew it in place.

• **L'eggs Sheer Energy Panty Hose** and **Oral-B Mint Waxed Floss.** To prevent animal pests from destroying growing fruits, cut off the feet from a clean, used pair of L'eggs Sheer Energy Panty Hose, slip a foot over an apple, pear, or mango, and seal the open end closed with a piece of Oral-B Mint Waxed Floss. The synthetic fibers keep birds, rodents, squirrels, and raccoons away, and the flexible hose expands as the fruit grows. You can also cut a section from a leg of the panty hose, tie one end closed with dental floss, cover the fruit, and then secure the open end shut.

• **Listerine.** Protect fruit trees from insects by pouring one-quarter cup Listerine into clean, empty, plastic gallon jugs suspended from branches. The scent from the Listerine repels the insects. Cease using this method after blossoms bloom to avoid chasing away pollinating bees.

• **Maxwell House Coffee** and **Bubble Wrap.** To make a fruit picker, use a pair of tin snips to carefully cut a V shape (approximately one inch tall) into the top rim of a clean, used Maxwell House Coffee can. With a pair of pliers, carefully bend the pointed corners slightly inward so that when you pick fruit with the can, the bent sides will hold the fruit in the can. Drill two one-quarter-inch holes in the opposite side of the can and drill similar holes in the end of a six-foot-long piece of pine (two inches by three-quarters inch). Wire the can to the wooden pole. Cut two or three pieces of Bubble Wrap to sit at the bottom of the can as a cushion for the picked fruit.

• **Q-Tips Cotton Swabs.** To guarantee a more ample harvest of peaches (or make up for a lack of pollinating insects during a wet or chilly spring), hand-pollinate peach blossoms by using a Q-Tips Cotton Swab to swipe the male flower's anthers and brush the pollen onto the central stigma of the female flower.

• **Reynolds Wrap** and **Oral-B Mint Waxed Floss.** To chase birds away from fruit trees, cut circles or star shapes from cardboard, wrap the cardboard cutouts in Reynolds Wrap, punch a hole through each shape, and then hang the glittering shapes from fruit trees with a loop of Oral-B Mint Waxed Floss strung through each hole. The sunlight, reflecting from the silvery shapes, frightens away birds.

• **Scotch Packaging Tape.** Wrap strips of Scotch Packaging Tape inside out around the bases of fruit trees to prevent ants from being able to climb up the trees and reach the fruit.

• **Slinky.** Scare birds away from fruit trees by hanging Slinky Juniors from their branches. The sunlight, reflecting from the silvery coils, frightens away birds.

• **Tabasco Pepper Sauce, McCormick Chili Powder,** and **Ivory Dishwashing Liquid.** To prevent mice from nibbling the bark of tender young fruit trees, mix three teaspoons Tabasco Pepper Sauce, one teaspoon McCormick Chili Powder, one-half teaspoon Ivory Dishwashing Liquid, and two cups water in a sixteen-ounce trigger-spray bottle. Spray the solution into the soil around the young trees.

• **Wilson Tennis Balls** and **Vaseline Petroleum Jelly.** To kill codling moths or the flies that lay apple maggot eggs, use an electric drill with a one-eighth-inch bit to drill a hole in several Wilson Tennis Balls. Screw an eye hook into the hole in each ball, spray-paint the balls red, coat each ball with Vaseline Petroleum Jelly, loop a piece of wire through each eye hook, and hang the balls in fruit trees. The moths and flies, lured to the fake fruit, get stuck in the gooey petroleum jelly and die. (Also see Ziploc Storage Bags below.)

• **Ziploc Freezer Bags.** To spur a fruit tree to bud fruit faster, fill Ziploc Freezer Bags with sand and hang them on the fruit tree's branches as weights to bend the branches down to approximately a 60-degree angle. The bent branches inhibit the growth of foliage, prompting the tree to rechannel that energy to grow fruit buds.

• **Ziploc Storage Bags.** To make the process of killing codling moths or the flies that lay apple maggot eggs less messy (see

Wilson Tennis Balls on page 92), place a Ziploc Storage Bag around the red ball and coat the plastic bag (instead of the ball) with the Vaseline Petroleum Jelly. This way, when the bags get coated with bugs, you can simply replace the bags.

• **Ziploc Storage Bags.** To store apples for months, punch a few holes in a Ziploc Storage Bag, place the fruit in the bag, and store in the refrigerator a few degrees above freezing.

• **Ziploc Storage Bags.** To prevent plum curculios from laying eggs on apples or to protect figs from frost, place a Ziploc Storage Bag over each young marble-sized fruit and staple it closed near the stem, enabling air to get in and moisture to get out.

STRANGE FACTS

• In 1753, Scottish naval surgeon James Lind, having discovered that citrus fruit prevents scurvy, published his findings in his *Treatise of the Scurvy*, urging the British Admiralty to add citrus juice to the naval diet. The British navy ignored Lind's prescription for forty-two years.

• The custom of giving an apple to the teacher originated in the days when the local community paid public school teachers whatever they could afford, frequently giving the teacher food or goods in lieu of cash.

• In 1964, the Kellogg Company and the Post Cereal Company, eager to cash in on the concept of freeze-dried foods popularized by the space program, added freeze-dried fruits to their cornflake cereals. However, consumers quickly discovered that the pieces of freeze-dried fruit in the cornflakes had to soak in milk for nearly ten minutes before they reconstituted, by which time the cornflakes were soggy and unappetizing.

• In 1965, V. Loveridge of Ross-o-Wye, Great Britain, grew the largest recorded apple in history, weighing three pounds, one ounce.

• According to historian Doris Kearns Goodwin, President Lyndon Johnson's passion for the grapefruit-flavored soda Fresca prompted him to have a soda fountain installed in the Oval Office that he could operate by pushing a button on his desk chair.

• Between 1978 and 1982, Beech-Nut executives—determined to save the company an estimated 250,000 dollars a year and boost profits—arranged for all bottles labeled Beech-Nut "100 percent" pure apple juice, consumed by babies, to be filled with a mixture of water and a bogus apple juice concentrate made solely from sugar and flavorings. After a trade association exposed this abhorrent fraud, the United States government fined Beech-Nut two million dollars for 215 violations of the Food, Drug, and Cosmetic Act. A criminal court sentenced former Beech-Nut president Niels Hoyvald and vice president John Lavery to one year in jail and fined each man 100,000 dollars.

• In 1984, J. and A. Sosnow of Tucson, Arizona, grew the largest recorded grapefruit in history, weighing 6 pounds, 8.5 ounces.

• The study of fruit is called pomology, a word derived from the Latin word *pomum*, meaning "fruit."

• In 1986, Silo, a discount electronics store chain, ran a television commercial in Seattle, Washington, and El Paso, Texas, offering a stereo system for "299 bananas." Dozens of customers lined up outside the stores with bags of bananas—compelling Silo to honor the offer, losing 10,465 dollars.

Growing Pains

WASHING FRUITS AND VEGETABLES

✗ **Arm & Hammer Baking Soda.** To clean pesticides and insects from fruits, wet the fruits and sprinkle them with a little Arm & Hammer Baking Soda, then rinse well.

✗ **Heinz White Vinegar.** To wash pesticides and insects from fruits, fill your kitchen sink with cold water, add three-quarters cup Heinz White Vinegar, and soak the fruits in the solution for five minutes. Then rinse clean with cold water.

Fungus

• **Arm & Hammer Baking Soda** and **Wesson Corn Oil.** To prevent fungal diseases like black spot and powdery mildew, mix one teaspoon Arm & Hammer Baking Soda and five drops Wesson Corn Oil in one quart water. Fill a trigger-spray bottle with the mixture and spray directly on the leaves of roses, houseplants, and cucurbit crops. Apply once a week for approximately two months. Reapply after rain. The USDA has approved baking soda as a fungicide. (Before treating the entire plant, test this oily formula on one of the plant's leaves and wait one day to make certain it doesn't burn the leaf.)

• **Arm & Hammer Baking Soda** and **Wesson Corn Oil.** To kill the rhizoctonia fungi that cause brownpatch (brown or yellow rings or patches of dead grass on your lawn), mix one tablespoon Arm & Hammer Baking Soda, one tablespoon Wesson Corn Oil, and one gallon water. Spray a light mist of the solution on your lawn, in addition to correcting any drainage problems and checking to make sure your fertilizer does not contain excess nitrogen. Consider aerating your lawn and adding a half-inch layer of compost. Compost contains the microbe trichoderma, which feeds on the rhizoctonia fungi.

• **Cascade**. To avoid spreading fungal diseases when transplanting seedlings or plants into pots, clean pots and flats thoroughly by soaking them for ten minutes in a bathtub filled with warm water and one tablespoon Cascade dishwashing powder, then scrubbing the pots in the solution with a stiff brush. Rinse clean and let the pots dry thoroughly in the sun.

• **Clorox**. Sterilize your pruning tools with a mixture of three-quarters cup Clorox Bleach in a gallon of water after each use to avoid spreading fungal diseases. Dip your pruning equipment into the disinfectant solution between cuts or at least between plants. When finished, soak the pruning shears in the solution for one hour, then rinse clean and dry.

• **Glad Trash Bags**. To get rid of the fungi causing rust spots on the leaves of geraniums, place the geranium plant inside a Glad Trash Bag, and set outside in the full sunlight for a few hours. The temperature inside the bag will quickly reach 90 degrees Fahrenheit, killing the fungi.

• **Grandma's Molasses**. Fight fungal diseases by dissolving one cup Grandma's Molasses in one gallon warm water in a bucket. Fill a trigger-spray bottle, small pressure sprayer, or pump sprayer with the solution and spray infected plants. The plants quickly absorb the molasses, which contains sugar to feed the plants and sulfur to kill the fungi.

• **Hydrogen Peroxide**. To prevent damping-off from killing seedlings, spray the affected part of the plants with a mixture of equal parts hydrogen peroxide and water.

• **Jell-O**. Fight off fungal diseases by adding one teaspoon powdered Jell-O (any flavor) to the soil of houseplants and covering the Jell-O with a light coat of soil. The gelatin helps the plants retain water, the nitrogen in Jell-O enhances plant growth, and the sugar feeds the microbes in the soil, producing more nutrients for the plant.

- **Listerine.** To avoid spreading fungal diseases, sterilize your pruning tools with Listerine after each use. In a bucket, mix one cup Listerine per gallon of water, and dip your pruning equipment into the antiseptic solution between cuts or at least between plants. When finished, soak the pruning shears in the solution for one hour, then rinse clean and dry.

- **McCormick Ground Cinnamon.** Fight mold, mildew, and mushrooms around peonies by lightly dusting McCormick Ground Cinnamon around each plant. Cinnamon contains a natural fungicide—ortho-methoxycinnamaldehyde—that prevents the growth of fungi.

- **Purell.** Disinfect pruning tools by coating the blades with Purell Instant Hand Sanitizer. The ethyl alcohol in Purell kills bacteria and fungi.

- **Reynolds Wrap.** Deter fungal diseases on squash or tomato plants by spreading sheets of Reynolds Wrap as mulch on the soil bed surrounding the plants. Check the plants daily to make sure the aluminum foil is not reflecting too much light back onto the plant, burning it.

- **Smirnoff Vodka.** Sterilize your pruning tools after each use with a mixture of two cups Smirnoff Vodka per gallon of water to avoid spreading fungal diseases. Dip your pruning tools into the alcohol solution between cuts or at least between plants. When finished, soak the pruning shears in the solution for one hour, then rinse clean and dry.

- **Star Olive Oil** and **Dr. Bronner's Peppermint Soap.** Prevent fungal diseases from attacking shiny-leaved fruit trees, vegetables, and flowers by mixing one teaspoon Star Olive Oil, one teaspoon Dr. Bronner's Peppermint Soap, and one gallon water in a bucket. Fill a trigger-spray bottle, small pressure sprayer, or pump sprayer with the solution and spray a fine mist on plant leaves early every morning for a week, then once a week, then once a month. Do not use this oil spray when the temperature goes below 32 degrees or above 85 degrees Fahrenheit. Before treating the entire plant, test this oil formula on one of the plant's leaves and wait one day to make certain it doesn't burn the leaf.

• **Tabasco Pepper Sauce, McCormick Garlic Powder,** and **Ivory Dishwashing Liquid.** Mix one-half teaspoon Tabasco Pepper Sauce, one-half teaspoon McCormick Garlic Powder, one drop Ivory Dishwashing Liquid, and two cups water in a sixteen-ounce trigger-spray bottle. Lightly mist any plants evidencing early symptoms of fungal disease (leaves with white powder, curling, or unusual patterns).

STRANGE FACTS

• In 1993, Montana chemists Don and Andrea Stierle found an alternative source for taxol, an expensive cancer-fighting chemical derived from yew trees. The source? A common unnamed tree fungus that produces taxol in minuscule quantities. Andrea named the fungus *Taxomyces andreanae,* and the University of

The Ancestry of Grandma's Molasses

Grandma's Original Molasses is made from 100 percent pure, natural sugarcane juices—clarified, reduced, and blended to achieve the right color and consistency (without any sugar extraction). Made from sugarcane grown in the West Indies, Grandma's Original Molasses is the only molasses made from premium quality, imported sugarcane.

• Americans used molasses, which was less expensive than sugar, as their principal sweetener until after World War I, when sugar prices plummeted.

• The founders of the colony of Georgia gave sixty-four quarts of molasses to each man, woman, and child who had settled in Georgia for one year.

• In England, any candy made of molasses was called toffee, which evolved into taffy in the American colonies.

• Rum is fermented principally from molasses. Before the Revolutionary War, the average American colonist drank four gallons of rum a year.

• With the Molasses Act of 1733, the British imposed a heavy tax on sugar and molasses imported into the American colonies from parts of the West Indies not under British control. The widespread evasion of this tariff prompted the British to repeal the act in 1764.

• Grandma's Molasses is the number-one brand of molasses in the United States.

Montana licensed it to Cytoclonal Pharmaceutics in Texas, which subsequently licensed it to Bristol-Myers Squibb. The chemical giant has yet to figure out how to trigger the fungus to mass produce taxol.

• Wood ear, a tree fungus used in making moo shu pork, is purportedly a great blood thinner.

• The rich topsoil in California's San Joaquin Valley harbors a fungus, *Coccidioides immitis*, whose dustborne microscopic spores cause "valley fever," a disease known to doctors as coccidioidomycosis. For five years before 1990, doctors reported an average of 450 cases a year. That number tripled to 1,208 in 1991. Two years later, the number skyrocketed to 4,541, with more than fifty estimated deaths—the worst epidemic of valley fever ever recorded.

• No one seems to know the origins of the phrase "There's a fungus among us."

• A specimen of the fungus *Armillaria ostoyae*, originating from a single fertilized spore, covers some 2,200 acres in the Malheur National Forest in eastern Oregon, making it the largest organism in the world.

• The mushroom is a fungus.

Garbage Cans

- **Clorox.** Disinfect garbage cans by washing them with a solution made from three-quarters cup Clorox Bleach to one gallon water. Let stand for five minutes, then rinse clean.

- **Epsom Salt.** Keep raccoons and woodchucks away from garbage cans by sprinkling a few tablespoons of Epsom Salt around the trash bins. Raccoons and woodchucks dislike the taste of Epsom Salt—and it will not harm them.

- **L'eggs Sheer Energy Panty Hose.** To secure plastic garbage bags inside your trash can, cut off the elastic top from a pair of L'eggs Sheer Energy Panty Hose and stretch the extra-large rubber band around the rim of the trash can to hold the lip of the plastic garbage bag in place.

- **McCormick Black Pepper.** Keep dogs, cats, raccoons, and squirrels out of your garbage cans by sprinkling McCormick Black Pepper around the trash bins. All these animals have a keen sense of smell. They smell the pepper and take off for someone else's garbage cans.

• **Tidy Cats.** To deodorize a garbage can, cover the bottom of the bin with one inch of unused Tidy Cats cat litter to absorb grease and moisture.

STRANGE FACTS

• In 1987, entrepreneur H. Wayne Huizenga, cofounder of Waste Management, Inc., the world's largest garbage collection and disposal company, decided to start peddling a different kind of product. For eighteen million dollars, he acquired a controlling interest in Blockbuster. By the end of the year, Huizenga bought out Blockbuster founder David Cook and began acquiring other video chains and converting them into Blockbuster stores. By 1990, Blockbuster had more than 1,500 stores. In 1994, Viacom bought Blockbuster for 7.6 billion dollars. Huizenga left Blockbuster to head Republic Waste Industries, returning to his love for genuine garbage.

• In September 1970, New Yorker A. J. Weberman peeked into the garbage cans sitting outside Bob Dylan's Greenwich Village townhouse, found an unsent letter to Johnny Cash, and began using the trash to write a scathing exposé on Dylan, coining the word "Garbology" and proclaiming himself the world's first "Garbologist." Weberman's 1980 book *My Life in Garbology*, unearths the dirt found in the trash cans of Dylan, Jackie Onassis, Martha Mitchell, Henry Kissinger, David Rockefeller, and Dustin Hoffman.

• Setting a world record, 19,924 volunteers cleaned up Wellington, New Zealand, on October 6, 1991, for the "Keep Wellington Beautiful" campaign.

• On March 19, 2000, Willie Fulgear of Los Angeles found fifty-two missing gold-plated Oscar statuettes in a Dumpster. Fulgear contacted authorities and collected a fifty-thousand-dollar reward for his honesty.

• Before escaped slave Frederick Douglass founded the *North Star*, an antislavery newspaper, and became the leading spokesman for American blacks in the nineteenth century, he worked as a garbage collector.

• To prevent the annual massacre of approximately forty million Christmas trees in the United States and the resulting disposal problems, environmental groups urge people to buy live potted fir trees (that can be planted outside after the holiday season) or reusable artificial trees.

• In French, the word for garbage is *ordures*.

Gardenias

- **Coca-Cola.** Watering gardenias with Classic Coke increases the acidity in the soil, which gardenias love, and boosts plant performance. The sugar in the Coke feeds microorganisms in the soil, increasing the organic matter in the soil.

- **Epsom Salt.** To increase the acidity of the soil, sprinkle a handful of Epsom Salt around gardenia plants.

- **Heinz White Vinegar.** To grow beautiful gardenias, occasionally water plants with a mixture of two tablespoons Heinz White Vinegar to one quart water. Gardenias love acid soil and grow best in soils with a pH below 6.5.

- **L'eggs Sheer Energy Panty Hose.** Using a pair of scissors, cut off the toe from the foot of a pair of used, clean L'eggs Sheer Energy Panty Hose, then cut one-inch strips from the leg, creating circular loops of panty hose. Use the loops to gently tie stems and thin plant trunks to stakes with a figure-eight loop.

- **Lipton Tea Bags.** Put Lipton Tea Bags (new or used) on top of the soil around gardenias and cover with mulch. Every time you water the plants, the nutrients from the decomposing tea leaves work their way into the soil, invigorating the gardenias.

- **Maxwell House Coffee.** Fertilize gardenias with Maxwell House Coffee grounds by working used grounds around the bases of these acid-loving plants once a month.

- **Nestea.** Mix up a quart of unsweetened Nestea instant iced tea according to the directions (without adding sugar or ice) and fertilize gardenias with the solution. Or simply sprinkle the powdered mix directly on top of the soil. As the tea decomposes, the nutrients work their way into the soil.

STRANGE FACTS

- Gardenias wilt quickly if placed in a vase because the stems do not take up water well. Display gardenias by floating the flowers in a shallow bowl of water.

- Gardenias, when given as a gift, symbolize ecstasy.

- The 1938 novel *Death Wears a White Gardenia*, by Zelda Popkin, marks the first of a series of mystery novels featuring Mary Carner, a young New York City department store detective, who, in this hard-boiled novel, investigates the murder of the store's credit manager.

- In the 1953 movie *The Blue Gardenia*, Anne Baxter stars as a woman who gets drunk and wakes up to find herself in a strange apartment with a dead man by her side.

- Actor Vincent Gardenia, who played Frank Lorenzo on *All in the Family*, appeared in the 1986 movie musical *Little Shop of Horrors*, the story of a man-eating plant hell-bent on world domination.

- The gardenia is named in honor of Scottish naturalist Alexander Garden, who collected botanical specimens in South Carolina before the Revolutionary War.

- In 1993, jazz greats Tito Puente and Woody Herman released the collaborative album *Blue Gardenia*.

Garlic

- **Forster Toothpicks.** To make a garlic clove easy to remove from a marinade, stick a Forster Toothpick into the clove before tossing it into the marinade.

- **Gerber Baby Food.** Store garlic cloves in clean, empty Gerber Baby Food jars and place in the freezer.

- **L'eggs Sheer Energy Panty Hose.** Store garlic by filling the foot of a pair of L'eggs Sheer Energy Panty Hose and hanging it high to keep the contents dry. The synthetic fibers of the panty hose also repel rodents and insects.

STRANGE FACTS

- Ancient Egyptians considered garlic to be a potent medicinal food.

- A hieroglyph representing garlic is engraved on the Pyramid of Cheops in Giza, Egypt. Archeologists believe the hieroglyph was meant to strengthen the builders of the pyramid and protect them from disease.

• Garlic should be pulled from the ground when 75 percent of the stems are dry and brown.

• In his play *A Midsummer Night's Dream*, first performed around 1595, Shakespeare wrote: "Eat no onions nor garlic, for we are to utter sweet breath."

• When planted as a companion, garlic seems to enhance the growth of roses, strawberries, fruit trees, cabbage, and tomatoes. However, as a companion plant, garlic seems to inhibit the growth of peas, beans, and asparagus.

SMELLY HANDS

✗ **Arm & Hammer Baking Soda.** To remove garlic smells from your hands, wash your hands with a small handful of Arm & Hammer Baking Soda.

✗ **Campbell's Tomato Juice.** Washing your hands with Campbell's Tomato Juice gets rid of garlic odors.

✗ **Colgate Toothpaste.** Squeeze a dollop of Colgate Regular Flavor Toothpaste into your palm and wash your hands under running water to deodorize the stench of garlic on your hands and leave them smelling minty fresh.

✗ **Downy.** Wash your hands as usual, then place one teaspoon Downy Fabric Softener in your cupped palm, rub your hands together well, and rinse clean. The surfactants in Downy make water a more efficient solvent, washing garlic oil from your hands.

✗ **Heinz White Vinegar.** To get rid of the smell of garlic on your hands, pour Heinz White Vinegar over your hands, rub them together well, then rinse with soap and water.

• In 1985, R. Kirkpatrick of Eureka, California, grew the largest recorded garlic in history, weighing two pounds, ten ounces.

• Fear of garlic is called *alliumphobia*.

• Tying the stems of a garlic plant in a knot a few days before harvesting helps dry out the stems and is believed to concentrate the garlic juice in the cloves.

• Elephant garlic bulbs weigh up to one pound.

• Garlic leaves are edible and can be used like chives.

• In German, the word for garlic is *Knoblauch*.

✂ **Huggies Baby Wipes.** After chopping garlic, clean your hands with Huggies Baby Wipes to eliminate the smell from your skin.

✂ **Jet-Dry.** Pour one teaspoon Jet-Dry in your cupped palm, wash your hands with soap and water, and rinse clean. The surfactants in Jet-Dry boost the efficacy of water as a solvent, washing garlic oil from your hands.

✂ **Jif Peanut Butter.** Use a dollop of Jif Peanut Butter—the top-selling peanut butter in America—to remove garlic smells from your hands.

✂ **Maxwell House Coffee.** Wash the smell of garlic from your hands with one teaspoon Maxwell House Coffee grounds and a little water.

✂ **Morton Salt.** To remove garlic odor from your hands, wet your hands, then rub one teaspoon Morton Salt between your hands, concentrating on your fingertips and nails. The salt absorbs garlic oil and gently exfoliates dead skin.

✂ **ReaLemon.** Washing your hands with ReaLemon lemon juice eliminates the smell of garlic like magic.

Coming Clean with Jet-Dry

In the 1960s, Ecolabs, a company founded in 1923 by Merritt J. Osborn to sell cleaning products to businesses and hospitals, introduced Jet-Dry, a blue-colored rinse agent. Jet-Dry contains a powerful surfactant that works during the dishwasher's rinse cycle to boost the solvency of water, preventing spots, film, and other mineral residue from depositing on dishes, glassware, and flatware.

Recognizing a strong consumer demand for a household rinse agent to prevent hard water stains from spotting tableware cleaned in the kitchen dishwasher, Reckitt Benckiser purchased Jet-Dry from Ecolabs, made Jet-Dry available to consumers through retail stores, and expanded the line, offering Jet-Dry in lemon, citrus vinegar, and orange. In 1997, to alert consumers that all dishwashers are built with a receptacle cap on the inside of the door to be filled once a month with Jet-Dry, New York advertising agency Margeotes Fertitta developed the cartoon character Mr. Cap, a personified dishwasher rinse agent cap.

- According to the United States Geological Survey, 85 percent of the United States water supply is hard water.

- Hard water is water that contains a high concentration of dissolved minerals, most notably calcium and magnesium.

- The minerals in hard water leave deposits—such as lime scale—in pipes, fixtures, appliances, and water heaters. These deposits reduce the effectiveness of cleaning products and make fixtures and equipment more difficult to clean, reducing their service life.

- Homeowners supplied with hard water tend to have discolored, bad-tasting water, more clogged pipes and plumbing fixtures, spotty dishes and glassware, problems getting their laundry clean and soft, soap scum, tangled hair, drier skin, and higher water heater bills.

- Dishwashers made by Maytag, General Electric, Frigidaire, and Bosch all contain rinse agent dispensers designed specifically for Jet-Dry.

- Jet-Dry, available in Baking Soda, Citrus Vinegar, and Lemon scents, is America's best-selling dishwasher rinse agent.

- New Jersey-based Reckitt Benckiser Inc., maker of Jet-Dry, also sells Lysol disinfectants, Wizard air fresheners, French's mustards, and Resolve carpet cleaners.

Germinating

- **Bounty, Saran Wrap,** and **Ziploc Storage Bags.** Cut a three-inch-wide strip from a sheet of Bounty Paper Towel, dampen it, and lay it on top of a strip of Saran Wrap. Place the seeds on top of the paper towel at the intervals recommended on the seed packet. Cover with another three-inch-wide strip of damp Bounty Paper Towel, then roll up the paper and plastic together, place in a Ziploc Storage Bag, and store in a warm place (on a windowsill, on top of a refrigerator). When the seeds begin to sprout, remove the Ziploc Storage Bag, unroll the Saran Wrap, and plant the strip of Bounty Paper Towels in a well-tilled garden bed. Cover with a fine layer of soil, and water thoroughly. The paper towel acts as a mulch to inhibit dehydration and soon dissolves, ensuring a perfectly spaced row of seedlings.

- **Carnation NonFat Dry Milk.** Fill a saltshaker with powdered Carnation NonFat Dry Milk and sprinkle over seeds planted in starter cups (see Coca-Cola, Dannon Yogurt, or Dixie Cups on page 110). Cover the powdered milk with a light coat of seed-starting mix. The milk gives the plants extra calcium.

• **Coca-Cola.** Remove the label from a clean, empty two-liter plastic Coca-Cola bottle, drill drainage holes in the bottom, cut the bottle in half with a pair of scissors, and use the bottom half as a planter for seedlings. Or, instead of cutting the bottle in half, lay the bottle on its side, cut a three-inch-wide access flap along the length of the bottle, and drill drainage holes in the other side of the bottle. Fill the bottle halfway with seed-starting mix and plant seeds inside.

• **Crayola Chalk.** Use a mortar and pestle to grind up a box of Crayola Chalk, and then sprinkle the chalk dust (calcium carbonate) on top of seed-starting mix in starter cups to give the plants added calcium.

• **Dannon Yogurt** and **Mr. Coffee Filters.** Using a drill with a one-eighth-inch bit, drill several drainage holes in the bottom of a clean, empty Dannon Yogurt cup (or use a hammer and a large nail to poke a hole in the center of the bottom creating a three-pronged crack radiating out from the center). Line the inside of the cup with a Mr. Coffee Filter, add seed-starting mix, and plant your tomato, pepper, or other seeds. An eight-ounce yogurt cup provides enough room for two or three seedlings of most vegetables. Plant at least three seeds, label the cup with the plant name, and after the seeds have germinated, thin down to one seedling per cup. When the seedling sprouts two full leaves, transplant the seedling with the coffee filter into your garden, where the coffee filter will decompose.

• **Dixie Cups.** To sprout seeds before planting in your garden, use a pencil to poke a hole in the center of the bottom of a Dixie Cup. Fill the cup halfway with seed-starting mix. Place the seed inside and cover with more seed-starting mix. Follow the directions on the seed packet for proper care, and be sure to label the plant name on the cup with an indelible marker. When the seedling is ready to plant in your garden, peel away the cup.

• **Forster Clothes Pins.** To identify a plant easily, use a Forster Clothes Pin to clip the seed packet (marked with the name of the plant, the number of seeds, and the date planted) to the seed-starting pot. (For more ways to label plants and seedlings, see page 161.)

• **Frisbee.** Use a clean, old Frisbee as a saucer for soaking seeds.

• **Glad Trash Bags.** To get seeds to germinate in cold soil, slice open the sides of black Glad Trash Bags to make long sheets and place the black plastic on the garden bed as mulch. Secure the plastic in place with stones, and then plant the seeds in holes in the black plastic at the proper planting intervals. The radiant heat created by the plastic warms the soil an additional 3 degrees Fahrenheit. The plastic sheets can be rolled up at the end of the season and reused the next year. Be certain to water beneath the impermeable plastic sheet with a drip line or soaker hose.

• **Hydrogen Peroxide.** To prevent damping-off from killing seedlings, spray the affected area with a mixture of equal parts hydrogen peroxide and water.

• **Huggies Baby Wipes.** Empty Huggies Baby Wipes boxes make excellent drainage trays for two small seed-starting pots.

• **Jell-O.** Fill a saltshaker with powdered Jell-O (any flavor) and sprinkle the Jello-O over seeds planted in seed-starting mix in starter cups (see Coca-Cola, Dannon Yogurt, or Dixie Cups on page 110). Cover the Jell-O powder with a light coat of seed-starting mix. The gelatin helps the plants retain water, the nitrogen in Jell-O enhances plant growth and hastens sprouting, and the sugar feeds the microbes in the soil, producing more nutrients for the plant.

• **Kodak 35mm Film Canister.** To chill seeds before sowing, wash clean, empty Kodak 35mm Film canisters with soap and warm water, rinse well, place seeds inside along with enough moist, sterile potting soil to fill the canister, and snap on the lid. Label and place in the refrigerator.

• **Lipton Tea Bags** and *USA Today.* Accelerate the germination of seeds by mixing two tablespoons cold, strong brewed Lipton

Tea into each pound of seed, cover, and set in the refrigerator for five days. The tannic acid softens the seeds' outer cover. Before sowing, spread the seed on pages from *USA Today* and let dry for a day or two.

- **Mr. Coffee Filters** and **Dannon Yogurt.** Place seeds evenly spaced inside a damp, unbleached, cone-shaped Mr. Coffee Filter. Place the filter upright inside a clean, empty Dannon Yogurt container with a clear, snap-on lid. Dampen the filter with a teaspoon of water and snap on the lid.

- **Nestea** and *USA Today.* Accelerate the germination of grass seeds by mixing up a quart of unsweetened Nestea instant iced tea according to the directions (without adding sugar or ice). Mix two tablespoons of the tea into each pound of seed, cover, and set in the refrigerator for five days. The tannic acid softens the seeds' outer cover. Before sowing, spread the seed on pages from *USA Today* and let the seed dry for a day or two.

- **Pampers.** To keep seedlings moist without daily watering, saturate a Pampers disposable diaper with water (until it cannot absorb any more water). Lay the wet diaper plastic-side down in the bottom of a tray liner for seedling flats and place the seed pot on top. Every four days, remove the pot and saturate the diaper with more water.

- **Reynolds Wrap** and **Charmin.** Make transplanting germinated plants a breeze by wrapping Reynolds Wrap around a cardboard tube from a used roll of Charmin Bath Tissue. Stand the tube on a tray, fill it with seed-starting mix, and plant the seed inside. When the seed sprouts, remove the Reynolds Wrap and plant the entire cardboard tube.

- **Reynolds Wrap** and **Scotch Packaging Tape.** Spread a long sheet of Reynolds Wrap on the shelf under your plant lights, set your seedling trays on top of it, then lift up the ends of the aluminum foil and use Scotch Packaging Tape to attach the ends to the outside cover of the fluorescent lights. The Reynolds Wrap focuses the light on the seedlings and helps retain heat.

• **Saran Wrap** and **Popsicle.** Lay a sheet of Saran Wrap over four Popsicle sticks inserted into a seed tray filled with seed-starting mix. The Saran Wrap creates a miniature greenhouse, providing enough humidity to keep the growing medium moist for germination. If too much moisture collects on the inside of the plastic, remove the Saran Wrap for a few hours to avoid fostering disease.

• **Ziploc Storage Bags.** Cover small seed flats with an open Ziploc Storage Bag until germination occurs to humidify the seed flats and prevent them from drying out. To avoid fostering disease, do not let too much moisture accumulate.

• **Ziploc Storage Bags** and **Scotch Magic Tape.** Make a miniterrarium by placing two inches of seed-starting mix in a Ziploc Storage Bag. Plant a seed in the soil, moisten with water, and use Scotch Magic Tape to tape the bag to a window that gets plenty of sunlight.

STRANGE FACTS

• In the New Testament, Jesus compares the kingdom of heaven to a mustard seed sowed in a field:

> Though it is the smallest of all your seeds, yet when it grows, it is the largest of garden plants of all and becomes a tree, so that the birds of the air come and perch in its branches (Matthew 13:31–32).

Mustard plants grow up to six feet tall.

• In the English nursery story "Jack and the Bean-Stalk," based on a worldwide myth, Jack's mother tosses magic beans out the window. By morning, the beans grow into a bean-stalk that reaches up into the clouds, making them the fastest-germinating beans of all time.

• The children's poem "Mary, Mary, quite contrary, how does your garden grow?" originated in the eighteenth century. Ecclesiastical tradition holds that the poem refers to the Virgin Mary. Secular tradition maintains that the poem concerns the moody

Inside Cracker Jack

In 1872, German immigrant F. W. Rueckheim opened a popcorn stand in Chicago, Illinois. Brisk business soon enabled Rueckheim to send to Germany for his brother Louis. F. W. Rueckheim & Bro. soon expanded into candy–making, and at the 1893 Columbian Exposition, the duo introduced a unique popcorn-and-peanut molasses-coated candy—the forerunner of Cracker Jack caramel-coated popcorn and peanuts. Unfortunately, the original candy kernels, while popular, stuck together in blocks—until 1896, when Louis discovered a secret process to keep them separate. Louis gave the molasses-covered treat to a salesman, who, after tasting it, exclaimed, "That's crackerjack!" F. W. Rueckheim immediately embraced the slang word (meaning excellent) and had it trademarked. In 1899, the Rueckheim brothers packaged Cracker Jack in a wax-sealed box that preserved the candy's freshness, enabling the brothers to ship their product to stores nationwide.

In 1912, the Rueckheim brothers added "a prize in every box" of Cracker Jack. Over the years, the "toy surprise inside" has included rings, yo-yos, whistles, charms, tops, plastic toys, miniature storybooks, superhero stick-ons, and tiny tattoos.

In 1964, Borden, Inc., based in Columbus, Ohio, bought the Cracker Jack Company. In 1997, Frito-Lay of Dallas, Texas, purchased Cracker Jack from Borden.

- In 1908, Jack Northworth wrote the lyrics to the song "Take Me Out to the Ball Game" during a thirty-minute subway ride, immortalizing Cracker Jack brand in the third line, "Buy me some peanuts and Cracker Jack." Albert Von Tilzer, who composed the music to the song, did not see a baseball game until more than twenty years after the song's release. Norworth witnessed his first baseball game in 1940 when the Brooklyn Dodgers honored him at Ebbets Field.

- In 1918, Sailor Jack and his dog, Bingo, first appeared on the Cracker Jack box. Sailor Jack was modeled after F. W. Rueckheim's grandson Robert, who had a dog named Bingo. Robert, who died of pneumonia shortly after the new box appeared, is buried in St. Henry's cemetery, near Chicago, under a headstone with a depiction of him in his sailor suit.

- In the 1961 movie *Breakfast at Tiffany's*, Holly Golightly, played by Audrey Hepburn, pays Tiffany's to engrave initials on a ring from a Cracker Jack box.

- The Cracker Jack Company maintains an archive of all the toys ever put in Cracker Jack boxes and displays some of the best toys at its Chicago headquarters.

- Since 1912, Cracker Jack has given out more than twenty-three billion toys.

- Collectors value some old Cracker Jack prizes as high as seven thousand dollars.

114

Mary, Queen of Scots, and her eccentric French custom of wearing gowns adorned with silver bells and cockle shells.

• In his 1759 novel *Candide*, French satirist Voltaire wrote, "We must cultivate our own garden."

• In July 1954, Harold Schmidt found seeds for the Arctic lupine in frozen silt at Miller Creek in the Canadian Yukon. Radiocarbon dating placed the seeds' origins somewhere between 13,000 B.C.E. and 8,000 B.C.E. The seeds, germinated in 1966, were the longest-viable seeds in recorded history.

• For a great science experiment for children, germinate seeds in a glass filled with Jell-O and observe the root structures. The Jell-O will also grow mold.

• All the sesame seeds in McDonald's hamburger buns are produced in Mexico.

Gloves

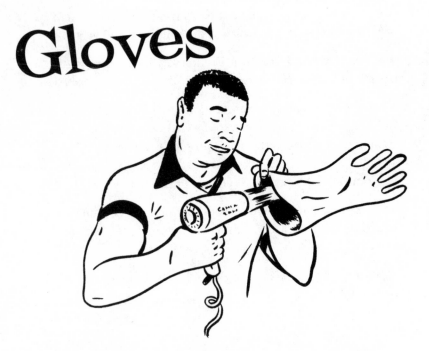

- **Arm & Hammer Baking Soda.** Sprinkle a little Arm & Hammer Baking Soda inside a pair of gloves to help them slip on more easily.

- **Conair Pro Style 1600 Hair Dryer.** Dry the insides of rubber gloves by inserting the nozzle of a Conair Pro Style 1600 hair dryer into a glove and blowing in warm air.

- **Coppertone.** Rubbing a few drops of Coppertone sunscreen into your hands before putting on rubber gloves helps them slide into gloves easily and effortlessly.

- **Johnson's Baby Powder.** To help rubber gloves slip on easily, sprinkle Johnson & Johnson Baby Powder inside the gloves.

- **Johnson & Johnson Cotton Balls.** Extend the life of plastic gloves by stuffing a Johnson & Johnson Cotton Ball into each fingertip of the gloves to prevent your fingernails from tearing through.

- **Kingsford's Corn Starch.** Sprinkling Kingsford's Corn Starch inside a pair of rubber gloves absorbs moisture, enabling your hands to slip inside almost effortlessly.

• **Lubriderm.** Applying Lubriderm your hands before putting on rubber gloves helps them slide into gloves smoothly.

• **Playtex Living Gloves.** When the fingertips of Playtex Living Gloves wear out, making the gloves impractical for housework, cut off the fingertips of the gloves and use them for gardening outdoors. You'll have more dexterity using fingertip-less gloves.

STRANGE FACTS

• The word *glove* originates from the Anglo-Saxon word *glof*, meaning "palm of the hand."

• During the Middle Ages, knights would attach women's gloves to their helmets to demonstrate love or devotion.

• During the Middle Ages, throwing down a glove signaled a challenge to a duel and was called "throwing down the gauntlet." Whoever picked up the glove accepted the challenge.

• William Shakespeare's father was a glove maker.

• German Kaiser Wilhelm II frequently attempted to conceal his withered arm by posing with his hand resting on a sword or by holding gloves.

• Right-handed people live an average of nine years longer than left-handed people do.

• Soldiers from every country in the world salute with their right hand.

• The Japanese word *karate* means "empty hand."

• The three major candidates in the 1992 United States presidential election—George Bush, Bill Clinton, and Ross Perot— were all left-handed.

• When terrorists sent letters filled with anthrax spores through the United States Postal Service in the wake of the attacks on the World Trade Center and Pentagon on September 11, 2001, sales of latex gloves skyrocketed.

• Paul McCartney and Ringo Starr, the only two left-handed Beatles, are the only two surviving Beatles.

Gnats

- **Dr. Bronner's Peppermint Soap.** Repel gnats by rubbing a few drops of Dr. Bronner's Peppermint Soap (the liquid variety) over your skin. Peppermint is a natural gnat repellent.

- **Johnson's Baby Oil.** Rubbing a thin coat of Johnson's Baby Oil on exposed skin forms a protective barrier against gnat bites. (If you have baby oil on your skin, stay out of the sun to avoid sunburn.)

- **Heinz Apple Cider Vinegar** and **Gerber Baby Food.** Put one table-spoon Heinz Apple Cider Vinegar in a clean, empty Gerber Baby Food jar, fill the jar with water, and set the jar near plants infested with fungus gnats for a few days. Attracted by the sweet vinegar, the fungus gnats fly to the rim of the jar, climb inside, and drown.

- **L'eggs Sheer Energy Panty Hose.** If swarming gnats are pestering you, pull the waist of a pair of clean, used L'eggs Sheer Energy Panty Hose over your head and down to your neck to make a see-through face mask. The synthetic fibers keep gnats out of your eyes, ears, nose, and mouth—although your neighbors may think you're getting ready to rob a bank, in which case you may have some explaining to do if the police show up at your door.

• **Smirnoff Vodka.** Mix one-half cup Smirnoff Vodka and 1.5 cups water in a sixteen-ounce trigger-spray bottle and spray on plant leaves in the cool of the day to kill fungus gnats on houseplants. Do not use alcohol on delicate plants like African violets. (Before treating the entire plant, test this alcohol formula on one of the plant's leaves and wait one day to make certain it doesn't burn the leaf.)

• **SueBee Honey.** Make homemade flypaper to attract gnats by simply smearing SueBee Honey (warmed in the microwave oven) over sheets of yellow construction paper.

• **Vicks VapoRub.** Apply Vicks VapoRub to your skin to repel gnats. The scent of eucalyptus repels the feisty pests.

STRANGE FACTS

• In the New Testament, Jesus admonishes, "You blind guides! You strain out a gnat but swallow a camel" (Matthew 23:24).

• In an episode of the television comedy series *Gilligan's Island*, when a rock 'n' roll group named the Mosquitoes visits the island, Gilligan, the Skipper, Mr. Howell, and the Professor form their own singing group called the Gnats.

• In his 1971 book, *A Separate Reality*, author Carlos Castaneda, seeking enlightenment with his teacher, Don Juan, through the use of peyote, describes finding himself being circled by a drooling 100-foot-tall gnat with spiked hair.

• In French, the word for gnat is *moucheron*. The French verb *moucher* means "to blow the nose."

• General Norman Schwarzkopf, recalling his preparations in 1990 for the Gulf War, told *Time* magazine, "By the middle of October, we had a completely robust strategic air campaign that was very executable, right down to a gnat's eyelash."

• In 1992, *Tonight Show* host Jay Leno told *Time* magazine that he has the attention span of a gnat.

Gophers and Moles

- **Bounce.** To repel gophers and moles, shove a few fresh sheets of Bounce Classic into the tunnel openings and then fill the openings with dirt. The fragrance (oleander, a natural repellent) repulses gophers and moles.

- **Castor Oil** and **Ivory Dishwashing Liquid.** Repel moles by mixing one-half cup Castor Oil, four tablespoons Ivory Dishwashing Liquid, and two gallons water and drenching the molehills with the solution.

- **Clorox.** To protect bulbs from gophers, cut the top half off a clean, empty Clorox Bleach jug, punch drainage holes in the sides and bottom of the bottom half of the jug, sink the jug into a flowerbed, fill it with soil, and plant your bulbs inside of it.

- **Glad Trash Bags.** Divert a mole away from your garden by creating a more inviting spot in your yard. Slice open the sides of black Glad Trash Bags to make long sheets and place the black plastic over a damp section of the yard from late winter through spring, securing the plastic in place with stones. (The black plastic will kill the grass and weeds in that spot, perhaps making an ideal spot—well aerated by the mole—for a future garden bed.)

- **Maxwell House Coffee.** Spreading Maxwell House Coffee grounds around your yard repels moles—and simultaneously fertilizes your lawn and garden.

- **Playtex Living Gloves.** When baiting a trap for gophers or moles, wear Playtex Living Gloves to avoid leaving a human scent on the trap or bait.

- **Reynolds Wrap, Glad Flexible Straws,** and **Scotch Magic Tape.** Planting pinwheels near gopher and mole tunnel openings creates enough noise and vibrations to chase away the animals. To make a pinwheel, cut a six-inch square of Reynolds Wrap, fold it in half diagonally, then fold it in half diagonally again. Open up folded square, poke a pinhole in the center, and cut along the diagonal folds toward the center, leaving an uncut X with one-inch legs in the center. Bend two opposite petals forward and the remaining two petals backward so that all four corners overlap the center hole. Push a straight pin through the four corners and the center hole, then poke the pin through the end of a Glad Flexible Straw, bend the sharp end down, and secure to the straw with Scotch Magic Tape.

- **Tidy Cats.** Pour used Tidy Cats into the mole or gopher tunnels. The creatures smell the scent of their natural enemy and quickly tunnel elsewhere.

- **Ziploc Freezer Bag.** Place a portable radio inside a gallon-size Ziploc Freezer Bag, turn the radio on, seal the bag shut, and place it near mole and gopher tunnels. The sounds of Paul Harvey, Aerosmith, or Eminem blaring from the radio will repel moles and gophers.

STRANGE FACTS

- When gophers push out dirt from their holes, they create a fan-shaped mound. Moles create a circular mound of dirt.

• Gophers—members of the rodent family—eat garden vegetables, buds, and roots. Moles—mammals with large finlike forelegs and sharp claws—eat worms and insects, rarely plants.

• Gopher tunnels can reach up to eight hundred feet in length.

• The 1960s Saturday-morning animated television show *Underdog* included a segment featuring *The Go Go Gophers*, starring two Native American gophers that schemed to keep their territory in Fort Gopher, run by Colonel Kit Coyote.

• A "gopher" is a native or resident of Minnesota, nicknamed the Gopher State.

• The word *gopher* is slang for an ambitious employee, trainee, or intern who does menial errands. The word is a humorous misspelling of the phrase "Go fer," meaning someone who will "go for" coffee.

• The word *mole* is slang for a spy.

• Simply flattening mole tunnels by stepping on them may chase moles into another yard.

• On the television series *The Love Boat*, the purser, played by actor Fred Grandy, was nicknamed Gopher. Grandy, the best man at David and Julie Nixon Eisenhower's wedding in 1968, was elected to four terms as a United States congressman representing the state of Iowa and ran an unsuccessful campaign to be the Republican nominee for governor of Iowa.

• Owls, hawks, skunks, gopher snakes, and king snakes all prey on gophers.

• While moles eat helpful earthworms, they also feed on destructive pests, including beetle grubs, wireworms, and cutworms. Moles also aerate the soil with their tunnels.

• In the 1980 comedy movie *Caddyshack*, Bill Murray stars as an assistant greens keeper at an exclusive golf club in pursuit of a wily gopher.

Grapes

• **Arm & Hammer Baking Soda** and **Wesson Corn Oil.** To protect grapes from fungi such as black rot, mix one teaspoon Arm & Hammer Baking Soda and five drops Wesson Corn Oil in one quart water. Fill a trigger-spray bottle with the mixture and spray directly on vines when the fruit starts to appear, then apply once a week for approximately two months. Reapply after rain. The USDA has approved baking soda as a fungicide. (Be sure to test the solution on a few grape leaves and watch for a day to make sure the formula does not burn the leaves.)

• **Bounce.** Stuff two Bounce Classic sheets into a small cotton sachet and tie the sachet to the stem of a grape cluster (after pollination) to protect it from birds and insects. The oleander fragrance in Bounce Classic repels insects and birds.

• **Forster Clothes Pins.** Secure grapevines to a trellis by simply attaching them to the trellis with Forster Clothes Pins.

• **L'eggs Sheer Energy Panty Hose.** Using a pair of scissors, cut off the toe from the foot of a pair of used, clean L'eggs Sheer En-

Everyone Loves a Slinky

In 1943, Richard James, a 29-year-old marine engineer working in Philadelphia's Cramp Shipyard, tried to figure out how to use springs to mount delicate meters for testing horsepower on World War II battleships. When a torsion spring fell off his desk and tumbled end over end across the floor, James realized he could create a new toy by devising a steel formula that would give the spring the proper tension to "walk."

After James found a steel wire that would coil, uncoil, and re-coil, his wife, Betty, a graduate of Pennsylvania State University, thumbed through the dictionary to find an appropriate name for the toy. She chose Slinky because it meant "stealthy, sleek, and sinuous."

In the summer of 1945, the Jameses borrowed five hundred dollars to pay a machine shop to make a small quantity of Slinkys. During the Christmas shopping season, they convinced a buyer from Gimbel's Department Store in downtown Philadelphia to provide counter space for four hundred Slinkys and let them demonstrate the new toy to customers. Richard James went alone, carrying a small demonstration staircase. Much to his astonishment, he sold all four hundred Slinkys in ninety minutes.

The Slinky became the hit of the 1946 American Toy Fair, and Slinky sales soared. The Jameses founded James Industries with a factory in Philadelphia to market their product. Richard James invented machines that could coil eighty feet of steel wire into a Slinky in less than eleven seconds.

In 1960, Richard James abandoned his business and family to join a religious cult in Bolivia, leaving Betty behind with six kids, a foundering Slinky business, and a huge debt (largely rung up by his donations to his spiritual leaders). Betty James relocated the Slinky factory to her home town of Hollidaysburg, Pennsylvania, devised a unique co-op advertising plan for the toy, and began marketing the Slinky with a simple jingle that infected the collective consciousness of the Baby Boom. She ran

ergy Panty Hose, then cut one-inch strips from the leg, creating circular loops of panty hose. Use the loops to gently tie grapevines to a trellis with a figure-eight loop.

• **L'eggs Sheer Energy Panty Hose** and **Oral-B Mint Waxed Floss.** To prevent birds or insects from destroying growing grapes, cut off the feet from a clean, used pair of L'eggs Sheer Energy Panty the company until 1998, when, at the age of eighty-three, she sold James Industries to Poof Products so she would have more time to spend with her six children and sixteen grandchildren.

• The original Slinky has seen only two changes since its inception in 1943. The prototype blue-black Swedish steel was replaced with less expensive, silvery American metal (specially coated for durability), and in 1973, the Slinky's ends were crimped for safety reasons.

• Slinky sales have totaled more than 250 million. That's roughly one Slinky for every man, woman, and child in the United States.

• The metal coil of a standard Slinky stretched out straight measures eight-seven feet in length.

• The Slinky jingle, broadcast on television continuously since 1962, is now one of the most recognizable toy jingles in America, recognized by nearly 90 percent of all adults.

• More than three million miles of wire have been used to make the classic Slinky since its inception.

That's enough wire to make a Slinky big enough to hold the earth and stretch to the moon and back.

• The Slinky is sold on every continent of the world except Antarctica.

• A Slinky is on exhibit in the Smithsonian Institution and in the Metropolitan Museum of Art.

• United States soldiers using radios during combat in Vietnam tossed the Slinky into trees to act as a makeshift antenna.

• In 1985, space shuttle astronaut Jeffrey Hoffman became the first person to play with a Slinky in space. He used the Slinky to conduct zero-gravity physics experiments while in orbit around the earth.

• The Slinky helps scientists understand the supercoiling of DNA molecules. Slinky and Shear Slinky, two computer graphics programs developed at the University of Maryland, use a Slinky model to approximate the double-helix coiling of DNA molecules.

• In 1999, the United States Postal Service introduced a Slinky stamp.

Hose, slip each foot over a cluster of grapes, and seal the open end closed with a piece of Oral-B Mint Waxed Floss. The synthetic fibers keep birds away, and the flexible hose expands as the grapes grow. You can also cut a section from a leg of the panty hose, tie one end closed with dental floss, cover the grapes, and then secure the open end shut.

• **Oral-B Mint Waxed Floss.** String pieces of dental floss across two stakes, along galvanized eye screws spaced up the sides of a wall, or around nails hammered around a door to make a trellis for grapevines.

• **Slinky.** Hang several Slinkys in a row from the side of the house or an overhang to give grapevines a trellis to slink their way up. You can also build a simple wood frame with legs and drape a dozen Slinkys across it so grapevines can grow around the coils.

• **Tabasco Pepper Sauce and McCormick Ground (Cayenne) Red Pepper.** To repel Japanese beetles from grapevines, mix two tablespoons Tabasco Pepper Sauce, two tablespoons McCormick Ground Red Pepper, and two cups water in a sixteen-ounce trigger-spray bottle. Spray the soil with the solution wherever Japanese beetles are giving you trouble.

• **Ziploc Storage Bags.** When grapes grow to the size of peas, use a hole puncher to punch a dozen holes in a gallon-size Ziploc Storage Bag, place the bag over the cluster of grapes, and zip the bag closed up to the stem to protect the grapes from birds, insects, and disease.

STRANGE FACTS

• Ancient Egyptian tomb paintings dating to 2440 B.C.E. portray Egyptians cultivating grapes.

• The phrase *sour grapes*, meaning "a show of disdain for something you cannot have," originated from Aesop's fable "The Fox and the Grapes," in which a fox, unable to reach a bunch of grapes, says, "I am sure the grapes are sour."

• The largest grapevine in recorded history was in Carpinteria, California, and yielded an average of 7.7 tons of grapes every year. The grapevine, planted in 1842, died in 1920.

• Grapevines generally bear between fifteen and eighty pounds of grapes every year for up to one hundred years.

- The song "The Battle Hymn of the Republic," written by Julia Ward Howe in 1861, includes the lyrics:

  Mine eyes have seen the glory of the coming of the Lord:
  He is trampling out the vintage where the grapes of wrath
  are stored.

- In the 1933 movie *I'm No Angel*, Mae West delivers her famous line, "Beulah, peel me a grape."

- The 1940 movie *The Grapes of Wrath*, based on John Steinbeck's 1939 novel, stars Henry Fonda and tells the story of farmers fleeing the poverty of the Oklahoma Dust Bowl only to find economic oppression in California.

- Birds tend to peck unprotected grapes; the damaged grapes then tend to attract bees and wasps.

- The Minor Thornton Ranch in Fresno, California, is the largest continuous vineyard in the United States, covering 5,200 acres and producing 6,500 tons of grapes every year.

- The 1968 song "I Heard It through the Grapevine," recorded by Marvin Gaye, hit number one on the charts and became Motown's best-charting single of the decade.

- A cluster of grapes yields between six and three hundred berries.

- When asked if he had ever taken a serious political stand on anything, comedian Woody Allen replied, "Yes, for twenty-four hours I refused to eat grapes."

- Nearly 80 percent of the grapes harvested in the world are used to make wine.

- According to *The Guinness Book of World Records*, the largest recorded bunch of grapes in history weighed 20 pounds, 11.5 ounces in May 1984 in Santiago, Chile. The grapes were 'Red Thompson' seedless.

- California grows roughly 90 percent of the grapes produced in the United States, providing 20 percent of the world's raisins and 10 percent of the world's table grapes.

Hand Cleaner

• **Alberto VO5 Conditioning Hairdressing.** Lightly coating your hands with Alberto VO5 Conditioning Hairdressing before gardening enables you to clean them off afterward without harsh scrubbing.

• **Arm & Hammer Baking Soda.** Clean dirt, grime, and oil from hands by sprinkling Arm & Hammer Baking Soda onto wet hands with liquid soap. Rub vigorously, rinse, and dry.

• **Barbasol Shaving Cream.** Rubbing Barbasol Shaving Cream between your hands will dissolve grime without water. Keep a can of it at the gardening workbench.

• **Blue Bonnet Margarine.** Rubbing Blue Bonnet Margarine between your hands cleans off grease and grime and leaves your hands smelling like popcorn.

• **Clairol Herbal Essences Shampoo.** A dab of Clairol Herbal Essences Shampoo and water cuts through the grime on your hands. Rinse well and dry.

- **Clorox.** Make a convenient outdoor sink by poking a small hole in the side of a clean, empty Clorox Bleach jug (near the bottom). Plug the hole with a golf tee, fill the jug with water, and simply remove the tee to wash your hands in a pleasant stream of water.

- **Coppertone.** Rub Coppertone sunscreen into your skin to remove grease, then wash clean with water.

- **Crisco All-Vegetable Shortening.** Clean grease and grime from your hands by rubbing in Crisco All-Vegetable Shortening. Then wash with soap and water.

- **Domino Sugar.** Sprinkle Domino Sugar on your hands, then lather with soap and water. The sugar acts like an abrasive, scrubbing grease from your skin.

- **Huggies Baby Wipes.** Keep a box of Huggies Baby Wipes nearby to wash your hands or remove stains from clothes while working in the garden. You can also use the wipes as emergency toilet paper.

- **Johnson's Baby Oil.** Before washing greasy hands, massage in Johnson's Baby Oil. Then wash with soap and water. The mineral oil dissolves grease.

- **L'eggs Sheer Energy Panty Hose.** Cut off a leg from a clean, used pair of L'eggs Panty Hose, place a bar of soap inside the foot, and tie a knot to secure the bar of soap in place. Then tie the free end of the panty hose leg to an outdoor water faucet so you always have a clean bar of soap available in the garden.

- **Miracle Whip.** Clean dirt, grease, and grime from your hands with a dollop of Miracle Whip. Rub the salad dressing—first introduced at the 1933 Chicago World's Fair—between your hands, let set for five minutes, then rinse clean with soap and water.

- **Morton Salt.** Sprinkle Morton Salt on your soapy hands to help dissolve grease. Salt breaks down many greases, and the abrasive grit helps scrub skin clean.

- **Noxzema.** To clean grease and grime from skin, rub a dab of Noxzema—originally sold as Dr. Bunting's Sunburn Remedy—into the skin and wash clean with soap and water.

- **Pam Original Cooking Spray.** If your hands get sticky and greasy, clean them with Pam Cooking Spray, dispensed from a convenient aerosol can containing no fluorocarbons.

- **Play-Doh.** Squeezing Play-Doh between your hands cleans grease, grime, and dirt from the skin.

- **ReaLemon.** Remove fruit or berry stains from your hands by rinsing your hands with ReaLemon lemon juice.

- **Skin-So-Soft.** Grease and grime come right off your hands if you rub Skin-So-Soft into the skin and then wash clean with soap and water.

- **Star Olive Oil** and **Domino Sugar.** Pour one teaspoon Star Olive Oil and one teaspoon Domino Sugar into the palm of your cupped hand and gently rub your hands together for several minutes. Wash your hands with soap and water, rinse thoroughly, and dry for amazingly clean and soft hands. The olive oil moisturizes your skin, while the sugar exfoliates.

- **Wesson Corn Oil** and **Ivory Dishwashing Liquid.** Place a dollop of Wesson Corn Oil in your palm, rub thoroughly all over your hands, then use the same amount of Ivory Dishwashing Liquid and rinse with water.

STRANGE FACTS

- Humans are the only primates that do not have pigment in the palms of their hands.

- Spiral staircases in medieval castles run clockwise to prevent an intruding knight from being able to brandish a sword with his right hand.

- President James Garfield could write in Latin with one hand while simultaneously writing in Greek with the other hand.

- The human hand contains twenty-seven bones.

- In 1963, advance orders of one million copies for the Beatles' fifth single record, "I Want to Hold Your Hand," immediately placed it at Number One in the Top Ten.

How Play-Doh Took Shape

In 1956, brothers Noah and Joseph McVicker of the Rainbow Crafts Company, a soap company in Cincinnati, Ohio, received United States patent number 3,167,440 for a soft, reusable, non-toxic modeling compound cleverly named Play-Doh. According to the Patent Office, the McVicker brothers originally invented Play-Doh as a wallpaper cleaner. The McVicker brothers obviously realized their invention made a better children's toy. In 1955, they tested Play-Doh in nursery schools, kindergartens, and elementary schools in Cincinnati.

First sold and demonstrated in the toy department of Woodward & Lothrop Department Store in Washington, D.C., the original cream-colored Play-Doh, packaged in a twelve-ounce cardboard can, became an immediate hit. In 1957, the Rainbow Crafts Company introduced Play-Doh in blue, red, and yellow. Three years later, the company introduced the Play-Doh Fun Factory.

In 1965, General Mills bought the Rainbow Crafts Company, folding Play-Doh into its Kenner Toy Company in 1970. The Tonka Corporation purchased Kenner in 1987, and four years later, Hasbro acquired Tonka and transferred Play-Doh to its Playskool division.

- One of the most recognized scents in the world is the smell of Play-Doh.

- The Play-Doh boy, pictured on every can of Play-Doh, is named Play-Doh Pete and was created in 1960.

- In 1986, the cardboard Play-Doh can, used for thirty years, was replaced with a tight-seal, easy-to-open plastic container to ensure the modeling compound a longer life.

- In 1992, Playskool introduced Sparkling Play-Doh and Glow-in-the-Dark Play-Doh.

- Kids eat more Play-Doh than crayons, fingerpaint, and white paste combined.

- To celebrate its fortieth birthday in 1996, Play-Doh introduced gold and silver Play-Doh.

- The formula for the original Play-Doh still remains top secret.

- Today, Play-Doh is sold in more than seventy-five countries.

- If rolled together, all the Play-Doh manufactured since 1956 would make a ball weighing more than 700 million pounds.

- More than two billion cans of Play-Doh have been sold since 1956.

- If all the Play-Doh made since 1956 was squeezed through the Fun Factory, it would make a snake that would wrap around the earth nearly three hundred times.

Harvesting

• **Bounty.** To prevent crushed fruits and berries from staining a harvesting basket, line the inside of the basket or bucket with several sheets of Bounty Paper Towels to absorb the juicy stains.

• **Clorox.** To make a hip bucket for harvesting fruits or berries, cut a large hole in the side of an empty, clean Clorox Bleach jug opposite the handle, then string your belt through the handle.

• **L'eggs Sheer Energy Panty Hose.** To make a net basket to pick fruits from high branches, use a pair of pliers to cut apart a wire clothes hanger, form a hoop approximately six inches in diameter, and attach the wire loop to the end of a ten-foot-long wooden pole. Cut off an entire leg from a pair of used, clean L'eggs Sheer Energy Panty Hose, stretch the open end of the leg around the hoop, and sew it in place.

• **Maxwell House Coffee** and **Bubble Wrap.** To make a fruit picker, use a pair of tin snips to carefully cut a V shape (approximately one inch tall) into the top rim of a clean, used Maxwell House Coffee can. With a pair of pliers, carefully bend the pointed corners slightly inward so that when picking fruit with the can, the bent sides will hold the fruit in the can. Drill two one-quarter-inch holes in the opposite side of the can and drill similar holes in the end of a six-foot-long piece of pine (two inches by three-quarters inch). Wire the can to the wooden pole. Cut two or three pieces of Bubble Wrap to sit at the bottom of the can as a cushion for the picked fruit.

STRANGE FACTS

• In the Bible, God tells Moses to announce to the Israelites: "When you reap the harvest of your land, do not reap to the very edges of your field or gather the gleanings of your harvest. Do not go over your vineyard a second time or pick up the grapes that have fallen. Leave them for the poor and the alien" (Leviticus 19:9–10).

• The lyrics to the 1908 song "Shine On, Harvest Moon" were written by Jack Northworth, who also wrote the lyrics to "Take Me Out to the Ball Game."

• In the 1929 Marx Brothers' movie *The Cocoanuts*, Groucho Marx tells Mrs. Potter, "I'll meet you tonight under the moon. Oh, I can see you now. You and the moon. You wear a necktie so I'll know you."

• In the Northern Hemisphere, a harvest moon is the full moon nearest the autumnal equinox of the sun (on September 22 or 23), giving farmers enough natural light to harvest their crops at night. In the Southern Hemisphere, the harvest moon occurs at the vernal equinox (on March 20 or 21).

• In the 1937 French film *Harvest*, directed by Marcel Pagnol, a poacher and a vagabond woman team up to bring a deserted village back to life.

• The world record for apple picking is held by George Adrian of Indianapolis, Indiana, who, on September 23, 1980, picked 15,830 pounds of apples in eight hours.

• Indian leader and nonviolence advocate Mahatma Gandhi said, "I have known many meateaters to be far more nonviolent than vegetarians."

• In Spanish, the word for harvest is *cosecha*—which also means crop.

Herbs

- **Bounty.** To dry large-leaved herbs, like basil, mint, and sage, re-move the leaves from the stem and place them in a single layer on top of a sheet of Bounty Paper Towel. To dry short-leaved herbs, place the entire stem on the paper towel, let dry, then strip the leaves from the stem.

- **Goodyear Tires.** Place an old Goodyear Tire on the ground, fill with potting soil, and plant herbs like lavender, oregano, sage, and thyme in the soil. The tire retains moisture and provides ex-cellent drainage.

- **Maxwell House Coffee.** To speed the germination of parsley seeds, soak the seeds in lukewarm water for several hours, let dry, and mix with dry Maxwell House Coffee grounds before sowing outdoors in one-quarter inch of soil. Cover the spot with a board to keep the seeds moist and cool until they sprout.

- **Saran Wrap.** To germinate basil, plant the seeds in a flat pan filled with seed-starting mix and cover the pan with a sheet of Saran Wrap to create a miniature green house.

- **Scotch-Brite Heavy Duty Scrub Sponges.** To grow herbs indoors, place a wet Scotch-Brite Heavy Duty Scrub Sponge on a plate with the abrasive side facing down and sprinkle parsley or alfalfa seeds over the sponge. Set the plate by a window that gets plenty of sunlight.

- **Smirnoff Vodka.** To preserve diced, fresh ginger in your refrigerator, peel and chop the ginger, put in a jar, top off with Smirnoff Vodka, and seal tightly. The ginger will last up to one year in your refrigerator.

- **Smirnoff Vodka** and **Mr. Coffee Filters.** Make a tincture of fresh herbs by filling a clean glass jar with the herbs and covering with Smirnoff Vodka. Seal tightly, let steep for two to three weeks, then strain through a Mr. Coffee Filter and store in a cool, dark place.

- **Star Olive Oil.** To store herbs and preserve their flavor, mix two firmly packed cups of chopped or pureed herb leaves and stems in one-half cup Star Olive Oil. Pack the mixture in airtight containers and freeze. (Never store herbs packed in oil in the refrigerator; unless frozen, the mixture can develop botulism.)

- **20 Mule Team Borax.** To prevent thyme from being burned in the summer sun, dissolve one tablespoon 20 Mule Team Borax in one gallon water and use this solution to water the thyme once in the spring.

- **Ziploc Freezer Bags.** To preserve the oils that give parsley its flavor, place freshly picked parsley in a Ziploc Freezer Bag and store in the freezer until ready to use.

- **Ziploc Freezer Bags.** Store rosemary by stripping the leaves from the branches and placing them in the freezer in a Ziploc Freezer Bag.

STRANGE FACTS

- Planting basil near tomato plants repels flies and worms and, according to folklore, produces stronger and healthier basil and tomato plants.

• The 1966 Simon and Garfunkel album *Parsley, Sage, Rosemary and Thyme* opens with the song "Scarborough Fair/Canticle," the lyrics of which pay homage to the herbs parsley, sage, rosemary, and thyme.

• Tea brewed from sage works as an antiseptic mouthwash and a digestive aid.

• The word *tarragon* stems from the Latin word for dragon because tarragon plants have serpentine root systems.

• Different varieties of thyme smell like coconut, caraway, lemon, and nutmeg.

• Planting horseradish near potatoes repels potato beetles.

• During the twelve days of Christmas, Greeks traditionally burn herbs in the fireplace to prevent mischievous goblins, called *kallikantzeri*, from dropping down the chimney to extinguish the fire or sour the milk. Hanging a cross wrapped in basil over a bowl of water also helps ward off the *kallikantzeri*, as does leaving chunks of meat outside the door as a bribe.

Hoses

- **Forster Toothpicks** and **Scotch Packaging Tape.** To mend a puncture in a garden hose, insert a Forster Toothpick into the hole, snap it off flush with the hose's outer skin, then wrap Scotch Packaging Tape around the spot. The wood toothpick will absorb water, swelling to seal the hole.

- **Goodyear Tires.** Store a hose by coiling it inside a used Goodyear Tire to prevent kinking in the line.

- **Krazy Glue.** Fix leaks in a garden hose by applying Krazy Glue to seal the hole or leaky valve stems.

- **Wrigley's Spearmint Gum.** Repair a small leak in a garden hose by patching the hole with chewed Wrigley's Spearmint Gum. During World War II, American soldiers used Wrigley's Spearmint Gum—received as an emergency ration—to patch gas tanks and jeep tires.

STRANGE FACTS

• Prior to the invention of the rubber hose, people used watering cans to water lawns, flowerbeds, and vegetable gardens.

• In 1860, the inventor of vulcanized rubber, Charles Goodyear, died, having failed to perfect a practical use for his invention and leaving his family with nearly 200,000 dollars in debt. Ten years later, Dr. Benjamin Franklin Goodrich, determined to cash in on rubber's untapped potential, founded the B. F. Goodrich Company in Akron, Ohio, and began producing the world's first rubber hoses.

• The 1970s television sitcom *Welcome Back, Kotter*, starring Gabe Kaplan and John Travolta, popularized the meaningless catchphrase "up your nose with a rubber hose."

• The 1983 movie *Strange Brew*, inspired by a popular sketch on the television comedy show *SCTV*, starred Rick Moranis and Dave Thomas as Bob and Doug McKenzie, two Canadian buddies who lambasted others as "hosers" and "hoseheads."

• A leaky hose can be used to make an inexpensive drip irrigation system or soaker hose. Simply use a hammer and nail to poke a series of holes along the length of the hose.

• In Italian, a hose is called a *tubo flessìbile*, which literally translates to "flexible tube."

Hot Caps

• **Clorox.** Cut off the bottom of an empty, clean Clorox Bleach jug and place the jug over seedlings. Take the cap off during the day and replace the cap at night. To anchor these hot caps, simply cut off the top of the handle, insert a sharp stick, and drive the stick into the ground.

• **Clorox.** Make radiant heat by filling several clean, empty Clorox Bleach jugs with water, sealing the caps tightly, and placing them in planting beds near your seedlings. During the day, the sun heats up the water in the jugs. At night, the heated water radiates warmth for the tender seedlings nearby. To make the jugs even more effective, spray-paint them flat black to absorb more heat.

• **Coca-Cola.** To make a hot cap, remove the label from a clean, empty two-liter plastic Coca-Cola bottle, cut the bottle in half with a pair of scissors, and place the top half of the bottle over seedlings. Remove the cap for ventilation during the day and replace it at night to retain heat and moisture.

• **Gatorade.** To make a hot cap, remove the label from an empty, clean bottle of Gatorade, the thirst quencher invented in 1965 by University of Florida nephrologist Dr. Robert Cade and named after the school's football team, the Florida Gators. Cut off the bottom of the bottle and place the top part over seedlings, pushing the bottle into the soil firmly. Take the cap off during the day and replace the cap at night.

• **Mott's Apple Juice.** To make a hot cap, remove the label from an empty, clean Mott's Apple Juice bottle, cut off the bottom, and place the bottle over seedlings, pushing it into the soil firmly. Take the cap off during the day and replace the cap at night.

• **Ocean Spray Cranberry Juice Cocktail.** To make a hot cap, remove the label from an empty, clean bottle of Ocean Spray Cranberry Juice Cocktail, introduced in 1930 as the world's first cranberry juice drink. Cut off the bottom and place the plastic bottle over seedlings, pushing it into the soil firmly. Take the cap off during the day and replace it at night.

STRANGE FACTS

• Most historians believe the song "Yankee Doodle" was written by a dapper British soldier, Dr. Richard Shuckburg, in 1755 during the French and Indian Wars, to ridicule American colonial militiamen's motley clothes, outdated equipment, and lack of military training. A Yankee Doodle is a ragamuffin country bumpkin from New England who sticks a feather in his cap to be stylish, but actually looks ridiculous. British soldiers sang the ditty as they marched to the battle of Concord, to demoralize the colonists. When the colonists won the battle, they adopted the derisive song as their own defiant patriotic cheer.

• Cap guns were invented after the United States Civil War ended in 1865. Gun manufacturers, determined to keep their factories operating, began making the toy cap guns that generated the sound of an explosive shot being fired. The caps themselves are simply small drops of gunpowder encapsulated between two strips of paper.

• The comic strip *Andy Capp*, created in 1957 by former British postal worker Reg Smythe, features the adventures of an unemployed English bloke who, always wearing his trademark cap, avoids doing household chores, hangs out with his mates at the local pub, and plays football, rugby, and snooker. Andy's long-suffering wife, Flo, constantly shows him the error of his ways. Smythe named his cartoon character Andy Capp after the Northern British pronunciation of the word *handicap*, because that's exactly what Andy is to his hard-working wife.

• A nightcap is an alcoholic beverage drunk just before bedtime or to cap off a festive evening.

• Why does director Ron Howard usually wear a baseball cap whenever he is interviewed on television? Howard, who had a full head of red hair when he played Opie Taylor on *The Andy Griffith Show* and Richie Cunningham on *Happy Days*, seems to wear the caps to hide the fact that he is now bald.

• In German, the word for cap is *mütze*.

Houseplants

- **Alberto VO5 Conditioning Hairdressing.** Clean houseplant leaves by applying a small dab of Alberto VO5 Conditioning Hairdressing to the leaves with a soft cloth.

- **Arm & Hammer Baking Soda.** Neutralize the acidity of potting soil by watering the soil once with a mixture of four tablespoons Arm & Hammer Baking Soda and one quart water.

- **Aunt Jemima Original Syrup.** Revive an ailing houseplant by adding two tablespoons Aunt Jemima Original Syrup at the base of the plant once a month.

- **Bounce.** To prevent the soil from leaking out of a planter, line the bottom of the planter with a used sheet of Bounce Classic. Water can drain through the dryer sheet without the sheet breaking down in the pot.

- **Canada Dry Club Soda.** Feed flat Canada Dry Club Soda to your houseplants. The minerals found in club soda are beneficial to plants.

• **Carnation NonFat Dry Milk.** Mix three ounces Carnation NonFat Dry Milk with two cups water and, using a soft cloth, wipe the milky solution on houseplant leaves to give them a fine gloss.

• **Castor Oil.** Rejuvenate a houseplant ailing from a nutrient deficiency by dribbling one tablespoon castor oil into the soil and then watering well.

• **Cool Whip.** Clean houseplant leaves by using a soft cloth to wipe Cool Whip on the leaves.

• **Depends.** If a planter is leaking excess water, set the pot inside a pair of Depends, creating a diaper for the plant. Conceal the Depends diaper by placing the pot inside a second, larger pot.

• **Epsom Salt.** For every foot of a houseplant's height, sprinkle one teaspoon Epsom Salt evenly around the base for better blossoms and deeper greening. Adding Epsom Salt to houseplant food will also enrich the color of any flowering plants and aid in disease-resistance. Or mix one tablespoon Epsom Salt in one gallon water and spray the mixture on the plant. Epsom Salt is magnesium sulfate, which lowers the pH of the soil and provides magnesium.

• **Geritol.** Revive an ailing houseplant by adding two tablespoons Geritol to the soil twice a week for three months. New leaves should begin to grow within the first month.

• **Heinz Apple Cider Vinegar.** To revive undernourished houseplants, mix one tablespoon Heinz Apple Cider Vinegar in one gallon water in a watering can and water your houseplants with the solution. The vinegar neutralizes the pH of the water, making vital nutrients in the water more available to the plants.

• **Heinz White Vinegar** and **Q-Tips Cotton Swabs.** To remove mealybugs from houseplants, dab the bugs with a Q-Tips Cotton Swab dipped in a mixture of equal parts Heinz White Vinegar and water.

- **Huggies Pull-Ups.** If your planter is leaking water, set the pot inside a pair of Huggies Pull-Ups, creating an absorbent diaper for the plant. Place the pot inside a second, larger pot to conceal the Pull-Up.

- **Ivory Dishwashing Liquid.** To repel insects (like aphids, whiteflies, and spider mites) from houseplants, put a drop of Ivory Dishwashing Liquid in a trigger-spray bottle, fill the rest of the bottle with water, shake well, and mist the leaves and soil of your houseplants.

- **Ivory Dishwashing Liquid.** If you put houseplants outside for sun or while away on vacation, you should kill any insects on the plants before bringing them back inside. Put a drop of Ivory Dishwashing Liquid in a trigger-spray bottle, fill the rest of the bottle with water, shake well, and mist the leaves and soil of the plant well to kill the insects.

- **Jell-O.** Work a few teaspoons of powdered Jell-O into the soil of houseplants to absorb water and prevent it from leaking out of the bottom of the pot. The absorbent gelatin also reduces how often you need to water the plants. The nitrogen in Jell-O enhances plant growth and hastens sprouting, and the sugar feeds the microbes in the soil, producing more nutrients for the plant.

- **L'eggs Sheer Energy Panty Hose.** To prevent the soil from leaking out of the bottom of a planter, place a used, clean pair of L'eggs Sheer Energy panty hose in the bottom of the pot. The panty hose still allow water to drain, without letting soil seep out.

- **L'eggs Sheer Energy Panty Hose.** Using a pair of scissors, cut off the toe from the foot of a pair of used, clean L'eggs Sheer Energy Panty Hose, then cut one-inch strips from the leg, creating circular loops of panty hose. Use the loops to gently tie stems and thin plant trunks to stakes with a figure-eight loop.

- **Lipton Tea Bags.** Before potting a houseplant, place several Lipton Tea Bags (new or used) on top of the drainage layer of pebbles, pottery shards, or panty hose (see L'eggs Sheer Energy Panty Hose above) at the bottom of the planter. The tea bags retain water and provide nutrients for the plant.

- **Lipton Tea Bags.** Put Lipton Tea Bags (new or used) on the soil around houseplants. Every time you water the plants, the nutrients from the decomposing tea leaves work their way into the soil.

- **Maxwell House Coffee.** Add used Maxwell House Coffee grounds to your houseplants to fertilize the soil. The smell of the coffee also repels cats from digging up the plants.

- **Miracle Whip** and **Bounty.** Using a Bounty Paper Towel, rub Miracle Whip on houseplant leaves to make them shine and to prevent dust from settling on them.

- **Murphy Oil Soap.** To kill pesky whiteflies on houseplants, mix one tablespoon Murphy Oil Soap in a gallon of water, pour into a trigger-spray bottle, and mist the infected plants.

- **Nestea.** Mix up a quart of unsweetened Nestea instant iced tea according to the directions (without adding sugar or ice) and fertilize houseplants with the solution. Or simply sprinkle the powdered mix directly on the soil. As the tea decomposes, the nutrients work their way into the soil.

- **Pampers.** Using a pair of scissors, carefully cut open a Pampers disposable diaper and mix the superabsorbent polymer flakes with the potting soil. The polymer flakes absorb three hundred times their weight in water, keeping the soil moist for your houseplant. The gelatinous polymer also stores nutrients, slowly feeding the plants.

- **Reynolds Wrap.** Increase the natural light for houseplants during the winter months by wrapping a sturdy piece of cardboard with Reynolds Wrap. Position the plant between the homemade mirror and the window, with the foil-covered side of the cardboard facing the window. The aluminum foil will reflect the sunlight, causing the plant to grow more evenly.

- **Reynolds Wrap.** Wrapping Reynolds Wrap around the bases of houseplant containers keeps humidity high and prevents the soil from drying out as quickly.

- **Saran Quick Covers.** To prevent water from dripping all over the floor while watering hanging plants, place a Saran Quick Cover around the bottom of the hanging planter before watering. The plastic cap catches the drips. Wait one hour before removing and save the Quick Cover to use the next time you water the plants.

- **Saran Wrap.** To revitalize a wilting houseplant, water the plant thoroughly and then loosely wrap Saran Wrap around the leaves and the base of the plant, creating a miniature greenhouse. Remove the plastic wrap after a few days.

- **Smirnoff Vodka** and **Q-Tips Cotton Swabs.** To remove mealybugs or scale from houseplants, dab the bugs with a Q-Tips Cotton Swab dipped in Smirnoff Vodka. Or mix one part Smirnoff Vodka to one part water in a trigger-spray bottle and spray the plants. Repeat two weeks later to kill any newly hatched mealybugs. (Before treating the entire plant, test this alcohol formula on one of the plant's leaves and wait one day to make certain the solution doesn't burn the leaf.)

- **Star Olive Oil** and **Bounty.** To shine the leaves of a houseplant, put a few drops Star Olive Oil on a Bounty Paper Towel and gently rub each leaf, then wipe off the excess oil.

- **Star Olive Oil.** Add two tablespoons Star Olive Oil at the root of ferns or palm plants once a month.

- *USA Today.* When watering houseplants with a mister, hold a section of *USA Today* behind the plant to avoid getting water on furniture or walls.

- **Windex.** Use a clean, empty Windex bottle as a mister for plants. Clean the bottle with dishwashing liquid and water to remove traces of any undesirable chemicals.

STRANGE FACTS

- Overwatering kills more houseplants than any other single cause. The leaves of an overwatered plant will wilt, turn yellow, and fall off. The base of the stem may also rot, a symptom of root damage.

• Underwatering a houseplant causes far less damage than overwatering. Revive a plant wilted from dryness by misting the leaves lightly, watering the soil, and placing the plant in direct sunlight.

• In 1848, German professor Gustav Theodor Fechner first suggested in his book *Nanna* that talking to plants helps them grow, insisting that plants have central nervous systems and possess emotions.

• In his 1882 book *The Power of Movement in Plants*, naturalist Charles Darwin noted the shared characteristics between primates and plants.

• In his 1906 book *Training of the Human Plant*, horticulturist Luther Burbank hypothesized that plants, while unable to understand spoken words, can telepathically comprehend the thoughts and emotions being expressed.

• The 1960 Roger Corman movie *Little Shop of Horrors*, costarring Jack Nicholson, tells the story of a meek florist who accidentally creates a man-eating plant. The movie, adapted into a campy off-Broadway musical, was in turn remade into the 1986 movie musical starring Rick Moranis and Steve Martin.

• In 1970, New York dentist George Milstein, convinced that exposing houseplants to gentle melodies could accelerate their growth, produced the record album *Music to Grow Plants By*. Studies verified that plants exposed to soft, classical music grow toward the source of the sound, while plants exposed to hard rock music tend to grow away from the source of the music, shrivel, and die.

• The cartoon strip *Doonesbury*, by Garry Trudeau, frequently features Zonker Harris at home talking to his plants.

Insects

- **Albers Grits.** Sprinkle a small mound of Albers Grits around the base of an anthill. Each ant will carry away one grit and eat it. After the ant drinks some water, the grit will expand, causing the ant's stomach to burst. (For more ways to kill ants, see page 1.)

- **Aunt Jemima Original Syrup.** Coating a few small pieces of cardboard with Aunt Jemima Original Syrup and placing them around the perimeter of the yard will attract wasps. The stinging insects will get stuck in the gooey syrup. (For more ways to kill or repel wasps, see page 279.)

- **Bounce.** Attach sheets of Bounce Classic to plant stakes to protect the plants from insects. The oleander fragrance in the Bounce Classic repels insects.

- **Bounce.** To repel mosquitoes while you're working in the garden, tie a sheet of Bounce Classic through one of your belt loops or the plastic flap in the back of your baseball cap. Oleander, the fragrance in Bounce Classic, repels insects. (For more ways to repel mosquitoes, see page 180.)

- **Coca-Cola.** To get rid of fruit flies, remove the cap from a two-liter bottle of Classic Coke (not diet or caffeine-free) and use an electric drill with a one-quarter-inch bit to drill a hole in the cap. Replace the cap on the bottle, leaving one inch of Classic Coke in the bottom of the bottle, and set outside. Fruit flies will crawl into the bottle to enjoy the Real Thing, but won't be able to get back out.

- **Con-Tact Paper.** Fold a long piece of Con-Tact Paper in half, with the sticky side out, and wrap around the bases of yew trees to trap black vine weevils.

- **Dixie Cups** and **Vaseline Petroleum Jelly.** To repel leafhoppers from lettuce heads, tack yellow plastic Dixie Cups upside down to short stakes in the lettuce patch and coat the cups with Vaseline Petroleum Jelly. The leafhoppers, attracted to the color yellow, get stuck in the gelatinous gunk on the cups.

- **Dr. Bronner's Peppermint Soap.** Mix one tablespoon Dr. Bronner's Peppermint Soap with two cups water in a sixteen-ounce trigger-spray bottle and spray on plants to repel aphids and caterpillars. The mint drives them away.

- **Dustbuster** and **Listerine.** Place a cotton ball moistened with Listerine inside the nozzle of the Dustbuster before inserting the bag, then use the Dustbuster to suck whiteflies, mites, and other small insects (like squash bugs or Mexican bean beetles) off leaves and out of the air. (Hold the Dustbuster lightly over the plant with one hand and hold the leaves with the other hand to prevent them from being sucked into the Dustbuster and ripped.) The antiseptic on the cotton ball will help kill the insects inside the Dustbuster. When you're finished, empty the pests into soapy water.

- **Forster Toothpicks.** Flick mealybugs from the undersides of plant leaves with a Forster Toothpick.

- **Glad Flexible Straws.** Protect seedlings from cutworms by cutting Glad Flexible Straws into 1.5-inch pieces, slitting each piece lengthwise, and then slipping a section around each stem before transplanting. The straws will prevent cutworms from destroying the plants, and as the plants grow, the cut straws will gently expand along with them. (For more ways to repel cutworms, see page 64.)

- **Gold Medal Flour.** To prevent or repel spider mites, mix 3.5 cups Gold Medal Flour and one-half cup buttermilk in five gallons water. Spray the plants with this solution.

- **Gold Medal Flour** and **L'eggs Sheer Energy Panty Hose.** To repel blister beetles, cabbageworms, and grasshoppers, cut off a leg from a clean, used pair of L'eggs Sheer Energy Panty Hose, fill it with three cups Gold Medal All-Purpose Flour (not self-rising), and tie a knot in the end. In the early morning, when dew is still on the plants, gently shake the infested plant leaves to knock off the insects, then shake the flour-filled panty-hose sachet to dust the plant leaves and top of the soil with flour. Grasshoppers and blister beetles gorge themselves on the flour and stop eating the plants. After two days, use a hose with a fine spray to wash the flour off the plant leaves.

- **Heinz Apple Cider Vinegar** and **Gerber Baby Food.** To kill fruit flies or fungus gnats, put one tablespoon Heinz Apple Cider Vinegar in a clean, empty Gerber Baby Food jar, fill the jar with water, and set the jar near fruit or infested plants for a few days. Attracted by the sweet vinegar, the insects fly to the rim of the jar, climb inside, and drown.

- **Heinz Apple Cider Vinegar** and **Grandma's Molasses.** Prevent codling moth larvae from destroying ripening apples by mixing one quart Heinz Apple Cider Vinegar and four ounces Grandma's Molasses in a blender, then filling clean, empty soda cans with the solution and hanging the cans from tree branches. The adult moths, attracted to the sweet solution, drown in it, and never get a chance to lay their eggs.

- **Heinz White Vinegar** and **Q-Tips Cotton Swabs.** To remove mealybugs from houseplants, dab the bugs with a Q-Tips Cotton Swab dipped in a mixture of equal parts Heinz White Vinegar and water.

- **Hula Hoops, Bubble Wrap,** and **Scotch Packaging Tape.** Building row covers can stop insects that spread diseases from infecting your crops. Make hoop supports by cutting Hula Hoops in half and inserting the legs firmly into the soil. Cover with a canopy made from sheets of Bubble Wrap and secure to the hoops with Scotch Packaging Tape, making sure the sheets of Bubble Wrap are high enough not to touch the plants. You can also secure the Bubble Wrap by staking the ends to the ground with wire. At the end of the season, roll up the Bubble Wrap to be used again the following year. (Be sure to monitor the temperatures inside this minigreenhouse to make certain you do not burn out your plants, or substitute sheer curtains for the Bubble Wrap.)

• **Ivory Dishwashing Liquid.** To repel insects from houseplants, put a drop of Ivory Dishwashing Liquid in a trigger-spray bottle, fill the rest of the bottle with water, shake well, and mist the leaves and soil of your houseplants.

• **Ivory Dishwashing Liquid.** To kill cucumber beetles, set out yellow pans filled with a mixture of one teaspoon Ivory Dishwashing Liquid per quart of water. The yellow color attracts the beetles, which then drown in the soapy water.

• **Ivory Dishwashing Liquid** and **Playtex Living Gloves.** Control moth larvae by mixing one teaspoon Ivory Dishwashing Liquid and one quart water in a bucket. Wearing a pair of Playtex Living Gloves (to avoid the stinging hairs of some larvae), pluck the moth larvae off your plants and drop them in the bucket of soapy water, which kills them.

• **Johnson's Baby Oil.** To prevent earworms from attacking a corn crop, fill an eyedropper with Johnson's Baby Oil and apply the mineral oil to the base of the ear a few days after the silk first emerges. Repeat every few days.

• **Kaopectate.** Get rid of grasshoppers by mixing one tablespoon Kaopectate in one gallon water and spraying the mixture on the lawn, plants, trees, or wherever else you do not want grasshoppers.

• **L'eggs Sheer Energy Panty Hose** and **Oral-B Mint Waxed Floss.** To prevent insects from destroying growing fruits and vegetables, cut off the feet from a clean, used pair of L'eggs Sheer Energy Panty Hose, slip a foot over an apple, pear, tomato, eggplant, cluster of grapes, or head of broccoli or cabbage, and seal the open end closed with a piece of Oral-B Mint Waxed Floss. The synthetic fibers keep insects away, and the flexible hose expands as the fruit or vegetable grows. You can also cut a section from a leg of the panty hose, tie one end closed with dental floss, cover the fruit or vegetable, and then secure the open end shut.

• **Listerine.** Protect gladiolas and freesia bulbs from thrips by soaking them for twelve hours in a mixture of 2.5 tablespoons Listerine in a gallon of water. Remove the bulbs from the Listerine dip and, without rinsing them off, plant them in your garden.

• **Listerine** and **Ivory Dishwashing Liquid.** Repel insects from plants by mixing one-half teaspoon Listerine (regular flavor), one-half teaspoon Ivory Dishwashing Liquid, and two cups water in a sixteen-ounce trigger-spray bottle. Use once every two weeks as an insecticide on fruit and vegetable gardens. (Be sure to test the solution on a few leaves of the plant and watch for a day to make sure the formula does not burn the leaves.)

• **McCormick Garlic Powder** and **Ivory Dishwashing Liquid.** Mix three tablespoons McCormick Garlic Powder, one-half teaspoon Ivory Dishwashing Liquid, and one quart water in a blender to create a concentrate. Pour two ounces of the concentrate into a sixteen-ounce trigger-spray bottle, fill the rest of the bottle with water, shake well, and spray plants to repel insects. (Choose the plants you intend to spray with garlic carefully; garlic also repels helpful insects.)

• **McCormick Ground (Cayenne) Red Pepper** and **Ivory Dishwashing Liquid.** To keep cabbageworms, cabbage loopers, and diamondback moth larvae at bay, dissolve one tablespoon McCormick Ground Red Pepper and six drops Ivory Dishwashing Liquid in two quarts water in a bucket. Let the solution sit overnight, then fill a trigger-spray bottle with the solution and mist cabbage plants once a week. The pepper spray repels moths, preventing the pests from laying eggs on the cabbage leaves.

• **Murphy Oil Soap.** To kill pesky whiteflies on plants, mix equal parts Murphy Oil Soap and water in a trigger-spray bottle and mist the infected plants. (For more ways to kill whiteflies, see page 293.)

• **Playtex Living Gloves.** If you wish to hand-pick insects from your garden but prefer not to touch them with your bare hands, wear a pair of Playtex Living Gloves.

• **Q-Tips Cotton Swabs.** To fight cabbageworms, use a wet Q-Tips Cotton Swab to wipe the yellowish oval eggs from the undersides of cabbage leaves.

• **Reynolds Wrap.** Place sheets of Reynolds Wrap on the ground between rows of plants and secure in place with rocks. In the sunlight, the glittering foil keeps away insects like thrips, aphids, and squash vine borers.

• **Simple Green.** Mix one teaspoon Simple Green with two cups water in a sixteen-ounce trigger-spray bottle. Shake well and spray insects. They die instantly.

• **Smirnoff Vodka** and **Q-Tips Cotton Swabs.** To keep aphids, mealybugs, scale, and whiteflies off a houseplant, wash any insects off the plant with tap water, then dab the leaves with a Q-Tips Cotton Swab dipped in Smirnoff Vodka. (Do not use alcohol on delicate plants like African violets.) Or mix four ounces Smirnoff Vodka and 1.5 cups water in a sixteen-ounce trigger-spray bottle and spray on plant leaves in the cool of the day. (Before treating the entire plant, test this alcohol formula on one of the plant's leaves and wait one day to make certain it hasn't burned the leaf.)

• **SueBee Honey.** Make homemade flypaper to attract flies and gnats by simply smearing SueBee Honey (warmed in the microwave oven) over sheets of yellow construction paper. (For more ways to repel gnats, see page 118.)

• **Tabasco Pepper Sauce, McCormick Garlic Powder,** and **Ivory Dishwashing Liquid.** To repel aphids, flea beetles, grasshoppers, spider mites, and thrips, mix two tablespoons Tabasco Pepper Sauce, two tablespoons McCormick Garlic Powder, three drops Ivory Dishwashing Liquid, and two cups water in a sixteen-ounce trigger-spray bottle. Spray the solution on plants.

The Dirt on Dustbuster

In the mid-1970s, Black & Decker launched the Mod-4, a battery-powered handheld tool with four attachable power-tool heads, including a minivacuum for cleaning up wood shavings in the workshop. Although *Fortune* magazine praised the Mod-4 as a terrific product, consumers perceived any tool powered by batteries as a toy and had little interest in owning a four-in-one power tool. Analysis did reveal, however, that consumers loved the idea of a cordless handheld vacuum. In fact, owners of the Mod-4 confessed that their wives would make off with the handheld vacuum for use in the house. Black & Decker, eager to diversify beyond power tools, decided to design a cordless handheld vacuum for women as a household product.

Carroll Gantz, a 1953 graduate of Carnegie Mellon Design School who had worked for seventeen years at the Hoover Company before joining Black & Decker as an industrial designer, invented the new handheld vacuum. Realizing that consumers neglected to keep battery-powered tools properly charged, Gantz devised a charging base as a holster to encourage consumers to keep the new product charging while not in use. Recognizing that the device would have to hang near an electrical outlet (rather than hidden in a closet), Gantz designed the handheld vacuum to be flat, square, and almond-colored, with a unique built-in nozzle. At the time, other handheld vacuums were cylindrical and brashly colored, had attachable nozzles, and

---

- **Tabasco Pepper Sauce** and **Wesson Corn Oil.** To repel insects from plants, pour two teaspoons Tabasco Pepper Sauce and one-half teaspoon Wesson Oil into a sixteen-ounce trigger-spray bottle. Fill the rest of the bottle with warm water and shake well. Spray on plants.

- ***USA Today.*** To repel Colorado potato beetles, place at least three inches of shredded *USA Today* around potato plants. The mulch attracts beneficial insects that will devour destructive Colorado potato beetles before they can make their way to the surface through the mulch.

- **Wesson Corn Oil.** To kill earwigs, fill a saucer with Wesson Corn Oil and set it in your backyard. Earwigs love oil, crawl into the saucer, and drown.

needed to be plugged into a wall socket. The company held a contest among its employees to find a name for the new product. The winning entry, submitted by an employee whose name has been lost to history, was Dustbuster.

In December 1978, Black & Decker test-marketed the Dustbuster in St. Louis, Missouri, selling out the entire stock of the new household device. In 1979, the company went into full production, selling more than one million Dustbusters by the end of the year—more than any other Black & Decker product sold in history.

• *National Geographic* magazine published a photograph of entomologists using a Dustbuster to catch rare insects without harming them.

• An original model of the Dustbuster is on display in the Smithsonian Institution in Washington, D.C.

• Dustbuster inventor Carroll Gantz convinced Black & Decker's attorneys to file a design patent to protect the shape and nozzle design of the Dustbuster.

• Black & Decker has sold more than 100 million Dustbusters. That's more than one Dustbuster for every household in the United States.

• The name Dustbuster provided the inspiration for the title of the 1984 comedy movie *Ghostbusters*, starring Dan Aykroyd, Bill Murray, Sigourney Weaver, and Harold Ramis.

• Dustbuster inventor Carroll Gantz worked at Black & Decker for fourteen years, headed the Carnegie Mellon Design School from 1987 to 1992, and holds thirty United States patents.

• **Wesson Corn Oil** and **Ivory Dishwashing Liquid.** To kill mealybugs on plants, mix one teaspoon Wesson Corn Oil, one teaspoon Ivory Dishwashing Liquid, and two cups water in a sixteen-ounce trigger-spray bottle. Spray infested plants thoroughly with the solution, coating the mealybugs well. The soap penetrates the protective coating of most mealybugs, killing them instantly. The oil suffocates the others. Repeat two weeks later to kill any recently hatched mealybugs. (Be sure to test the solution on a few leaves of the plant and watch for a day to make sure the formula does not burn the leaves.)

• **Wesson Corn Oil** and **Ivory Dishwashing Liquid.** Mix two tablespoons Wesson Corn Oil, one teaspoon Ivory Dishwashing Liquid, and one quart water in a bucket. Pluck unwanted insects from your garden and toss them into the solution, or position trays filled with the soapy solution under plants and shake the branches. The oil prevents the insects from crawling out of the soapy solution, which kills them. To spray this solution directly on plants, mix two teaspoons Ivory Dishwashing Liquid with one-quarter teaspoon Wesson Corn Oil and one gallon water. Pour the mixture into a trigger-spray bottle and spray the plants. (Be sure to test the solution on a few leaves of the plant and watch for a day to make sure the formula does not burn the leaves.)

• **Wilson Tennis Balls** and **Vaseline Petroleum Jelly.** To kill codling moths or the flies that lay apple maggot eggs, use an electric drill with a one-eighth-inch bit to drill a hole in several Wilson Tennis Balls. Screw an eye hook into the hole in each ball, spray-paint the balls red, coat them with Vaseline Petroleum Jelly, and hang them in fruit trees. Moths and flies, lured to the fake fruit, get stuck in the gooey petroleum jelly and die. (See Ziploc Storage Bags below.)

• **Wrigley's Spearmint Gum.** To keep weevils out of flour, place a stick of Wrigley's Spearmint Gum in your flour canister. Weevils, repulsed by mint, stay out of the flour, and the gum does not flavor the flour.

• **Ziploc Storage Bags.** To make the process of killing codling moths and flies less messy (see Wilson Tennis Balls above), place a Ziploc Storage Bag around each red ball and coat the plastic bag (instead of the ball) with Vaseline Petroleum Jelly. This way, when the bags get coated with bugs, you can simply replace the bags.

• **Ziploc Storage Bags.** Prevent plum curculios from laying eggs on apples by placing a Ziploc Storage Bag over each young marble-sized fruit and stapling it closed near the stem, enabling air to get in and moisture to get out.

STRANGE FACTS

• According to entomologists, at least 95 percent of the insects in our yards and gardens are beneficial or harmless. The ground beetle, for instance, devours cutworms, slugs, and snails. Spined soldier bugs eat Colorado potato beetle larvae, Mexican bean beetles, and various destructive caterpillars.

• A 1551 version of the Bible mistranslated the verse "Thou shalt not be afraid for the terror by night" (Psalm 91:5) as "Thou shalt not be afraid of any buggies at night."

• In 1869, a naturalist in Medford, Massachusetts, imported gypsy moth caterpillars from France in the hopes of cross-breeding the gypsy moth with the American silk moth to create a silkworm capable of making a durable thread. Descendants of those gypsy moth caterpillars frequently defoliate millions of acres of trees in New England.

• Apples or pears usually fall from trees due to an infestation of insects.

• In the 1904 children's book *The Marvelous Land of Oz*, the first sequel to *The Wonderful Wizard of Oz*, author L. Frank Baum introduces the Woggle-Bug, an insect the size of a man.

• During World War II, the United States used DDT (dichloro-diphenyl-trichloroethane)—first prepared as an insecticide in 1939 by Swiss chemist Paul Mueller—to fight an epidemic of typhus fever in Naples, Italy, by killing the body lice that carry the disease.

• Scientists estimate the existence of more than thirty million species of insects.

• The heaviest insect in the world is the Goliath beetle of equatorial Africa, which measures up to 4.33 inches in length and weighs up to 3.5 ounces—or slightly more than the weight of three AA batteries.

• The longest insect in the world is the walkingstick, which can grow up to 15.75 inches in length.

• Although the United States Environmental Protection Agency banned the use of DDT in 1972, fruits and vegetables imported into the United States frequently carry residues of DDT and other pesticides banned in the United States.

Japanese Beetles

• **Heinz Apple Cider Vinegar.** Place a bucket filled with equal parts Heinz Apple Cider Vinegar and water under plants infested with Japanese beetles and knock the insects into the acid solution. The vinegar kills the pests.

• **Heinz White Vinegar.** Since Japanese beetle larvae hate alkaline soil, water your lawn and plants in the fall with a mixture of two tablespoons Heinz White Vinegar to one quart water to raise the pH level. (Before adding vinegar to soil, make certain that the plants in your garden do well in acid soil.)

• **Johnson's Baby Oil** and **McCormick Garlic Powder.** Mix one bottle of Johnson's Baby Oil with two tablespoons McCormick Garlic Powder in a trigger-spray bottle. Shake well, then spray the bases of fruit trees, rose bushes, and berry bushes to prevent Japanese beetles from attacking.

• **McCormick Garlic Powder** and **Ivory Dishwashing Liquid.** Mix three tablespoons McCormick Garlic Powder, one-half teaspoon Ivory Dishwashing Liquid, and one quart water in a blender to create a concentrate. Pour two ounces of the concentrate into a sixteen-ounce trigger-spray bottle, fill the rest of the bottle with water, shake well, and spray rose bushes, fruit trees, and berry bushes to repel Japanese beetles.

• **Playtex Living Gloves.** If you wish to hand-pick Japanese beetles from your garden but prefer not to touch them with your bare hands, wear a pair of Playtex Living Gloves.

• **Tabasco Pepper Sauce, McCormick Ground (Cayenne) Red Pepper, and Ivory Dishwashing Liquid.** To repel Japanese beetles from roses and grapevines, mix two tablespoons Tabasco Pepper Sauce, two tablespoons McCormick Ground Red Pepper, three drops Ivory Dishwashing Liquid, and two cups water in a sixteen-ounce trigger-spray bottle. Spray the soil with the solution wherever Japanese beetles are giving you trouble.

• *USA Today.* Place an open sheet of *USA Today* under infested plants before 7 A.M., then shake the plants, sending the beetles falling onto the sheet of newspaper. Pour the beetles into a soapy solution (see Wesson Corn Oil below).

• **Wesson Corn Oil and Ivory Dishwashing Liquid.** Mix two tablespoons Wesson Corn Oil, one teaspoon Ivory Dishwashing Liquid, and one quart water in a bucket. Pluck unwanted insects from your garden in the early morning or evening and toss them into the solution (or hold the bucket under the branches and shake them). The oil prevents the insects from crawling out of the soapy solution, which kills them.

STRANGE FACTS

• Scientists believe that the Japanese beetle first entered the United States in 1916 inside the root of a nursery plant imported from Japan. The Japanese beetle causes an estimated twenty million dollars' worth of damage every year.

• Adult Japanese beetles live for only two months. The grubs, however, live burrowed in the soil for roughly nine months, eating plant roots, until they enter the pupa stage.

• The back of all Japanese beetles is rimmed by twelve white spots.

- Japanese beetles are rarely found west of the Mississippi River.

- Japanese beetles love beans, corn, raspberries, apple trees, grapevines, and roses.

- The enlarged jaws of some male stag beetles look like the horns of a male deer and are nearly double the size of the insect.

- In his classic children's book, *Fox in Socks*, Dr. Seuss describes a battle that takes place between beetles with paddles inside a bottle sitting on top of a poodle eating noodles.

- The Volkswagen Beetle is nicknamed the Bug because of its beetle-like shape.

- John Lennon and Stuart Sutcliffe named their band the Beatles, changing the letter *e* to *a* to give the word a double meaning—the same way the name of the rock group the Crickets played off cricket the game and cricket the insect. After achieving worldwide fame, the Beatles met the Crickets, who had no idea cricket was a game in England. George Harrison speculated that Sutcliffe, who admired Marlon Brando, took the name from a scene in the movie *The Wild One*, where Lee Marvin, referring to a group of motorcycle chicks, says, "The Beetles have missed you." Lennon said he changed the e to an a, "because 'beetles' didn't mean two things on its own. When you said it, people thought of crawly things; and when you read it, it was beat music."

- A Volkswagen Beetle appears on the cover of the Beatles' 1969 album *Abbey Road*. Its license plate reads "28IF." Some fans, convinced that the Beatles had planted clues on their record albums to suggest that Beatle Paul McCartney was dead, claimed the figures on the plate revealed McCartney's age *if* he were still alive. When *Abbey Road* was released, however, Paul McCartney was twenty-seven years old—not twenty-eight. Photographer Ian Macmillan insisted that the Volkswagen just happened to be parked there.

Labels

- **Avery Laser Labels, Forster Toothpicks,** and **Glad Flexible Straws.**
Use an indelible marker to write the name of the plant and the
date of sowing on a self-sticking Avery Address Label and adhere it to the seed-starting pot or around a Forster Toothpick or
Glad Flexible Straw inserted into the soil.

- **Clorox.** Using a pair of scissors, cut strips of white plastic from
a clean, used Clorox Bleach jug to make plant marking stakes.
Use indelible marker to write the name of the plant and the date
of sowing and insert into the soil.

- **Con-Tact Paper** and **Oral-B Mint Waxed Floss.** Write the name of the
vegetable, herb, or flower and the date of planting on an index
card and cover the card with clear Con-Tact Paper to laminate the
card. With a hole puncher, punch a hole in the card, loop a piece of
Oral-B Mint Waxed Floss through the hole, and secure it to a stem
loosely. Or do the same with the original seed packet.

- **Dannon Yogurt.** With a pair of scissors, cut clean, empty
Dannon Yogurt containers into strips. Use an indelible marker to

write the name of the plant and the date of sowing or planting on the blank side of each plastic strip and insert into the soil.

• **Forster Clothes Pins.** Using an indelible marker, write the plant name, number of seeds, and the date on a Forster Clothes Pin and clip to the seed-starting pot. Or use a Forster Clothes Pin to clip the seed packets marked with the appropriate information to the seed-starting pot.

• **Glad Flexible Straws.** To make a stake in the garden to attach labels, simply insert one end of a Glad Flexible Straw into the soil.

• **Oral-B Toothbrush.** Pushing one end of an old Oral-B Toothbrush into the soil of a garden creates a stake to which you can easily attach a label.

• **Popsicle.** Use clean, used Popsicle sticks as plant markers, writing the appropriate information on the sticks with an indelible marker.

• **Post-it Notes.** Using an indelible marker, write the name of the plant and the date of sowing on a Post-it Note and adhere it to a seed-starting pot as a temporary label.

• **Scotch Packaging Tape** and **Oral-B Mint Waxed Floss.** Write the name of the vegetable, herb, or flower and the date of planting on an index card and cover the card with strips of Scotch Packaging Tape to laminate it. With a hole puncher, punch a hole in the card, then loop a piece of Oral-B Mint Waxed Floss through the hole and secure it to a stem loosely. Or do the same with the original seed packet.

• **Ziploc Storage Bags.** Display empty seed packets from flowers and vegetables on small stakes stuck in the ground. Cover each paper packet with a Ziploc Storage Bag to protect the packet from the elements.

STRANGE FACTS

• Novelist Charles Dickens—author of *Oliver Twist* (1839), *A Christmas Carol* (1843), David Copperfield (1850), *A Tale of*

Two Cities (1859), and *Great Expectations* (1861)—worked at the age of twelve in a London factory pasting labels on bottles of shoe polish.

• In French, the word for label is *étiquette.*

• In his 1869 novel *War and Peace,* Russian author Leo Tolstoy wrote, "In historical events great men—so called—are but the labels that serve to give a name to an event, and like labels, they have the least possible connection with the event itself."

• In 1935, R. Stanton Avery, using an old washing machine motor and parts from a sewing machine, developed a machine to produce self-adhesive labels. He named his company Kum-Kleen Products, eventually changing the name to the Avery Adhesive Label Corporation.

• Record companies, in response to pressure from Tipper Gore's Parents' Music Resource Center, now place warning labels on records containing explicit lyrics to alert parents that the songs might be inappropriate for minors. Critics argue that the labels, nicknamed Tipper Stickers, have backfired, prompting kids to buy the controversial CDs because of the parental advisory label.

• In August 1995, before a crowd of forty visitors on the Ben & Jerry's factory tour, the tour leader announced that a pint of ice cream labeled with the name "Rebecca" had been found on the production line. The tour leader handed the container to a female visitor named Rebecca, who opened it to find a diamond engagement ring. The other visitors showered the happy couple with rainbow-colored sprinkles.

Lawn Mowers

- **Bounce.** A sheet of Bounce Classic makes an excellent disposable air filter for use with any gasoline-powered lawn mower. Simply fit one or two Bounce Classic sheets in place to protect the air-intake opening.

- **Coca-Cola.** To make a funnel for refueling your lawn mower, cut a clean, empty two-liter Coca-Cola bottle in half and use the capless top half.

- **Forster Clothes Pins.** To hold a plastic leaf bag open when raking leaves, use two or three Forster Clothes Pins to clip one side of the bag to a chain link fence. This way, you can hold the other side open to fill the bag with leaves easily.

- **Jif Peanut Butter.** Lubricate a lawn mower by putting a dollop of Jif Peanut Butter (creamy, not chunky) on the blade shaft. The peanut oil provides excellent lubrication.

- **L'eggs Sheer Energy Panty Hose.** Improvise a filter for a lawn mower by cutting a large piece from a pair of clean, used L'eggs

Sheer Energy Panty Hose and folding the nylon into four layers. Attach the nylon to the carburetor intake horn with duct tape.

• **Maxwell House Coffee.** To protect the bark at the base of a small tree from being damaged by a lawn mower, use a can opener to remove the bottom of a clean, empty Maxwell House Coffee can, use a pair of tin snips to split the can open lengthwise, then wrap this metal sleeve around the base of the tree.

• **Maybelline Crystal Clear Nail Polish.** Prevent screws on a lawn mower from vibrating loose by coating the ends of the screws with Maybelline Crystal Clear Nail Polish.

• **Mr. Coffee Filters.** To filter sediment from gasoline when filling a lawn mower, place a Mr. Coffee Filter over the mouth of the plastic portable gas canister and screw on the threaded cap. The gas pours slowly, but the coffee filter strains out any sediment. Change the Mr. Coffee Filter at least once a year.

• **Pam Original Cooking Spray.** To prevent cut grass from sticking to lawn mower blades, spray the underside of the lawn mower with Pam Cooking Spray before mowing the lawn.

• **Slinky.** Tired of scarring young trees and plants when mowing the lawn? Wrap a Slinky around the trunk of that young tree or plant, mow the grass around it, then slip off the Slinky and put it on the next tree.

• **Turtle Wax.** Prevent grass cuttings from building up underneath your lawn mower by waxing the underside of the lawn mower with Turtle Wax.

• **WD-40.** If your lawn mower refuses to start up, spray WD-40 in the carburetor/air cleaner and pull the draw cord.

• **WD-40.** Prevent cut grass from sticking to the blades of a lawn mower by spraying WD-40 on the blades and the underside of the lawn mower housing before cutting the grass.

STRANGE FACTS

• In 1830, British inventor Ferrabee Budding invented the world's first hand-pushed lawn mower by adapting parts from a rotary sheering machine used to cut the nap off cotton cloth.

• In 1911, American army colonel Edwin George, using a gasoline engine from a washing machine, invented the world's first gasoline-powered lawn mower.

• The modern-day reel lawn mower weighs some twenty pounds and, unlike motorized models, is quiet and nonpolluting and cuts grass evenly without splitting the ends. Using a reel lawn mower also gives you a healthy workout—without the expense of joining a gym.

• During tournaments held at the professional croquet court at Sonoma-Cutrer Vineyards in California, the 84-foot-by-105-foot lawn is mowed three times a day to exactly three-sixteenths inch with a lawn mower outfitted with precision blades.

• Turf farmer Jay Edgar Frick of Monroe, Ohio, owns the widest lawn mower in the world. "The Big Green Machine," a lawn mower sixty feet wide, can mow an acre of grass per minute.

• Gasoline-powered lawn mowers are not required by law to meet the same emissions standards as automobiles.

• Mowing your lawn for one hour with a conventional gasoline-powered lawn mower creates more air pollution than driving a new car from New York City to Washington, D.C.

• According to the United States Environmental Protection Agency, gasoline-powered lawn mowers cause 5 percent of the nation's air pollution.

• Electric and rechargeable lawn mowers use approximately five dollars' worth of electricity over the course of a year. Rechargeable models quietly mow up to ninety minutes on a single charge and start up at the push of a button.

Lawns

• **Arm & Hammer Baking Soda.** To repair yellow burn spots on a lawn caused by dog urine, dissolve one cup Arm & Hammer Baking Soda in one gallon water in a watering can and saturate the urine spots every three days. The baking soda neutralizes the acidity of the urine and simultaneously deodorizes the area of the lawn, preventing the offending dog from recognizing the spot. (For more tips on repelling cats and dogs, see page 39.)

• **Arm & Hammer Baking Soda** and **Wesson Corn Oil.** To kill the Rhizoctonia fungi that cause brownpatch (brown or yellow rings or patches on your lawn that die), mix one tablespoon Arm & Hammer Baking Soda, one tablespoon Wesson Corn Oil, and one gallon water. Spray a light mist of the solution on your lawn. You should also correct any drainage or excessive watering problems and check to make sure the fertilizer you're using doesn't contain too much nitrogen. In addition, consider aerating the lawn and adding a one-half-inch layer of compost. Compost contains the microbe trichoderma, which feeds on the Rhizoctonia fungi. (For other ways to kill fungi that attack lawns, see page 95.)

• **Budweiser, Epsom Salt, Ivory Dishwashing Liquid**, and **Listerine**. Mix one cup Budweiser, one cup Epsom Salt, one cup Ivory Dishwashing Liquid, and one cup Listerine in a one-quart jar. Spray this on up to 2,500 square feet of lawn with a hose-attached sprayer in May and again in late June.

• **Heinz White Vinegar.** To prevent grass from growing in crevices, pour Heinz White Vinegar in sidewalk cracks and between bricks.

• **Ivory Dishwashing Liquid.** To determine whether cutworms are responsible for rapidly growing bare patches in your lawn, mix one tablespoon Ivory Dishwashing Liquid and one gallon water in a bucket and drench one square yard with the soapy solution. If cutworms rise to the surface, you've identified the problem.

• **Lipton Tea Bags.** To repair a bare patch on the lawn, place moist Lipton Tea Bags (new or used) on the spot and sprinkle the tea bags with grass seed. The wet tea provides moisture and nutrients for the grass seed, and the tea bags themselves eventually decompose.

• **Lipton Tea Bags.** Before sowing grass seed, brew a strong pot of Lipton Tea, let cool, and soak the seed in the liquid for an hour. The tannic acid softens the seeds' outer cover.

• **Maxwell House Coffee.** Fertilize your entire lawn with Maxwell House Coffee by simply sprinkling used coffee grounds (or fresh grounds, if you want to be extravagant) over your yard. Coffee grounds are full of nutrients that boost the performance of grass. Coffee may keep your lawn up all night, but you can always use the decaf.

• **Maxwell House Coffee.** To spread grass seed or fertilizer, punch holes in the bottom of an empty Maxwell House Coffee can with a hammer and a punch, fill with grass seed or fertilizer, cover with the plastic lid, and shake the can as you walk around your lawn or garden.

• **Morton Salt.** To kill grass in cracks and crevices, sprinkle Morton Salt on the unwanted grass. Salt is a corrosive that kills plants.

- **Nestea** and *USA Today.* Accelerate the germination of grass seed by mixing up a quart of unsweetened Nestea instant iced tea according to the directions (without adding sugar or ice). Mix two tablespoons of the premixed tea into each pound of seed, cover, and set in the refrigerator for five days. The tannic acid softens the seeds' outer cover. Before sowing, spread the seed to dry for a day or two on pages from *USA Today* on the garage or basement floor.

- **Nestea.** Repair a bare patch on the lawn by covering the bare spot with one inch of unsweetened Nestea instant iced tea, moistening with water, and sprinkling with grass seed. The wet tea provides moisture and nutrients for the seeds.

- **Reynolds Wrap.** To grow your own sheets of sod, line a plastic flat with a sheet of Reynolds Wrap (with the foil hanging over one lip to enable excess water to drain away). Fill the flat with soil, sprinkle with grass seed, set outside, and water frequently. Within a few weeks, you'll have a thick sheet of turf.

- **20 Mule Team Borax.** To kill Creeping Charlie on your lawn, mix exactly five teaspoons 20 Mule Team Borax and one quart water and fill a pump sprayer. Spray the solution evenly over the trouble spots—the amount above should cover a twenty-five-square-foot area of lawn. (The borax may cause the grass to yellow temporarily.) (For more ways to kill weeds, see page 289.)

- *USA Today.* To get rid of a lawn, cover the grass in late summer with a layer of wet newspaper at least one inch thick, held in place with stones. Keep the newspaper wet. In the fall, cover the newspaper with six to twelve inches of leaves and keep wet, allowing the newspaper and leaves to decompose through the winter. In the spring, cover the remaining leaves and newspaper with one foot of soil.

STRANGE FACTS

- In his poem *Leaves of Grass,* Walt Whitman wrote, "I believe a leaf of grass is no less than the journey-work of the stars."

• The fastest growing grass in the world is bamboo, growing up to three feet in a single day.

• In the 1960 comedy movie *The Grass Is Greener*, Cary Grant and Deborah Kerr star as a married couple experimenting with extramarital affairs.

• Love grass is purple.

• In 1963, Josef Kaiser of Germany manufactured the world's first grass skis—for skiing down grassy slopes.

• Bluegrass, a style of country music, is named after the bluegrass of Kentucky, which is nicknamed the Bluegrass State.

• On his 1975 album *Today*, Elvis Presley sings "The Green, Green Grass of Home," written by J. Curly Putnam.

• Newspaper columnist Erma Bombeck wrote a best-selling book called *The Grass Is Always Greener over the Septic Tank*, which was made into a movie in 1978 starring Carol Burnett and Charles Grodin.

• In 1997, President Bill Clinton bestowed White House intern Monica Lewinsky with a hardcover edition of Walt Whitman's *Leaves of Grass*.

Lettuce

- **Bounty** and **Ziploc Storage Bags.** To prolong the life of harvested lettuce heads, wrap the heads in sheets of Bounty Paper Towel, seal in a gallon-size Ziploc Storage Bag, and store in the refrigerator.

- **Conair Pro Style 1600 Hair Dryer.** To dry lettuce leaves after rinsing, set a Conair Pro Style 1600 hair dryer on cool and blow-dry the wet leaves.

- **Dixie Cups** and **Vaseline Petroleum Jelly.** To repel leafhoppers from lettuce heads, tack yellow plastic Dixie Cups upside down to short stakes in the lettuce patch and coat the cups with Vaseline Petroleum Jelly. The leafhoppers, attracted to the color yellow, get stuck in the Vaseline on the cups.

- **Hula Hoops** and **Forster Clothes Pins.** To build row covers to shade lettuce from the hot summer sun, make hoop supports by cutting Hula Hoops in half and inserting the legs firmly into the soil. Cover with a canopy made from lace curtains or nylon netting and secure to the hoops with Forster Clothes Pins.

- **McCormick Black Pepper.** To keep rabbits away from lettuce beds, sprinkle McCormick Black Pepper in your garden around and over the lettuce heads. Rabbits have a keen sense of smell and are repelled by the scent of pepper. After it rains, be sure to re-pepper the garden.

- **Tabasco Pepper Sauce, McCormick Garlic Powder,** and **Ivory Dishwashing Liquid.** To repulse rabbits from nibbling at growing lettuce heads, mix two tablespoons Tabasco Pepper Sauce, two tablespoons McCormick Garlic Powder, three drops Ivory Dishwashing Liquid, and two cups water in a sixteen-ounce trigger-spray bottle and mist the lettuce. (Be sure to wash all vegetables thoroughly before preparing or eating—unless, of course, you enjoy spicy lettuce.)

- **Wonder Bread.** When storing lettuce in a plastic bag, place a slice of Wonder Bread in the bag to absorb moisture and retain freshness longer.

- **Ziploc Storage Bags.** To toss a salad quickly and neatly, place all the ingredients in a gallon-size Ziploc Storage Bag, add salad dressing, and seal the bag. Shake the bag until the salad is tossed and coated with dressing.

STRANGE FACTS

- Archeologists speculate that people began farming lettuce in Persia as early as 550 B.C.E.

- In the 1909 children's book *The Tale of the Flopsy Bunnies*, author Beatrix Potter wrote, "It is said that the effect of eating too much lettuce is 'soporific.'"

- The giant African snail, a land snail the size of a baseball, has eighty thousand rasping teeth and can devour an entire head of lettuce in one feeding.

- Lettuce, a key ingredient in most diets, contains few calories but provides calcium, iron, and vitamin A.

• Television commercials for Burger King, advertising the slogan "Have It Your Way," featured the jingle, "Hold the pickles, hold the lettuce, special orders don't upset us."

• California grows nearly 75 percent of all the lettuce grown in the United States.

• In German, the word for lettuce is *Kopfsalat*, which literally means "head salad."

Melons

- **Arm & Hammer Baking Soda.** Protect melon plants from mildew by spraying the leaves twice during the season (mid-July and again mid-August) with a mixture of one tablespoon Arm & Hammer Baking Soda and one gallon water.

- **Carnation NonFat Dry Milk.** To prevent blossom-end rot on melon plants (caused by drought or excessive rain), sprinkle a handful of Carnation NonFat Dry Milk around the base of the plant and gently mix into the soil. Repeat every few weeks. Carnation NonFat Dry Milk adds calcium to the soil.

- **Coca-Cola.** Cut a two-inch-diameter hole in the bottom of a clean, empty two-liter bottle of Coca-Cola. Drill a one-sixteenth-inch hole in the cap (one-eighth-inch for clay soil). Plant the capped bottle upside-down in the middle of a melon hill. Fill the bottle with water every four days by placing a hose in the hole. For greater saturation, drill roughly a dozen holes in the top rounded part of the bottle before burying it.

- **Crayola Chalk.** To prevent diseases caused by calcium deficiency, use a mortar and pestle to grind up a box of Crayola Chalk and then sprinkle the chalk dust (calcium carbonate) over the soil around the melon plants.

- **Glad Trash Bags.** To protect melons from weeds and simultaneously enhance their growth, slice open the sides of black Glad Trash Bags to make long sheets and place the black plastic over the melon patch as mulch, securing the plastic in place with stones. Cut slits into the plastic to accommodate seeds or transplants. The radiant heat created by the plastic warms the soil an additional 3 degrees Fahrenheit. You can roll up the plastic sheets at the end of the season and reuse them the next year. Be certain to water beneath the impermeable plastic sheet with a drip line or soaker hose.

- **Hula Hoops** and **Scotch Packaging Tape.** Building row covers over melon seedlings creates a warm microclimate and helps keep away insect pests. Make hoop supports by cutting Hula Hoops in half and inserting the legs firmly into the soil. Cover with a canopy made from old, sheer curtains or old, white bedsheets and secure the curtains to the hoops with Scotch Packaging Tape, making sure the fabric doesn't touch the seedlings. At the end of the season, roll up the curtains so you can use them again the following year.

- **Maxwell House Coffee.** To grow better melons, raise the melons off the ground by resting them on top of upside-down, empty Maxwell House Coffee cans pushed into the soil. The metal cans accumulate heat, making the fruit ripen earlier; they also help repel insects.

STRANGE FACTS

- The need for melons that could withstand the rigors of being transported across the country prompted farmers to breed melons with tougher skins. Consequently, sweeter, more succulent varieties of melon are now difficult, if not impossible, to find in the United States.

• Mao Tse-tung, Chairman of China's Communist Party, chewed melon seeds.

• On the comedy album *The 2,000-Year-Old Man*, when Carl Reiner asks Mel Brooks to name the greatest invention of all time, Brooks replies, "cantaloupe."

• On June 24, 1989, in Luling, Texas, Lee Wheelis achieved a world record by spitting a watermelon seed 68 feet, 9.125 inches.

• Planting melon seeds with their pointy tip downward yields better sprouting.

• In 1990, B. Carson of Arrington, Tennessee, grew the largest recorded watermelon in history, weighing 262 pounds.

• In 1991, G. Daughtridge of Rocky Mount, North Carolina, grew the largest recorded cantaloupe in history, weighing sixty-two pounds.

• To determine whether a watermelon is ripe for harvesting, knock on the melon with your knuckles. A ripe watermelon sounds hollow.

• The rock group Blind Melon, best known for their smash hit "No Rain," appeared on the cover of *Rolling Stone* after their debut album went triple platinum.

• The children's book *Melonhead*, by Michael deGuzman, tells the story of a boy with a head the size of a melon.

• During his comedy stage act, Gallagher smashes a watermelon with a sledgehammer, prompting audience members to don raingear.

• On his late-night television talk show, David Letterman has dropped watermelons from atop tall buildings and had a steam-roller run over watermelons.

Mildew

• **Arm & Hammer Baking Soda, Wesson Corn Oil,** and **Ivory Dishwashing Liquid.** To prevent powdery mildew on plants, mix one teaspoon Arm & Hammer Baking Soda, five drops Wesson Corn Oil, and one drop Ivory Dishwashing Liquid in one quart water. Fill a trigger-spray bottle with the mixture and spray directly on roses, houseplants, and cucurbit crops. The baking soda changes the pH of the leaves, inhibiting fungi growth. Apply once a week for approximately two months. Reapply after rain. The USDA has approved baking soda as a fungicide. (Before treating the entire plant, test this oily formula on one of the plant's leaves and wait one day to make certain the solution doesn't burn the leaf.)

• **Arm & Hammer Baking Soda** and **Murphy Oil Soap.** To kill powdery mildew on plants, mix one teaspoon Arm & Hammer Baking Soda and one-quarter teaspoon Murphy Oil Soap in one quart water. Fill a trigger-spray bottle with the solution and spray directly on plants at the first sign of powdery mildew. Spray once a week until the daytime temperature exceeds 70 degrees Fahrenheit. Baking soda, approved by the USDA as a fungicide, changes the pH of the leaves, inhibiting fungi growth. (Before treating the entire plant, test this formula on one of the plant's leaves and wait one day to make certain it doesn't burn the leaf.)

• **Clean Shower.** Clean mold and mildew from plastic porch furniture by spraying the furniture and the pads with Clean Shower, then wiping clean. The nontoxic, environmentally safe rinsing agents in Clean Shower stop the growth of mold and mildew on contact.

• **Clorox.** To clean mold and mildew from outdoor siding, tile, brick, stucco, and patios, mix three-quarters cup Clorox Bleach per gallon of water. Wearing rubber gloves, scrub the affected area with the solution to kill and remove the mold and mildew.

• **Heinz White Vinegar.** To get rid of mildew stains on patio furniture, spray full-strength Heinz White Vinegar on the chairs and tables, then wipe clean. Vinegar cleans woven-strap lawn furniture without the decay caused by bleach.

• **McCormick Ground Cinnamon.** Fight mildew around peonies by lightly dusting McCormick Ground Cinnamon around the base of each plant. Cinnamon contains a natural fungicide—ortho-methoxycinnamaldehyde—that prevents the growth of fungi.

• **Tide** and **Clorox.** To clean mildew from vinyl-coated polyester cushions for outdoor furniture, mix one cup liquid Tide with one cup Clorox in three gallons water. Submerge the cushions in the solution, scrub with a soft-bristled brush, rinse well, and let dry in the sun.

STRANGE FACTS

• Powdery mildew appears on plants as circular patches of white powder, often crumpling and distorting plant leaves. The spores of this fungus establish themselves on dry leaves without moisture.

• Plants susceptible to powdery mildew include bee balm, crabapples, crape myrtle, dahlias, delphinium, English oak, euonymus, hackberries, honeysuckles, lilac, phlox, privets, roses, and zinnias.

• In his play *King Lear*, first performed around 1605, Shakespeare wrote, "the foul fiend Flibbertigibbet . . . mildews the white wheat, and hurts the poor creatures of earth."

• In his 1964 book *In His Own Write*, John Lennon wrote:

> I'm a moldy moldy man
> I'm moldy thru and thru
> I'm a moldy moldy man
> You would not think it true.

• In German, the word for mildew is *Schimmel*.

• In 1997, the funk band Fambooey, named after an episode of *Soul Train*, released the album *Live at Club Mildew*.

Mosquitoes

- **Bounce.** To repel mosquitoes while you're working in the garden, tie a sheet of Bounce Classic through one of your belt loops or the plastic flap on the back of your baseball cap. Oleander, the fragrance in Bounce Classic, repels mosquitoes. If one sheet of Bounce Classic doesn't work for you, fill your other belt loops with sheets of Bounce Classic, turning yourself into an interesting fashion statement.

- **Ivory Dishwashing Liquid.** One teaspoon Ivory Dishwashing Liquid per gallon of water in rain barrels and other pools of still water kills any developing mosquito larvae.

- **Lemon Joy.** To kill swarming mosquitoes, mix two or three drops of Lemon Joy in a bowl of water and place the bowl on the patio. Mosquitoes will converge on it, get stuck in the soapy solution, and die.

- **Listerine.** Repel mosquitoes by rubbing Listerine (original, not Cool Mint) on your skin. The thyme in Listerine keeps mosquitoes away.

- **Pam Original Cooking Spray.** Mosquito eggs, larvae, and pupae incubate in still water. Eliminating pools of still water helps reduce the proliferation of mosquitoes. If you can't drain pools of still water from holes in large tree trunks, spray the water surface with a fine coat of Pam Cooking Spray so the vegetable oil can smother any developing mosquito larvae.

- **Skin-So-Soft.** This skin cream also happens to double as the best mosquito repellent available, according to *Outdoor Life*, *Field & Stream*, and "Dear Abby." Put one tablespoon Skin-So-Soft in a sixteen-ounce trigger-spray bottle and fill with water. Shake well, then spray on yourself to keep mosquitoes away. You can also spray the Skin-So-Soft solution on screen doors and around doorjambs and windows.

- **Star Olive Oil.** If you can't drain small pools of still water from holes in large tree trunks, add a few drops of Star Olive Oil to the puddle until a fine film of oil coats the surface. The oil slick will smother any developing mosquito larvae.

- **Vicks VapoRub.** Apply Vicks VapoRub to your skin to repel mosquitoes. Mosquitoes hate the scent of eucalyptus.

- **Wesson Corn Oil.** Adding a few drops of Wesson Corn Oil to small pools of still water in large tree trunks creates a thin oil slick on the water surface that smothers any developing mosquito larvae.

STRANGE FACTS

- The strip of land comprising the east coast of Nicaragua and the northeast coast of Honduras is called the Mosquito Coast. The Mosquito Coast is named after the Mosquito Indians, who inhabited the area, not the insect.

- In the 1986 movie *The Mosquito Coast*, based on the novel by Paul Theroux, Harrison Ford stars as an inventor who moves his family to the Mosquito Coast to live like the Swiss Family Robinson.

- After gorging itself on blood, the anopheles mosquito rests for up to twenty-four hours.

- Mosquitoes spread some of the worst diseases known to man, including encephalitis, malaria, and yellow fever.

• The buzzing sound of the mosquito is generated by its beating wings, which flutter approximately one thousand times per second. Female mosquitoes make a higher-pitched buzzing sound than males, which helps males find mates.

• Changing the water frequently in birdbaths prevents mosquito infestations. Mosquito eggs, larvae, and pupae incubate in still water.

• The female mosquito lays up to one thousand eggs during its lifetime.

• The average male mosquito lives between ten and twenty days. The average female mosquito lives more than thirty days.

• The dragonfly feeds on mosquitoes and can fly as fast as sixty miles per hour.

• The word *mosquito* is Spanish for "little fly."

• Only the female mosquito "bites," and to do so, she inserts six needlelike stylets from her proboscis through the victim's skin, shoots saliva into the blood to prevent clotting, and then drinks the blood. Most people are allergic to mosquito saliva, and the swelling and itching are an allergic reaction.

• The town of Clute, Texas, hosts an annual three-day "Great Texas Mosquito Festival," which includes a Mosquito Calling Contest and the Mosquito Legs Contest. The festival's organizers call themselves the SWAT team.

MOSQUITO BITES

✗ **Alka-Seltzer.** Dissolve two Alka-Seltzer tablets in a glass of water, saturate a cotton ball with the solution, and apply to the mosquito bite for twenty minutes (unless you're allergic to aspirin, an ingredient in Alka-Seltzer).

✗ **Aqua Net Hair Spray.** A quick spritz of Aqua Net Hair Spray on a mosquito bite stops the itching pain.

✗ **Arm & Hammer Baking Soda** and **Q-Tips Cotton Swabs.** Make a paste of Arm & Hammer Baking Soda and water, apply to the affected area with a Q-Tips

Cotton Swab, and let dry. The sodium bicarbonate absorbs some of the mosquito saliva from the bite while simultaneously neutralizing the alkalinity, stopping the itch.

✗ **Ban Antiperspirant.** A quick swipe of Ban Antiperspirant over the mosquito bite seems to magically relieve the itching. The aluminum chloride in the antiperspirant apparently dries up the mosquito saliva in the skin.

✗ **Bayer Aspirin.** Wet the skin around the mosquito bite and rub a Bayer Aspirin tablet over the spot (unless, of course, you're allergic to aspirin). Salicin, the active ingredient in aspirin, helps control inflammation.

✗ **BenGay.** Applying a dab of BenGay to a mosquito bite soothes the itching. The menthol seems to do the trick.

✗ **Colgate Toothpaste.** A dab of Colgate Regular Flavor Toothpaste on a mosquito bite relieves the itch instantly. The glycerin in the toothpaste dries up the mosquito secretions in the skin.

✗ **Green Giant Sweet Peas** and **Bounty.** Applying an ice pack to a mosquito bite anesthetizes the sting and prevents swelling. Use a plastic bag of frozen Green Giant Sweet Peas as an ice pack. The sack of peas conforms to the shape of your body. If the bag of peas feels too cold, place a Bounty Paper Towel between your skin and the bag.

✗ **Heinz White Vinegar.** Saturate a cotton ball with Heinz White Vinegar and dab mosquito bites with the cotton ball to relieve the itch.

✗ **Ivory Soap.** Wet a bar of Ivory soap and gently rub it over the mosquito bite. When the soap dries, the skin will feel anesthetized.

✗ **Lipton Tea Bags.** Press a damp Lipton Tea Bag against the mosquito bite to let the tannic acid in the tea soothe the pain and relieve the swelling.

✗ **Listerine.** Use a cotton ball to apply Listerine to the mosquito bite. The antiseptic neutralizes the mosquito saliva and stops the itching.

* **Miracle Whip.** Rubbing a dab of Miracle Whip over a mosquito bite miraculously relieves the itching, perhaps explaining why it's called Miracle Whip.

* **Morton Salt.** Mix a teaspoon of Morton Salt with enough water to make a paste and apply to the mosquito bite. The salt water absorbs the mosquito saliva from the skin.

* **Orajel.** Relieve the itch from a mosquito bite by dabbing some Orajel directly on the skin to anesthetize the area.

* **Phillip's Milk of Magnesia.** Dabbing Phillip's Milk of Magnesia on a mosquito bite stops the itching, thanks to the antacid and drying agents.

* **Popsicle.** Apply an icy Popsicle to the mosquito bite to relieve the itching and swelling.

* **Preparation H.** Rubbing a dab of Preparation H over a mosquito bite soothes the itching and quickly relieves the swelling of any unsightly welts.

* **Vicks VapoRub.** The eucalyptus and menthol in Vicks VapoRub relieves itching when rubbed on a mosquito bite.

* **Ziploc Storage Bags** and **Bounty.** Applying a Ziploc Storage Bag filled with ice to a mosquito bite anesthetizes the sting and relieves swelling. If the bag of ice feels too cold, place a Bounty Paper Towel between your skin and the bag.

MOSS

- **Budweiser** and **Domino Sugar.** Mix one can of Budweiser beer, one-half teaspoon Domino Sugar, and a few patches of moss in a blender. Puree and then paint the slurry one-quarter-inch thick on walls, masonry planters, or fountains to initiate a mossy patina.

- **Carnation Condensed Milk** and **Karo Corn Syrup.** To encourage moss to grow on a stone wall, brick walkway, or terra-cotta pot, mix one can Carnation Condensed Milk and one cup water, spray the area with the solution, and wait a few weeks. Or mix one can Carnation Condensed Milk with one tablespoon Karo Corn Syrup and two cups moss in a blender. Pour or paint the slurry wherever you want moss to grow.

- **Clorox.** To clean slippery moss and algae from brick or stone paths, mix three-quarters cup Clorox Bleach in one gallon water in a bucket and, wearing rubber gloves, scrub the area to remove the moss and algae and help prevent regrowth.

- **Dannon Yogurt.** Grow moss by mixing one cup Dannon Plain Yogurt, one cup water, and a handful of common lawn moss in a blender for thirty seconds. Paint this mixture on flowerpots or pour it between the cracks in a stone sidewalk. Within a few weeks, you'll have attractive new moss decorating your planters or a green mossy carpet between sidewalk stones to prevent weeds from taking root.

- **Reddi-wip.** To get moss to grow on a stone wall, brick walkway, or terra-cotta pot or between sidewalk stones, spray the area with Reddi-wip and wait a few weeks for moss to grow.

STRANGE FACTS

- The moss family contains approximately 23,000 different true mosses.

- The best known moss is sphagnum moss, which holds twenty times its own weight in water.

- Spanish moss, a tropical plant found hanging from trees in Georgia, Alabama, Mississippi, Louisiana, and Florida, is neither a true moss nor a parasite. This flowering plant is actually a member of the pineapple family.

- Peat moss is partly decayed sphagnum moss.

- Roman philosopher Publilius Syrus's maxim "A rolling stone gathers no moss," coined in the first century B.C.E., provided the inspiration for the name of the rock 'n' roll group The Rolling Stones and the magazine *Rolling Stone*.

- Playwright and director Moss Hart won the 1937 Pulitzer Prize with George S. Kaufman for their play *You Can't Take It With You*. Hart also wrote the script for *Gentleman's Agreement*, which won the 1947 Academy Award for best movie.

- In the 1973 movie *The Paper Chase*, starring Timothy Bottoms and John Houseman, one of the law students in James Hart's study group is named Moss.

- In the 1992 movie *Glengarry Glen Ross*, written by David Mamet and adapted from his 1983 Pulitzer Prize–winning play of the same name, one of the real estate salesmen, played by Ed Harris, is named Moss.

• Kate Moss, one of the most recognized and highest paid supermodels of the 1990s, was discovered at the age of fourteen in New York's John F. Kennedy International Airport while returning home with her family from a vacation in the Bahamas.

Sweet Talk on Domino Sugar

In 1807, brothers William and Frederick Havemeyer immigrated to the United States from England to start a cane sugar refinery in lower Manhattan. Five generations of Havemeyers supervised the company's growth and expansion throughout the nineteenth century, adopting the most progressive methods of cane sugar refinement in the industry. In 1899, Henry Havemeyer organized the American Sugar Refining Company, which produced nearly all of the sugar in the United States at that time. The company, renamed Amstar Corporation, eventually became Tate & Lyle North American Sugars, Inc., which today owns the Domino Sugar brand.

• The word *domino* refers to the game played with a set of small rectangular wooden or plastic blocks that have one of their faces divided into halves, each half being either blank or marked by one to six dots resembling those on dice. Ironically, a domino is also a country expected to react politically to events as predicted by the domino theory, which derogatorily describes many sugar-producing countries.

• The average American uses ninety pounds of sugar every year.

• Sugar is used for mixing concrete.

• *Sugar* is slang for "money."

• During World War II, GIs called a letter from one's sweetheart a "sugar report."

• The hit song "Sugar Sugar," by the Archies, was the number three best-selling single in 1969, topping the Rolling Stones' "Honky Tonk Woman" and the Beatles' "Get Back."

• In 1975, Amstar Corporation (maker of Domino Sugar) sued Domino's Pizza for trademark infringement. Domino's Pizza won the legal battle.

Mulch

• **Bubble Wrap.** Place long sheets of Bubble Wrap with the bubble side down on vegetable beds as mulch, securing the plastic in place with stones or weights (see Clorox below). Cut slits in the plastic to accommodate seeds or transplants. The radiant heat created by the plastic warms the soil an additional 3 degrees Fahrenheit. The sheets of Bubble Wrap can be rolled up at the end of the season and reused the next year. Make sure to water beneath the impermeable plastic sheet with a drip line or soaker hose.

• **Clorox.** Secure plastic or aluminum mulch covers in place by filling clean, empty Clorox Bleach jugs with water, replacing the caps securely, and using the jugs as weights. The water-filled jugs double as solar-powered radiant heaters. During the day, the sun heats up the water in the jugs. At night, the heated water radiates warmth for the tender seedlings nearby. To make the jugs even more effective, spray-paint them flat black to absorb more heat.

• **Glad Trash Bags.** Slice open the sides of black Glad Trash Bags to make long sheets and place the black plastic on vegetable beds as mulch, securing the plastic in place with stones. Cut slits into the plastic to accommodate seeds or transplants. The radiant heat created by the plastic warms the soil an additional 3 degrees Fahrenheit. You can roll the plastic sheets up at the end of the season and reuse them the next year. Be certain to water beneath the impermeable plastic sheet with a drip line or soaker hose.

• **Lipton Tea Bags.** Put Lipton Tea Bags (new or used) on the soil around plants in garden beds and planters. Cover the tea bags with mulch. Every time you water the plants, the nutrients from the decomposing tea leaves work their way into the soil.

• **Reynolds Wrap.** Place sheets of Reynolds Wrap around plants and secure in place with stones or bricks. Aluminum foil reflects sunlight, repelling pests and insects. The aluminum foil mulch can be reused repeatedly and ultimately recycled.

• *USA Today.* To make mulch for your garden, shred a copy of *USA Today*, place in your garden bed, and wet down thoroughly. Or, to prepare a new bed in the late summer or early fall, lay several sheets of newspaper over the lawn or soil bed and cover with two inches of compost.

STRANGE FACTS

• Mulch—any loose material placed over the soil—insulates the soil from temperature extremes, prevents damage from frost, reduces evaporation of moisture from the soil, prevents weeds, protects fallen fruit from being damaged, provides plants with nutrients, adds organic matter to the soil, and can enhance the appearance of a garden.

• For Christmas, IKEA leases Christmas trees to customers, who get their deposit back if they return the trees after the holiday season to be ground into mulch.

• Straw and hay are not the same thing. Straw is the dried stems of grains such as wheat, rye, oats, and barley. Hay is dried grasses or other plants.

• The phrases "That's the last straw" and "That's the straw that broke the camel's back," originated with Archbishop John Bramhall, who, in 1655, wrote: "It is the last feather that breaks the horse's back."

• Every July, during the annual Moose Dropping Festival in Talkeetna, Alaska, a weather balloon takes off into the sky carrying a sack filled with one thousand numbered pellets of moose dung. When the dung is dropped, the spectator holding the ticket for the numbered pellet that lands closest to a two-inch X marked on the ground wins one thousand dollars.

• In an episode of the television comedy *The Larry Sanders Show*, Larry, played by Gary Shandling, reluctantly does several commercials for the Garden Weasel, a tool used to turn weeds into "valuable mulch."

Onions

• **Colgate Toothpaste.** To remove the stench of onion from your hands, squeeze a dollop of Colgate Regular Flavor Toothpaste into your palm and wash your hands under running water, leaving your hands smelling minty fresh. (For more ways to clean onion odor from your hands, use the tips on washing away the smell of garlic on page 106.)

• **L'eggs Sheer Energy Panty Hose.** To store onions, cut off a leg from a used, clean pair of L'eggs Sheer Energy Panty Hose, insert one onion and slide it down to the bottom, tie a knot after it, and repeat until you either run out of onions or panty hose leg. Then hang the onions in a cool, dark place with good ventilation. Use a pair of scissors to snip off the bottom onion as needed.

• **Reynolds Wrap.** To prolong the life of onions, wrap individual green onions in a sheet of Reynolds Wrap.

• **Wrigley's Spearmint Gum.** Chewing a piece of Wrigley's Spearmint Gum while peeling onions can help prevent your eyes from tearing.

STRANGE FACTS

• The onion originated in Mongolia.

• According to folklore, the number of skins on an onion at harvest tells how cold the coming winter will be. If the layers are few and thin, the winter will be mild. If the layers are numerous and thick, the winter will be fierce.

• An onion plant lives for only two years.

• In her 1966 poem "Cut," Sylvia Plath sarcastically revels over accidentally cutting her thumb while trying to slice an onion.

• "Green Onions," the instrumental rock 'n' roll song recorded by Booker T. & The M.G.'s, can be heard on the soundtrack of the 1973 movie *American Graffiti*.

• The song "Glass Onion" on the Beatles' 1968 *White Album* lampoons overzealous Beatles fans who obsessively comb the group's lyrics for meanings that are not there.

• In 1984, N. W. Hope of Tempe, Arizona, grew the largest recorded onion in United States history, weighing 7.5 pounds.

Patio Furniture

- **Arm & Hammer Baking Soda.** To clean plastic or metal patio furniture, sprinkle Arm & Hammer Baking Soda on a damp sponge, wipe clean, and dry.

- **Armor All.** Using Armor All to shine up resin patio furniture prevents dirt from settling on the furniture, making it easier to clean.

- **Barbasol Shaving Cream.** Spray Barbasol Shaving Cream on plastic patio furniture and scrub with a brush, wet rag, or sponge. Kids especially love to lather up the patio table with shaving cream. Then simply hose down the children and the furniture.

- **Carnation NonFat Dry Milk.** Paint wooden patio furniture by mixing three cups Carnation NonFat Dry Milk and one cup water until it's the consistency of paint. Then add food coloring or pigment (available at art supply stores) to make whatever hue you desire. Thin the paint by adding more water; thicken the paint by adding more powdered milk. Brush on as you would any other paint. Let the first coat dry for at least twenty-four hours before adding a second coat. Let the second dry for three days. American colonists painted their homes with milk. They would boil berries in milk that would thicken and color the milk. Once it dries, milk paint is incredibly durable. It won't wash off. Plus, you can have milk and cookies while you paint. Just try doing that with regular latex.

• **Cascade.** To clean patio furniture, dissolve one-quarter cup Cascade dishwashing powder in one gallon very hot water. Scrub, then wipe clean with a dry cloth. Cascade is spot-resistant and contains water-softening agents, so everything gets shiny clean without rinsing.

• **Clean Shower.** Clean mold and mildew from plastic porch furniture by spraying the furniture and the pads with Clean Shower, then wiping clean. The nontoxic, environmentally safe rinsing agents in Clean Shower stop the growth of mold and mildew on contact.

• **Clorox.** Mix three-quarters cup Clorox Bleach with one gallon water and fill a trigger-spray bottle with the solution. Spray the solution on plastic lawn chairs and tables and wipe dry with a clean cloth.

• **Coca-Cola.** Strip paint off metal patio furniture by covering the paint for one week with a bath towel saturated with Coca-Cola. Add more Coke every day to keep the towel wet. The paint strips off effortlessly.

• **Crisco All-Vegetable Shortening.** To preserve a wooden bench or any other wooden patio furniture, apply Crisco All-Vegetable Shortening to the wood and buff with a clean, soft cloth. The oils in the shortening give wood a healthy, protective shine.

• **Heinz White Vinegar.** To get rid of mildew stains on patio furniture, spray full-strength Heinz White Vinegar on the chairs and tables, then wipe clean. Vinegar cleans woven-strap lawn furniture without the decay caused by bleach.

• **Kiwi Shoe Polish.** Use Kiwi Shoe Polish to stain wooden patio furniture to a high polish. Repeat to achieve a deeper color. Kiwi Shoe Polish is less expensive than stain and easier to apply, and it leaves a high-gloss finish.

- **Pam Original Cooking Spray.** To clean oil and dirt from wooden lawn furniture, spray the wood with Pam Cooking Spray and buff with a soft cloth.

- **Pledge.** Spray plastic lawn chairs and tables with a light coat of Pledge and buff with a clean cloth. The Pledge keeps the plastic shiny and smooth so dirt no longer sticks to the furniture.

- **Rit Dye.** Stain wooden patio furniture by mixing up Rit Dye according to the directions on the box and using a sponge brush to give wood one coat of the mixture. Let dry, then sandpaper the wood, if desired, to achieve an antique look.

- **Spam** and **L'eggs Sheer Energy Panty Hose.** Polish wooden patio furniture with Spam. The animal oils in Spam polish furniture—without attracting insects or leaving any odor. Simply rub a block of Spam over the wood and buff with a used, clean pair of L'eggs Sheer Energy Panty Hose.

- **Tide** and **Clorox.** To clean mildew from vinyl-coated polyester cushions for outdoor furniture, mix one cup liquid Tide with one cup Clorox Bleach in three gallons water. Submerge the cushions in the solution, scrub with a soft-bristled brush, rinse well, and let dry in the sun.

- **Turtle Wax.** Giving aluminum garden furniture a coat of liquid Turtle Wax rejuvenates the luster of the metal.

- **Wilson Tennis Balls.** To prevent metal patio chairs from noisily scraping along the concrete patio floor, carefully cut a two-inch slit in four Wilson Tennis Balls and put one ball on the bottom of each leg of the chair. The tennis balls eliminate the noise problem.

STRANGE FACTS

- The ancient Egyptians built pyramids containing everything the dead king would need in the afterlife—including furniture.

- When asked for his advice on acting, Spencer Tracy replied, "Just know your lines and don't bump into furniture."

• In the 1973 science fiction movie *Soylent Green*, starring Charlton Heston, every apartment comes equipped with a woman whose profession is known as "furniture."

• The town of Manilus, New York, holds an annual chair race in which contestants push someone in a chair down the town's main street.

• Using only his teeth, Jack Del Rio of Chicago, Illinois, could lift two tables and six chairs.

• Archie Bunker's chair, as seen on the television series *All in the Family*, is on exhibit in the Smithsonian Institution in Washington, D.C.

Taking a Shine to Pledge

In 1886, Samuel C. Johnson—a carpenter in Racine, Wisconsin, whose customers were more interested in his floor wax product than his parquet floors—gave up carpentry, founded S. C. Johnson & Son, and began manufacturing floor care products. By the time his son, Herbert Fiske Johnson, died in 1928, annual sales exceeded five million dollars. Herbert's two children, Herbert Jr. and Henrietta Louis, inherited 60 percent and 40 percent of the company. In 1954, with annual sales topping $45 million, Herbert Jr.'s son Samuel Curtis Johnson joined the company. He introduced Raid insecticide, Off! insect repellent, Pledge aerosol furniture polish, and Glade aerosol air freshener. In 1987, S. C. Johnson & Son went public as Johnson Worldwide Associates, Inc., but the Johnson family retained the majority of the stock and voting control.

• The brand name *Pledge* apparently signifies the act of binding or securing furniture with a protective finish.

• S. C. Johnson & Son, better known as Johnson Wax because of its popular floor wax products, is one of the largest makers of consumer chemical specialty products in the world.

• S. C. Johnson & Son operates a charitable foundation and also gives five percent of its pretax profits to charity every year.

• Chairman Samuel Curtis Johnson, whose great-grandfather founded the company, controls 60 percent of S. C. Johnson & Son.

• Pledge is available in Lemon and Country Garden Potpourri.

Peppers

• **Campbell's Tomato Soup.** Protect pepper plants in your garden with clean, empty Campbell's Tomato Soup cans. With a can opener, remove the bottom of the soup can. Push the metal cylinder into the soil around young pepper plants to fend off cutworms, grubs, and other pests. The can will also shelter the sprouting plants from the wind.

• **Carnation NonFat Dry Milk.** To prevent blossom-end rot on peppers caused by drought or excessive rain, sprinkle a handful of Carnation NonFat Dry Milk powder around the base of the plant and gently mix into the soil. Repeat every few weeks. Carnation NonFat Dry Milk adds calcium to the soil.

• **Crayola Chalk.** To prevent diseases caused by calcium deficiency, use a mortar and pestle to grind up a box of Crayola Chalk and then sprinkle the chalk dust (calcium carbonate) over the soil around the pepper plant.

• **Goodyear Tires.** To protect pepper plants in your garden, lay Goodyear tires on top of the soil and plant peppers inside them.

The tires will shelter the sprouting plants from the wind, and the dark rubber will absorb heat from the sun and warm the soil.

- **L'eggs Sheer Energy Panty Hose** and **Oral-B Mint Waxed Floss.** To prevent squirrels or raccoons from destroying growing pepper plants, cut off the feet from a clean, used pair of L'eggs Sheer Energy Panty Hose, slip a foot over an individual pepper, and seal the open end closed with a piece of Oral-B Mint Waxed Floss. The synthetic fibers keep squirrels and raccoons away, and the flexible hose expands as the peppers grow. You can also cut a section from a leg of the panty hose, tie one end closed with dental floss, cover the pepper, and then secure the open end shut.

- **Mr. Coffee Filters.** To plant pepper seedlings, dip a Mr. Coffee Filter in water and wrap it around each plant stem. The paper wrapping keeps the plant moist and deters cutworms.

- **Oral-B Mint Waxed Floss.** To hang up chile peppers to dry and make a decorative wall hanging at the same time, tie a group of three peppers together by the stems with a long piece of Oral-B Mint Waxed Floss. Repeat until you've created several groups of three, then tie all the strings together to create a multilevel string of chile peppers that can be braided around each other. Hang from a door frame or ceiling rafter.

- **Playtex Living Gloves.** When picking, handling, or preparing chile peppers, wear Playtex Living Gloves to protect your hands from being burned by the fiery alkaloid capsaicin.

- **Reynolds Wrap.** Before planting a pepper seedling, wrap the stem loosely with a four-inch tube of Reynolds Wrap, giving the seedling room to grow. Plant the seedling with two inches of the foil in the soil. The foil tube will protect the pepper plant from cutworms.

- **Ziploc Storage Bags.** If you don't have a pair of gloves to protect your hands from being burned by the capsaicin when picking, handling, or preparing chile peppers, wear a pair of Ziploc Storage Bags over your hands.

STRANGE FACTS

• If hot chile peppers and sweet bell peppers are planted near each other in a garden, cross-pollination may occur, causing the bell peppers to be spicier.

• Tabasco Pepper Sauce, invented in 1868, is made by mixing crushed peppers and salt in white oak barrels and letting the concoction age for up to three years.

• Dr Pepper, invented in 1885, is purportedly named after a Virginia physician, Dr. William R. Pepper, whose daughter, Minerva, captured the heart of local pharmacist Wade B. Morrison. Customers at Morrison's Old Corner Drug Store in Waco, Texas, familiar with the story of the short-lived romance, named Morrison's bittersweet soft drink after Dr. Pepper.

• Chile peppers, unlike other peppers, contain higher levels of capsaicin, the alkaloid responsible for the fiery taste. The spicy compound is not found in any other plant.

• The alkaloid capsaicin found in peppers is proven to numb pain when applied topically. Capsaicin enters nerves and temporarily depletes them of the neurotransmitter that sends pain signals to the brain.

• In 1912, pharmacologist Wilbur Scoville devised an organoleptic test to rate the hotness of peppers. The mildest bell peppers rate zero; habanero peppers score between 200,000 and 300,000 units.

• The Beatles 1967 concept album *Sgt. Peppers Lonely Hearts Club Band* contains the song "A Day in the Life," which was banned by the BBC because of its overt reference to drugs.

• In the 1975 movie *The Great Waldo Pepper*, Robert Redford stars as a daredevil barnstorming pilot who longs to fly in World War I dogfights.

• In 1987, R. Allen of Gillespie, Illinois, grew the tallest recorded pepper plant in United States history, measuring eight feet, one inch tall.

Poison Ivy

- **Glad Trash Bags.** Slice open the sides of black Glad Trash Bags to make long sheets and place the black plastic over the poison ivy, securing the plastic in place with stones so no light can reach the plant. After a week, the poison ivy should be dead and you can carefully remove the plastic.

- **Morton Salt.** Pouring Morton Salt on poison ivy on a dry, sunny day kills the plant.

- **Playtex Living Gloves** and **Glad Trash Bags.** Wearing a pair of Playtex Living Gloves, place your hand and arm inside a Glad Trash Bag and use the plastic bag like an enormous glove to pull the poison ivy and its roots from the ground. Carefully remove the trash bag inside out, capturing the poison ivy inside. Secure tightly and dispose in the trash. Remove and hose down the gloves with water, without letting the urushiol—the oil from the poison ivy now on the gloves—come in contact with your skin.

- **Smirnoff Vodka.** Mix one ounce Smirnoff Vodka and two cups water in a sixteen-ounce trigger-spray bottle. Saturate the poison ivy. The vodka dehydrates the ivy, killing it.

• **20 Mule Team Borax.** Pour 20 Mule Team Borax directly on the roots of the poison ivy to kill the plant.

• *USA Today.* Thoroughly wet a section of *USA Today* so the pages cling together and place the soggy newspaper mat over the poison ivy, anchoring in place with rocks or soil so no light can reach the plant. After a week, the poison ivy should be dead and you can carefully remove the newspaper.

STRANGE FACTS

• The 1985 made-for-TV movie *Poison Ivy* stars Michael J. Fox as a counselor at Camp Pinewood who falls in love with the camp nurse, played by Nancy McKeon (best remembered as Jo Polniaczek on the television comedy *The Facts of Life*).

• Merely taking off your shoes after walking through poison ivy can give you the poison ivy rash. When urushiol—the oil from the poison ivy (which is now on your shoes)—comes in contact with your hands, it rapidly penetrates the skin and combines with skin proteins to trigger an allergic reaction.

• Pouring boiling water over small patches of poison ivy kills the plant.

• Urushiol oil—one of the most potent external toxins known to man—is similar to carbolic acid.

• Urushiol on tools, gloves, clothes, or boots retains its potency for up to one year.

• In the 1992 movie *Poison Ivy*, Drew Barrymore stars as a psychotic teenager named Ivy who, taken in by a wealthy family and determined to take control of the household, slowly seduces the father.

POISON IVY RASH

⚹ **Arm & Hammer Baking Soda.** To soothe a poison ivy rash, make a paste of Arm & Hammer Baking Soda and water, and apply to the affected skin.

⚹ **Balmex.** Apply Balmex to the affected skin to relieve the burning pain and dry any oozing sores.

⚹ **Carnation NonFat Dry Milk** and **Morton Salt.** Mix ten ounces Carnation NonFat Dry Milk powder and twenty-five ounces water in a two-quart container. Fill up the rest of the container by adding ice cubes, then sprinkle two tablespoons Morton Salt over the ice. Saturate a washcloth (or a Stayfree Maxi Pad) in the ice-cold milky solution and apply to the infected area for twenty minutes, three or four times daily.

⚹ **Cascade.** Fill your cupped palm with a handful of Cascade dishwashing powder and scrub affected skin in the shower. The phosphates in the dishwashing powder cleanse the urushiol oil from skin and dry any inflammations.

⚹ **Cutex Nail Polish Remover.** Within thirty minutes of contact with poison ivy, wash the contaminated skin with soap and water, then use a cotton ball to apply Cutex Nail Polish Remover to the area. According to the *New York Times*, the acetone in the nail-polish remover will remove some of the urushiol—the oil in poison ivy that rapidly penetrates the skin and combines with skin proteins to trigger an allergic reaction—thus reducing the severity of the itching and possibly preventing a rash altogether.

⚹ **Dr. Bronner's Peppermint Soap.** Coat the affected skin area with Dr. Bronner's Peppermint Soap and cover with a warm, damp washcloth. The peppermint helps relieve itching.

⚹ **Epsom Salt.** To soothe a poison ivy rash, make a paste of Epsom Salt and water, and apply to the affected skin.

⚹ **Heinz White Vinegar** and **Morton Salt.** Pour Heinz White Vinegar over the affected area, sprinkle lightly with Morton Salt, let dry, then brush clean. Repeat if itching recurs or if the rash begins oozing. The vinegar and salt treatment should dry up the rash within two days.

✗ **Kingsford's Corn Starch.** To soothe a poison ivy rash, make a paste of Kingford's Corn Starch and water, and apply to the affected skin.

✗ **Listerine.** Douse the affected area with Listerine and scrub well. This antiseptic treatment will sting but should stop the itching immediately.

✗ **Nestea.** Mix one tablespoon Nestea instant iced tea and one tablespoon water into a paste and, using a cotton ball, dab the paste on the affected area to dry and soothe the rash. Or, if the rash is extreme, pour the entire jar of Nestea instant iced tea into a bathtub, fill the bath with water, and soak in the tea. The tannic acid in the tea relieves poison ivy rash. It's not exactly what the company meant when they advertised "Take the Nestea Plunge," but you'll certainly feel soothed and refreshed.

✗ **Preparation H.** Applying this hemorrhoid ointment to poison ivy relieves the burning and swelling and clears up the rash.

✗ **Quaker Oats** and **L'eggs Sheer Energy Panty Hose.** Using a blender, grind one cup Quaker Oats into a fine powder. Cut off a foot from a clean, used pair of L'eggs Sheer Energy Panty Hose, fill with the powdered oats, and tie a knot in the nylon. Hang the "oatmeal tea bag" from the spigot in the bathtub, fill the tub with warm water, and soak for thirty minutes for an inexpensive and soothing oatmeal bath. You can also use the oatmeal sachet as a gentle washcloth.

✗ **ReaLemon.** Apply ReaLemon over the affected areas of skin to soothe itching and alleviate the rash.

✗ **Smirnoff Vodka.** If you come into contact with poison ivy, soak a washcloth (or Stayfree Maxi Pad) with Smirnoff Vodka and saturate the affected area of skin to remove the urushiol. Then wipe down your hands and the bottle.

✗ **Windex with Ammonia-D.** Within thirty minutes of contact with poison ivy, spray the contaminated skin with Windex, then wash with soap and water. The ammonia and soaps in Windex remove some of the urushiol, the oil in poison ivy that rapidly penetrates the skin and combines with skin proteins to trigger an allergic reaction.

Potatoes and Avocados

• **Campbell's Tomato Soup.** Protect potatoes in your garden with clean, empty Campbell's Tomato Soup cans. With a can opener, remove the bottoms of the soup cans. Push a metal cylinder into the soil around each young potato plant to fend off cutworms, grubs, and other pests. The can will also shelter the sprouting plants from the wind.

• **Forster Toothpicks.** To root a potato or avocado, securely insert four Forster Toothpicks equidistantly around the middle of the potato or avocado. (If necessary, use a nail to punch starter holes in the avocado.) Fill a glass with water and set the potato or avocado in the glass so the toothpicks allow only the bottom half of the potato or avocado to sit in the water. Place the glass on a window ledge to get sunlight. Change the water every few days and monitor the water level. After several weeks, when roots and shoots appear, pot up the potato or avocado.

• **Glad Trash Bags.** To control Colorado potato beetles, slice open the sides of black Glad Trash Bags to make long sheets, place the black plastic over the ground beneath the plants, and gently sweep over the plants with a broom to send the beetles tumbling into the plastic sheets.

• **Goodyear Tires.** To protect potato plants in your garden, place an old Goodyear Tire around each potato plant. The tires will shelter the sprouting plants from the wind, and the dark rubber will absorb heat from the sun and warm the soil. To yield up to five times more potatoes, fill the tire with soil. When the plant sprouts, stack a second old Goodyear Tire on top of the first and fill with soil. When the plant sprouts through the soil again, stack a third old Goodyear Tire on top of the second and fill with soil. Check the soil daily to see if it needs watering (the heat retained by the rubber tires dries out the soil quickly). To harvest, simply unstack the tires.

• **Heinz White Vinegar.** To prevent potato tubers from being disfigured by common scab, keep the soil slightly acid by watering the plant with a mixture of two tablespoons Heinz White Vinegar per quart of water.

• **Hula Hoops, Bubble Wrap,** and **Scotch Packaging Tape.** Building row covers can stop flea beetles that spread viruses from infecting your potato crop. Make hoop supports by cutting Hula Hoops in half and inserting the legs firmly into the soil. Cover with a canopy made from sheets of Bubble Wrap and secure to the hoops with Scotch Packaging Tape, making sure the sheets of Bubble Wrap are high enough not to touch the plants. You can also secure the Bubble Wrap by staking the ends to the ground with wire. At the end of the season, roll up the Bubble Wrap to be used again the following year. (Be sure to monitor the temperatures inside this minigreenhouse to make certain you do not burn out your plants, or substitute sheer curtains for the Bubble Wrap.)

• **Ivory Dishwashing Liquid.** Control Colorado potato beetles by mixing one teaspoon Ivory Dishwashing Liquid and one quart water in a bucket. Pluck the larvae off your plants and drop them in the bucket of soapy water, killing them.

• **McCormick Food Coloring.** To make colorful mashed potatoes, add a few drops of food coloring and mix well, creating a festive holiday food (green mashed potatoes for St. Patrick's Day, orange for Halloween, and red, white, and blue for the Fourth of July).

• **Smirnoff Vodka** and **Q-Tips Cotton Swabs.** The tips of avocado plants tend to attract aphids and mealybugs. Dip a Q-Tips Cotton Swab in Smirnoff Vodka to remove the pests. (For more ways to combat aphids, see page 7.)

• *USA Today.* To prevent weeds around potato plants, hoe between well-established plants, lay down a two-sheet-thick layer of *USA Today*, and top with a thin layer of soil to hold the paper in place. The newspaper mulch blocks weeds while simultaneously giving the potato plants a nutritious boost.

• *USA Today.* To repel Colorado potato beetles, place at least three inches of shredded *USA Today* around potato plants. The mulch attracts beneficial insects that will devour destructive Colorado potato beetles before they can make their way to the surface through the mulch.

STRANGE FACTS

• The potato originated in the Peruvian and Bolivian Andes, where farmers cultivated and crossbred it as early as 200 C.E.

• The Incas invented freeze-dried potatoes. They left potatoes out for several days, allowing them to continually freeze by night and thaw by day. They squeezed out the remaining moisture by hand and then dried the potatoes in the sun.

• In the sixteenth century, while Spanish explorers introduced the potato to Europe, English explorers brought the potato to the British Isles, where it became the principal crop of Ireland. Today, Russia grows nearly 30 percent of the world's potatoes, more than any other country.

• During colonial times, New Englanders—convinced that raw potatoes contained an aphrodisiac that induced behavior that shortened a person's life—fed potatoes to pigs as fodder.

• After serving as ambassador to France, Thomas Jefferson brought the recipe for French-fried potatoes to America, where he served them to guests at his Monticello home, popularizing French fries in the United States.

• From 1847 to 1850, potato blight (a fungal disease) swept across Ireland, destroying the country's entire potato crop for four consecutive years. The resulting famine killed more than one million people. Since then, Ireland has imported blight-resistant strains of the potato from South America.

• Vincent Van Gogh's 1885 painting *The Potato Eaters* portrays a family of five peasants gathered around a table eating potatoes. "I have tried to emphasize that those people eating their potatoes in the lamplight," Van Gogh wrote in a letter to his brother, Theo, "have dug the earth with those very hands they put in the dish, and so it speaks of manual labor, and how they have honestly earned their food."

• The leaves of the potato plant are poisonous if eaten.

• The eyes in a potato are the indents where sprouts grow. You can grow potatoes by chopping up a seed potato into chunks with at least two or three eyes, letting the chunks dry in the sun for twenty-four hours, and then planting them.

• Store-bought potatoes are frequently treated with a sprouting inhibitor. If you plant them, they may not grow.

• 'All Blue', 'Purple Peruvian', and 'Purple Viking' are potato varieties that have bright purple skin.

• In the lyrics to the 1937 hit song "Let's Call the Whole Thing Off," Ira Gershwin enunciates the different pronunciations for the word *potato*. His brother George Gershwin wrote the music.

• In 1946, the first toy commercial aired on television. The toy advertised was Mr. Potato Head.

• Placing the pit of an avocado in freshly made guacamole prevents the dip from turning brown.

• In 1963, J. East of Spalding, Great Britain, grew the largest recorded potato in history, weighing seven pounds, one ounce. In 1982, J. Busby of Atherstone, Great Britain, tied that record.

• When Pope John Paul II visited Miami, Florida, a local T-shirt maker translated the phrase "I Saw the Pope" into Spanish by incorrectly using the feminine *la papa* instead of the masculine *el pape*, which made the T-shirts read: "I saw the potato."

• Of the fruits most commonly eaten raw, the avocado has the most nutritional value, with 741 calories per edible pound, 2.2 percent protein, and vitamins A, C, and E.

• In 1992, while helping with a spelling bee at the Luis Munoz Rivera School in Trenton, New Jersey, Vice President Dan Quayle prodded sixth-grader William Figueroa, who had correctly spelled the word *potato* on the blackboard, to add one more letter—an "e" at the end.

• In India, McDonald's offers the McAloo Tikki burger, a spicy vegetarian patty made of potatoes and peas.

Potted Plants

• **Arm & Hammer Baking Soda.** Neutralize the acidity of potting soil by watering the soil once with a mixture of four table-spoons Arm & Hammer Baking Soda and one quart water.

• **Aunt Jemima Original Syrup.** Revive an ailing plant by adding two tablespoons Aunt Jemima Original Syrup at the base of the plant once a month.

• **Bounce.** To prevent the soil from leaking out of a planter, line the bottom of the planter with a used sheet of Bounce Classic. The dryer sheet allows water, but not soil, to drain through—and won't break apart when it gets wet.

• **Bounty.** Use the cardboard tube from a roll of Bounty Paper Towels to create additional drainage in a strawberry pot. Pour a few inches of fine gravel into the bottom of the pot, place the cardboard tube in the pot, and fill with gravel. Fill the rest of the pot with potting mix and remove the cardboard tube, leaving behind a column of gravel to help with drainage.

- **Bubble Wrap** and **Scotch Packaging Tape.** To protect plastic, wood, and fiberglass planters left outside during the winter months, wrap the planter with Bubble Wrap and secure in place with Scotch Packaging Tape. The extra insulation helps protect both the plant and the planters. Or before planting, cut a piece of Bubble Wrap to fit around the inside of a terra-cotta pot before filling with soil to insulate plant roots and prevent constant freezing and thawing. (To allow for drainage, do not line the bottom of the planter.)

- **Canada Dry Club Soda.** Feed flat Canada Dry Club Soda to potted plants. The minerals in club soda are beneficial to plants.

- **Cascade.** To avoid spreading diseases when transplanting seedlings or plants into pots, clean pots and flats thoroughly by soaking them for ten minutes in a bathtub filled with warm water and one tablespoon Cascade dishwashing powder, then scrubbing the pots in the solution with a stiff brush. Rinse clean and let dry thoroughly in the sun.

- **Castor Oil.** Rejuvenate a potted plant ailing from a nutrient deficiency by dribbling one tablespoon castor oil into the soil and then watering well.

- **Clorox.** Mix three-quarters cup Clorox Bleach per gallon of water in a bucket and use this solution to disinfect recycled plastic and clay pots, planters, and seed-starting trays. Let soak for an hour, then rinse and dry.

- **Coca-Cola.** Remove the label from a clean, empty two-liter plastic Coca-Cola bottle, drill drainage holes in the bottom, cut the bottle in half with a pair of scissors, and use the bottom half as a planter for flowers.

- **Dannon Yogurt.** Using an electric drill with a one-quarter-inch bit at a slow speed, drill a hole in the center of the bottom of a clean, empty Dannon Yogurt cup to create a drainage hole in this perfect planter.

- **Depends.** If a planter is leaking excess water, set the pot inside a pair of Depends, creating a diaper for the plant. Conceal the

Depends diaper by placing the pot inside a second, larger, empty pot.

• **Epsom Salt.** For every foot of a potted plant's height, sprinkle one teaspoon Epsom Salt evenly around the plant's base for better blossoms and deeper greening. Adding Epsom Salt to plant food will also enrich the color of any flowering plants and aid in disease resistance. Or mix one tablespoon Epsom Salt in one gallon water and spray the mixture on the plant. Epsom Salt is magnesium sulfate, which lowers the pH of the soil and provides much-needed magnesium.

• **Forster Clothes Pins.** Secure plants to a trellis by simply attaching the stems with Forster Clothes Pins.

• **Geritol.** Revive an ailing plant by adding two tablespoons Geritol to the soil twice a week for three months. New leaves should begin to grow within the first month.

• **Glad Trash Bags.** Store extra potting mix in a Glad Trash Bag for future use. Organic potting soil mix stays fresh for several months.

• **Glad Trash Bags** and **Bubble Wrap.** To help outdoor potted plants survive the winter, place the pot inside a Glad Trash Bag, then fill the bag with Bubble Wrap to insulate the plant roots and the pot (to prevent cracking). Seal the bag tightly around the trunk of the plant and set the pot on top of a wood block so it is raised off the ground.

• **Heinz Apple Cider Vinegar.** To revive undernourished plants, mix one tablespoon Heinz Apple Cider Vinegar in one gallon water in a watering can and water potted plants with the solution. The vinegar neutralizes the pH of the water, making vital nutrients in the water more available to the plants.

• **Heinz White Vinegar** and **Scotch-Brite Heavy Duty Scrub Sponges.** To remove mineral deposits or hard water stains from a planter, mix equal parts Heinz White Vinegar and water in a bucket, and scrub with a Scotch-Brite Heavy Duty Scrub Sponge.

• **Huggies Baby Wipes.** Empty Huggies Baby Wipes boxes make excellent drainage trays for two small potted plants.

• **Huggies Pull-Ups.** If your planter is leaking water, set the pot inside a pair of Huggies Pull-Ups, creating an absorbent diaper for the plant. Place the pot inside a second, larger pot to conceal the Pull-Up.

• **Jell-O.** Work a few teaspoons of powdered Jell-O into the soil of potted plants to absorb water and prevent it from leaking out of the bottom of the pot. The absorbent gelatin also reduces how often you need to water the plants. The nitrogen in Jell-O enhances plant growth and hastens sprouting, and the sugar feeds the microbes in the soil, producing more nutrients for the plant.

• **L'eggs Sheer Energy Panty Hose.** To prevent the soil from leaking from the bottom of a planter, place a used pair of L'eggs Sheer Energy Panty Hose in the bottom of the pot, allowing water, but not the soil, to drain.

• **L'eggs Sheer Energy Panty Hose.** Using a pair of scissors, cut off the toe from the foot of a pair of used, clean L'eggs Sheer Energy Panty Hose, then cut one-inch strips from the leg, creating circular loops of panty hose. Use the loops to gently tie stems, vines, and thin plant trunks to garden stakes with a figure eight loop.

• **Lipton Tea Bags.** Place Lipton Tea Bags (new or used) on the soil around plants in planters. Cover the tea bags with mulch. Every time you water the plants, the nutrients from the decomposing tea leaves work their way into the soil.

• **Lipton Tea Bags.** Before potting a plant, place several Lipton Tea Bags (new or used) on top of the drainage layer of pebbles, pottery shards, or panty hose (see L'eggs Sheer Energy Panty Hose above) at the bottom of the planter. The tea bags retain water and provide nutrients for the plant.

• **Maxwell House Coffee.** Maxwell House Coffee grounds are full of nutrients that plants love. Instead of throwing out the used coffee grounds after you make a pot of coffee, give them to your potted plants. Just work the grounds into the soil.

• **Mr. Coffee Filters.** To prevent soil from leaking through the drainage holes of a seed-starting pot, line the bottom of the pot with a Mr. Coffee Filter.

• **Nestea.** Mix up a quart of unsweetened Nestea instant iced tea according to the directions (without adding sugar or ice) and fertilize potted plants with the solution. Or simply sprinkle the powdered mix directly on top of the soil. As the tea decomposes, the nutrients work their way into the soil.

• **Pampers.** Using a pair of scissors, carefully cut open a Pampers disposable diaper, and pot a plant by alternating potting soil with the superabsorbent polymer flakes from the diaper. The polymer flakes absorb three hundred times their weight in water, reducing how often you need to water your potted plants. The gelatinous polymer also stores nutrients, slowly feeding the plants.

• **Reynolds Wrap.** Before leaving town for a few days, wrap clay pots with Reynolds Wrap to prevent the soil from drying out.

• **Saran Quick Covers.** To prevent water from dripping all over the floor when you are watering a hanging plant, place a Saran Quick Cover around the bottom of the hanging planter before watering. The plastic cap catches the drips. Wait one hour before removing and save the Quick Cover to use the next time you water the plant.

• **Star Olive Oil.** Add two tablespoons Star Olive Oil at the bases of ferns or palm plants once a month.

• *USA Today.* To help keep a potted plant moist if you are planning to be away on vacation longer than a week, cut a doughnut shape from a section of *USA Today*, then dampen the newspaper ring with water, water the plant well, and place the newspaper ring on top of the soil, around the plant. The dampened ring of newspaper will reduce the loss of moisture from the soil while you're gone.

STRANGE FACTS

• Planters Peanuts, founded in 1906 in Wilkes-Barre, Pennsylvania, by Italian immigrants Amedeo Obici and Mario Peruzzi, owes its success to Obici's ingenious invention: the world's first motorized peanut-roasting machine.

• Mr. Peanut was designed in 1916 by a Suffolk, Virginia, school-child who won five dollars in a contest sponsored by Planters Peanuts.

• Terra-cotta, a fired brownish orange clay usually used to fashion planters and roofing tiles, literally means "baked earth" in Italian.

• The creepy 1956 science fiction movie *Invasion of the Body Snatchers* stars Kevin McCarthy as a scientist who discovers that vegetable pods from outer space are duplicating and then destroying humans at an alarming rate.

• In 1974, Chinese peasants digging a well twenty miles east of the city of Xian uncovered an underground vault housing thou-sands of terra-cotta sculptures of life-size warriors and their horses in battle formation, following Emperor Qin Shi Huang—entombed nearby—into the afterlife. The terra-cotta warriors and the emperor had been buried undisturbed since 210 B.C.E. In 1976, archeologists found two more underground vaults of terra-cotta warriors.

• Soaking a terra-cotta pot in water for a few minutes before filling it with soil prevents the clay from absorbing moisture from the soil.

• The 1978 low-budget science fiction movie *The Plants Are Watching* tells the story of a clairvoyant woman who uses her uncanny ability to read the minds of plants to find a murderer.

• In 1996 alone, K-mart stores sold 83,000 tons of potting soil.

Pruning

• **Clorox.** Disinfect your pruning tools with a mixture of three-quarters cup Clorox Bleach in a gallon of water after each use to avoid spreading fungal or bacterial diseases. Dip your pruning equipment into the disinfectant solution between cuts or at least between plants. When finished, soak the pruning shears in the solution for one hour, then rinse clean and dry.

• **Coppertone.** A few drops of Coppertone on the sap-stained blades of pruning shears, when rubbed with a clean cloth, removes the sticky residue.

• **Crisco All-Vegetable Shortening.** Clean sap from the blades of pruning shears with a few dabs of Crisco All-Vegetable Shortening. Wipe the shortening off with a cloth.

• **Cutex Nail Polish Remover.** Clean sap or resin from pruning shears by rubbing the blades with a cloth dipped in Cutex Nail Polish Remover.

- **DAP Caulk.** Seal the ends of pruned stems and branches with DAP Caulk to protect the plant against insects and excessive moisture.

- **Dial.** To help saw blades glide easily while trimming a tree, rub a bar of Dial antibacterial soap over the blade and saw teeth. The soap acts as a lubricant and also kills bacteria that might harm the tree.

- **Elmer's Glue-All.** Use Elmer's Glue-All to seal the ends of pruned stems and branches to guard against insects and excessive moisture loss.

- **Forster Clothes Pins.** Use a Forster Clothes Pin as a clamp to hold the stems of thorny plants to avoid pricking your fingers when pruning.

- **Jif Peanut Butter.** Clean sap from the blades of pruning shears with a few dabs of Jif Peanut Butter and a clean cloth. The oil in peanut butter dissolves sap.

- **Johnson's Baby Oil.** A few drops of Johnson's Baby Oil dissolves tree sap from pruning shears and can also be used to lubricate the pivot joint on the shears.

- **Listerine.** To avoid spreading fungal and bacterial diseases among your plants, sterilize your pruning shears with Listerine after each use. Mix one cup Listerine per gallon of water in a bucket and dip your pruning equipment into the antiseptic solution between cuts or at least between plants. When finished, soak the pruning shears in the solution for one hour, then rinse clean and dry.

- **Lysol.** To prevent viruses from tainting the blades of your pruning shears and spreading diseases to your plants, spray the tool with Lysol. The disinfectant kills germs on contact, killing any viruses.

- **Miracle Whip.** Clean sap from the blades of pruning shears with a few dabs of Miracle Whip and a clean cloth.

- **Noxzema.** In a pinch, a dollop of Noxzema rubbed into the blades of pruning shears with a clean cloth removes stubborn sap.

- **Pam Original Cooking Spray.** Lubricate the pivot joint of pruning shears with Pam Cooking Spray so the blades clench together easily. The cooking spray also removes sap from shears.

- **Purell.** Disinfect pruning tools by coating the blades with Purell Instant Hand Sanitizer. The ethyl alcohol in Purell kills bacteria and fungi.

- **Smirnoff Vodka.** Sterilize your pruning tools with a mixture of two cups Smirnoff Vodka per gallon of water after each use to avoid spreading fungal diseases. Dip your pruning tools into the alcohol solution between cuts or at least between plants. When finished, soak the pruning shears in the solution for one hour, then rinse clean and dry.

- **Vaseline Petroleum Jelly.** Lubricating the pivot area of pruning shears with Vaseline Petroleum Jelly—a product found in virtually every home in the United States—helps the tool work more efficiently.

- **WD-40.** Oil the pivot joint of your pruning shears with a quick shot of WD-40, the water-displacement formula originally developed for the aerospace industry to prevent corrosion on Atlas Missile nosecones.

STRANGE FACTS

- Pruning helps prevent disease from spreading, improves the quality and quantity of fruit, and extends bloom time of flowers.

- The biblical book of Isaiah contains the verse:

  They shall beat their swords into plowshares, and their spears into pruning hooks: nation shall not lift up sword against nation, neither shall they learn war any more (Isaiah 2:4).

- In William Shakespeare's play *Measure for Measure*, first performed around 1604, Pompey says, "Sir, she came in great with child, and longing, saving your honour's reverence, for stewed prunes."

Purely Purell

During World War II, Jerry and Goldie Lippman, working in an Akron, Ohio, rubber plant that made lifeboats for the American military, cleaned graphite, tar, and carbon black from their hands with a benzene-based hand cleaner used by auto mechanics to remove grease.

After the war, Jerry, determined to find a healthier way for rubber workers to clean their hands, collaborated with Clarence Cook of Kent State University to invent a grease-cutting liquid soap that could be used with or without water. The Lippmans turned all their attention to making and selling the new heavy-duty liquid hand cleaner they named Gojer (*Go* for Goldie, *Jer* for Jerry), which later became Go-Jo and evolved into the present-day Gojo. Jerry made the product at night in an old washing machine tub in the couple's garage and sold it to maintenance garages during the day from the back of his car.

Unfortunately, garage owners thought the new hand cleaner was too expensive to purchase for their workers. Undaunted, Jerry developed a portion-control dispenser for the hand cleaner, receiving a patent for his invention in 1952. The dispenser boosted sales of Gojo, which soon dominated the heavy-duty hand cleaner market for institutional use. Gojo developed a full line of healthy skin care products, including Purell Instant Hand Sanitizer, introduced in the 1980s for use by health-care and food-service workers. A dollop of Purell rubbed between the hands briskly until dry (approximately fifteen seconds) instantly sanitizes skin without rinsing or drying. In 1996, the high demand for Purell among professionals using the product at work prompted Gojo to make Purell Instant Hand Sanitizer available to consumers through retail stores.

• In 1947, Jerry Lippman bought the company's first piece of heavy-duty mixing equipment: a used bread-dough mixer. The mixer replaced the old washing machine tub he had been using to mix Gojo.

• Purell kills germs on contact, but once it evaporates, Purell has no residual germ-killing effect.

• The ethyl alcohol in Purell destroys the walls of germ cells, causing germs to die and fall off your skin.

• According to the August 1995 issue of the *American Journal of Infection Control*, "Alcohols applied to the skin are among the safest known antiseptics."

• Purell evaporates from the skin, leaving virtually no residue or stickiness.

• More than 80 percent of all infectious illnesses are spread by the hands. Good hand hygiene helps stop the spread of illness.

• The first recorded use of the phrase "Nipped i' the bud" appears in Sir John Suckling's 1646 play titled *The Tragedy of Brennoralt.*

• In his 1734 poem *An Essay on Man,* Alexander Pope wrote:

Worth makes the man, and want of it the fellow;
The rest is all but leather or prunella.

• On the television comedy *The Andy Griffith Show,* Deputy Sheriff Barney Fife overzealously enforces the law and frequently urges his fellow citizens of quaint Mayberry to "Nip it in the bud."

• In the 1979 movie *Being There,* based on the novel by Jerzy Kosinsky, Peter Sellers stars as simple-minded gardener Chauncey Gardiner, who becomes a greatly admired political insider when his innocent remarks about gardening are interpreted as profound insights. The President of the United States asks him, "Do you think we can stimulate growth through temporary incentives?" Chauncey replies, "As long as the roots are not severed, all is well and all will be well in the garden."

• The phrase "lead someone up the garden path" means to mislead or delude.

• The Canadian town of Whitehorse, in Yukon Territory, hosts an annual "Chain Saw Chuck," in which contestants compete to see who can hurl a chain saw the longest distance.

Pumpkins

- **Arm & Hammer Baking Soda** and **Wesson Corn Oil.** To prevent fungal diseases on pumpkins, mix one teaspoon Arm & Hammer Baking Soda and five drops of Wesson Corn Oil in one quart water. Fill a trigger-spray bottle or sprayer with the solution and spray directly on pumpkins.

- **Clorox.** To kill bacteria and fungi on pumpkins after you've cut them from the vine, mix three-quarters cup Clorox Bleach and one gallon water, and dip the pumpkin in the solution. Then store the pumpkin in a cool, dry place.

- **L'eggs Sheer Energy Panty Hose.** To save space, grow a pumpkin vine on a trellis and, when the fruits begin to grow, slip each one inside a leg cut from a pair of L'eggs Sheer Energy Panty Hose. Tie the free end of the hose to one of the laths to support the growing pumpkin. The synthetic fibers keep insects away, and the flexible hose expands as the pumpkin grows.

- **Reddi-wip.** Spraying one-half cup Reddi-wip Whipped Cream around the base of pumpkin plants every three weeks gives the fruits a soft, creamy orange color.

- **Vaseline Petroleum Jelly.** To deter thieves from stealing decorative pumpkins from your front porch, coat the exterior of the pumpkins with a thin coat of Vaseline Petroleum Jelly to make them difficult to grip.

STRANGE FACTS

- Most Americans carve jack-o'-lanterns from 'Connecticut Field' pumpkins, a direct descendant of the original pumpkins grown by Native Americans.

- In his 1883 poem "When the Frost Is on the Punkin," James Whitcomb Riley wrote:

  O, it sets my heart a-clickin' like the tickin' of a clock,
  When the frost is on the punkin and the fodder's in the shock.

- In the 1904 children's book *The Marvelous Land of Oz*, the first sequel to *The Wonderful Wizard of Oz*, author L. Frank Baum introduces Jack Pumpkinhead, a man made from sticks with a jack-o'-lantern head and brought to life by a magical powder.

- The *Jack-O-Lantern*, the campus humor magazine founded in 1908 at Dartmouth College, boasts such famous alumni as Dr. Seuss, Buck Henry, Chris Miller, and Robert Reich.

- In the popular 1950 Walt Disney animated movie *Cinderella*, Cinderella's fairy godmother turns a 'Rouge Vif D'Etampes' pumpkin—developed in France during the late nineteenth century—into a coach. When French writer Charles Perrault told the Cinderella story in his book *Tales of Mother Goose*, published in 1697, the 'Rouge Vif D'Etampes' pumpkin did not yet exist.

- On October 8, 1997, a large pumpkin mysteriously appeared sitting atop the pointy tip of the famous bell tower at Cornell University. No one came forth to take credit for the prank, and no one could figure out how the pranksters had managed to get a pumpkin, estimated to weigh sixty pounds, pinned atop the 173-foot tower—where it sat undisturbed for several weeks.

Rabbits

- **Gatorade.** To protect a small plant from hungry rabbits, cut off the bottom of an empty, clean Gatorade bottle and place the uncapped bottle over the plant, pushing it into the soil. Remove the bottle when the weather gets too warm. (For other plastic containers that make excellent protective covers, see pages 139 and 140.)

- **Grandma's Molasses** and **Morton Salt.** Grow a patch of clovers and wildflowers in a corner of your yard to give rabbits something to eat other than your vegetables and flowers. To attract the rabbits to your alternative salad bar, spray the patch with a mixture of one cup Grandma's Molasses, one tablespoon Morton Salt, and one gallon water.

- **McCormick Black Pepper.** To keep rabbits away from flowerbeds and vegetable gardens, sprinkle McCormick Black Pepper in your garden around and over bean plants, carrots, lettuce, peas, ornamentals, strawberries, and the bark of apple trees. Rabbits are repelled by the scent of pepper. After it rains, be sure to re-pepper the garden.

- **Reynolds Wrap** and **Scotch Packaging Tape.** To prevent rabbits from chewing the bark of a tree, wrap a piece of Reynolds Wrap loosely around the tree trunk and secure with Scotch Packaging Tape. The shiny foil and the rattling noise will keep rabbits away.

- **Tabasco Pepper Sauce, McCormick Garlic Powder,** and **Ivory Dishwashing Liquid.** Mix two tablespoons Tabasco Pepper Sauce, two tablespoons McCormick Garlic Powder, three drops Ivory Dishwashing Liquid, and two cups water in a sixteen-ounce trigger-spray bottle. Apply this solution to beans, carrots, lettuce, peas, ornamentals, strawberries, and the bark of apple trees to repel rabbits. (Be sure to wash all vegetables thoroughly before preparing or eating—unless, of course, you enjoy spicy vegetables.)

STRANGE FACTS

- Rabbits eat weeds, most notably crabgrass, dandelions, knotweed, and ragweed. Rabbits also eat poison ivy—without any ill effects.

- Rabbits are born blind and without fur, while hares, which are larger and have longer ears than rabbits, are born with vision and fur.

- The Belgian hare is actually a rabbit, and the jackrabbit is actually a hare.

- The Easter bunny originated, according to English historian Venerable Bede (672–735 C.E.), with the Anglo-Saxons, who worshipped the pagan goddess Eastre, symbolized by the hare.

- In Lewis Carroll's 1865 novel *Alice's Adventures in Wonderland*, Alice sees a White Rabbit remove a watch from its waistcoat-pocket and exclaim "Oh dear! Oh dear! I shall be too late!" She follows the rabbit into a large hole and falls down a seemingly endless well, beginning her adventures in Wonderland.

• In the classic 1902 children's book *The Tale of Peter Rabbit*, by Beatrix Potter, Peter Rabbit sneaks away from his siblings—Flopsy, Mopsy, and Cotton-Tail—and, against his mother's warning, squeezes under the gate into Mr. McGregor's garden.

• In the 1937 novel *Of Mice and Men*, by John Steinbeck, farm workers Lennie and George raise rabbits.

• Mel Blanc, the talented voice-over artist who provided the voice of Bugs Bunny, hated carrots.

• In the 1950 movie *Harvey*, Jimmy Stewart stars as Elwood P. Dowd, a drunk who befriends a six-foot-tall invisible rabbit named Harvey.

• Author John Updike wrote a series of best-selling novels—*Rabbit, Run* (1960), *Rabbit Redux* (1971), *Rabbit Is Rich* (1981), and *Rabbit at Rest* (1990)—featuring Harry Angstrom, a car salesman in Brewer, Pennsylvania, who was nicknamed Rabbit as a boy.

• In television commercials for Trix cereal, an animated rabbit is constantly told, "Silly Rabbit, Trix are for kids." The concept for the Trix Rabbit was created by Chris Miller, who later wrote for *National Lampoon* and cowrote the 1978 comedy movie *National Lampoon's Animal House*.

Rodents

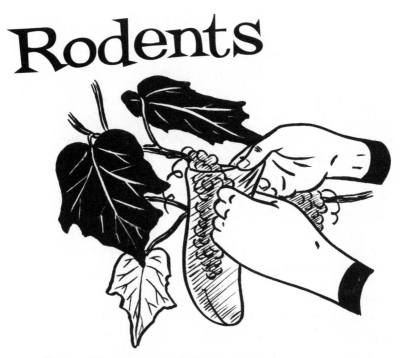

• **Bounce.** Deter mice and rats by placing sheets of Bounce Classic around bags of seed, attached to stakes in the garden, or around stored equipment. The oleander fragrance in Bounce Classic repels rodents.

• **Castor Oil.** To repel mice and rats, mix one-half cup castor oil and two gallons water and use the solution to water your vegetable garden. The castor oil enriches the soil while simultaneously repulsing rodents.

• **Clorox.** To protect bulbs from rodents, cut the top half off a clean, empty Clorox Bleach jug, punch drain holes in the sides and bottom of the bottom half of the jug, sink the jug into a flowerbed, fill with soil, and plant bulbs inside it.

• **Dannon Yogurt.** Protect bulbs from tunneling voles by planting the bulbs inside clean, empty Dannon Yogurt cups drilled with drainage holes.

• **Dannon Yogurt.** Repel rodents by mixing one tablespoon blood meal and one tablespoon water in a clean, empty Dannon

Yogurt container. Stand several of these yogurt cups throughout your garden, placing a rock in each cup to anchor it in place. The fetid aroma of blood meal keeps rodents at bay. Cover the yogurt cups when working in the garden.

• **L'eggs Sheer Energy Panty Hose** and **Oral-B Mint Waxed Floss.** To prevent rodents from destroying growing vegetables, cut off the feet from a clean, used pair of L'eggs Sheer Energy Panty Hose, slip a foot over a tomato, eggplant, bunch of grapes, or head of broccoli or cabbage, and seal the open end closed with a piece of Oral-B Mint Waxed Floss. The synthetic fibers keep rodents away, and the flexible hose expands as the vegetable grows. You can also cut a section from a leg of the panty hose, tie one end closed with dental floss, cover the vegetable, and then secure the open end shut.

• **McCormick Black Pepper.** Before you add layers of kitchen waste to your compost bin, sprinkle the foods with McCormick Black Pepper. The pungent aroma and taste of the pepper helps repel rodents from your compost pile.

• **McCormick Ground (Cayenne) Red Pepper.** Deter rodents from digging up bulbs by sprinkling McCormick Ground Red Pepper around bulb plantings.

• **Reynolds Wrap** and **Scotch Packaging Tape.** Protect a young tree from rodents by wrapping the bottom of the tree with Reynolds Wrap and securing with Scotch Packaging Tape.

• **Tabasco Pepper Sauce, McCormick Garlic Powder,** and **Wesson Corn Oil.** Mix four tablespoons Tabasco Pepper Sauce, four tablespoons McCormick Garlic Powder, and one-half teaspoon Wesson Corn Oil in one quart water. Fill a trigger-spray bottle with the solution and apply to plants to repel rodents. (Be sure to wash all vegetables thoroughly before preparing or eating— unless, of course, you enjoy spicy vegetables.)

• **Tabasco Pepper Sauce, McCormick Chili Powder,** and **Ivory Dishwashing Liquid.** Mix three teaspoons Tabasco Pepper Sauce, one teaspoon McCormick Chili Powder, one-half teaspoon Ivory

Dishwashing Liquid, and two cups water in a sixteen-ounce trigger-spray bottle. Spray the solution into the soil around freshly planted bulbs, tulip beds, and young trees to repel squirrels, chipmunks, and mice.

• **Tidy Cats.** Pour used Tidy Cats into mole, gopher, or groundhog tunnels. The creatures smell the scent of their natural enemy and quickly tunnel elsewhere. (For more ways to repel gophers and moles, see page 120.)

STRANGE FACTS

• The shrew looks like a mouse with a long pointy snout but is actually among the smallest known mammal in the world. Shrews are beneficial to gardens, eating harmful insects and grubs. A shrew eats up to three times its own weight every day.

• Field mice, with their big round ears, will not harm your garden. They merely eat grain.

• The vole, a close relative of the lemming, can wreak havoc on a garden, eating up to its own weight (between 1 and 2.5 ounces) in vegetable matter every day.

• Daffodil bulbs are poisonous to voles.

• Mice and rats, which carry serious diseases like plague and typhus, damage crops.

• Planting tulip bulbs an extra four to six inches deeper than the recommended depth may protect them from field voles, which tend to dig shallow tunnels. Surrounding tulip bulbs with daffodil bulbs, which contain foul-tasting, poisonous alkaloids, may also fend off pesky rodents.

• All 1,690 species of rodents have two upper and lower chisel-like teeth called incisors.

• The largest rodent in the world is the capybara of South America, which grows up to four feet long.

Roses

• **Arm & Hammer Baking Soda** and **Wesson Corn Oil.** To prevent roses from getting powdery mildew and black spot, mix one teaspoon Arm & Hammer Baking Soda and five drops Wesson Corn Oil in one quart water. Fill a trigger-spray bottle with the solution and spray directly on leaves. Apply once a week for approximately two months. Reapply after rain. The USDA has approved baking soda as a fungicide. (Before treating the entire plant, test this oily formula on one of the plant's leaves and wait one day to make certain it doesn't burn the leaf.)

• **Arm & Hammer Baking Soda** and **Ivory Dishwashing Liquid.** To cure black spot, mix two teaspoons Arm & Hammer Baking Soda and four drops Ivory Dishwashing Liquid in one gallon water. Spray the solution over the entire rosebush and repeat every five days until the spots disappear.

• **Clorox.** Prepare rosebushes for the onset of winter by cutting off the top and bottom from two clean, empty Clorox Bleach jugs. Cut open the remaining plastic cylinders with a slit up one

side and wrap the two jugs around the base of the plant to form a collar. Fill with mulched leaves and compost.

• **Clorox.** Sterilize your pruning tools with a mixture of three-quarters cup Clorox Bleach in a gallon of water after each use to avoid spreading fungal diseases. Dip your pruning equipment into the disinfectant solution between cuts or at least between plants. When finished, soak the pruning shears in the solution for one hour, then rinse clean and dry. (For more ways to disinfect pruning shears, see page 215.)

• **Elmer's Glue-All.** To ward off borers, prune canes below the infested stems and branches, then use Elmer's Glue-All to seal the pruned ends to guard against insects and excessive moisture loss.

• **Forster Clothes Pins.** Use Forster Clothes Pins as clamps to hold the stems of thorny roses to avoid pricking your fingers when cutting flowers.

• **Gatorade.** Give your rosebushes the potassium they love by watering the plants with Gatorade, which contains 1 percent potassium.

• **L'eggs Sheer Energy Panty Hose.** Using a pair of scissors, cut off the toe from the foot of a pair of used, clean L'eggs Sheer Energy Panty Hose, then cut one-inch strips from the leg, creating circular loops of panty hose. Use the loops to gently tie the trunk of the rosebush to a garden stake with a figure-eight loop.

• **Lewis Labs Brewer's Yeast Flakes.** Stimulate everblooming roses to flower throughout the summer by saturating the roots of each bush immediately after the first blooming with a solution of two tablespoons Lewis Labs Brewer's Yeast Flakes dissolved in one gallon water.

• **Lipton Tea Bags.** Place Lipton Tea Bags (new or used) on top of the soil around rose bushes. Cover the tea bags with mulch. Every time you water the plants, the nutrients from the decomposing tea leaves work their way into the soil.

- **Maxwell House Coffee.** Maxwell House Coffee grounds are full of nutrients and the acidity that roses love. Instead of throwing out the used coffee grounds after you make a pot of coffee, give them to your rosebushes in the garden. Simply work the grounds into the soil.

- **Nestea.** Mix up a quart of unsweetened Nestea instant iced tea according to the directions (without adding sugar or ice) and fertilize rose bushes with the solution. Or simply sprinkle the powdered mix directly on the soil. As the tea decomposes, the nutrients work their way into the soil.

- **Reynolds Wrap.** Place sheets of Reynolds Wrap on the ground around rosebushes and secure the foil in place with rocks. The light reflected by the foil can hasten the blooming of roses.

- **Tabasco Pepper Sauce** and **McCormick Ground (Cayenne) Red Pepper.** To repel Japanese beetles from roses, mix two table-spoons Tabasco Pepper Sauce, two tablespoons McCormick Ground Red Pepper, and two cups water in a sixteen-ounce trigger-spray bottle. Spray the soil with the solution wherever Japanese beetles are giving you trouble.

- *USA Today.* Rid rosebushes of Japanese beetles by placing an open sheet of *USA Today* under plants before 7 A.M. and shaking the plants to send the beetles falling onto the sheet of news-paper. Pour the beetles into soapy water. (For more ways to get rid of Japanese beetles, see page 158.)

- **Vaseline Petroleum Jelly.** Fight off borers by pruning just below the infested stems and branches, then seal the pruned ends with a dab of Vaseline Petroleum Jelly to guard against in-sects and excessive moisture loss.

STRANGE FACTS

- Red roses, when given as a gift, symbolize love.

- In his play *Romeo and Juliet*, first performed in 1596, William Shakespeare wrote, "What's in a name? That which we call a rose by any other name would smell as sweet."

• The nursery rhyme "Ring around the Rosey" refers to the Great Plague of London that killed more than seventy thousand people between 1664 and 1665. An early symptom of the plague was a red circular rash ("Ring around the rosey"), and people would carry herbs in their pockets ("a pocket full of posies") in the hopes of warding off the disease.

• In Lewis Carroll's 1865 children's book *Alice's Adventures in Wonderland*, three gardeners, having accidentally planted a white rose tree instead of a red one, hastily paint the white roses with red paint—in the hopes that the Queen of Hearts won't discover their mistake and have them beheaded.

• In her 1913 poem "Sacred Emily," Gertrude Stein wrote "A rose is a rose is a rose."

• The White House Rose Garden, located just outside of the Oval Office, was first planted with roses in 1919 by Ellen Wilson, the first wife of Woodrow Wilson. President John F. Kennedy had the Rose Garden redesigned to accommodate outdoor ceremonies. In 1971, President Richard Nixon's daughter Tricia was married in the Rose Garden.

• Organically grown roses are edible—as are nasturtiums, pansies, tulips, violets, hollyhocks, lavender, and daylilies.

• While breeders have yet to develop a genuine blue rose, the flower called the blue rose, more commonly known as prairie gentian, looks like a small, deep blue rose.

• From the time of Marilyn Monroe's death in 1962 until his own death in 1999, Joe DiMaggio—Monroe's second husband—had fresh red roses delivered to her grave three times a week.

• The almond, a nut that looks like a peach pit, belongs to the rose family.

• The largest rose tree in the world can be found in Tombstone, Arizona. The 'Lady Banks' rose tree, standing nine feet tall with a trunk forty inches thick, was grown from a cutting that came from Scotland in 1884.

Sap

- **Coppertone.** A dollop of Coppertone—the sunscreen invented in 1944 by Miami physician Dr. Benjamin Green to protect soldiers stationed in the South Pacific during World War II from sunburn—removes sap when rubbed between your hands.

- **Crisco All-Vegetable Shortening.** Clean sap off hands and tools with a few dabs of the vegetable shortening that gets its name from a clever combination of the suggested names *Krispo* (the word *crisp* combined with the suffix *-o*) and *Cryst* (onomatopoeia for the hissing and crackling sound foods make while being fried).

- **Jif Peanut Butter.** Clean sap from hands and garden tools with a dollop of Jif Peanut Butter. The peanut oil dissolves the gums in the sap.

- **Johnson's Baby Oil.** If you get covered with sap, Johnson's Baby Oil dissolves the sticky substance from hair, skin, clothes, and garden tools.

- **Miracle Whip.** When Kraft Foods introduced Miracle Whip at the 1933 Chicago World's Fair, the company had no idea that the salad dressing could be used to remove sap from hands and tools.

• **Noxzema.** A dollop of Noxzema—the skin cream originally sold in 1914 as Dr. Bunting's Sunburn Remedy—removes sap from hands.

• **Pam Original Cooking Spray.** If you get sap stuck on your hands or in your hair, spray Pam Cooking Spray on the sticky spot, rub it in, then wash in soapy water. The cooking oil dissolves the sap almost immediately.

• **Skin-So-Soft.** Wash sap from skin and hair with Skin-So-Soft. The hand and body lotion launched by Avon in 1962 dissolves sap instantly.

• **WD-40.** Clean sap from gardening equipment with a spritz of WD-40. Wait a few minutes for the petroleum distillates to dissolve the sap, then wipe clean. (For more ways to clean sap from tools, see page 215.)

STRANGE FACTS

• In the 1932 Marx Brothers' movie *Horse Feathers*, Groucho Marx, starring as professor Quincey Adams Wagstaff, asks Chico, "Why don't you bore a hole in yourself and let the sap run out?"

• In 1987, D. D. Soejarto, a plant researcher from the University of Illinois, extracted a sap sample from an unfamiliar species of tree in the Malaysian rain forest. Years later, Soejarto developed a compound from the sap in his laboratory that seemed to inhibit the AIDS virus. In 1992, Soejarto returned to Malaysia to extract more sap—only to discover that the tree had been cut down for lumber.

• The words *sap* and *saphead* are both slang for fool or someone easily duped.

• The yellow-bellied sapsucker, a member of the woodpecker family, makes holes in trees to drink the sap.

• Cane sugar is made from the sap of sugarcane. Maple syrup is derived from the sap of the maple tree. The milky juice of rubber trees provides the raw material for making rubber. Gum arabic is made from the dried sap of the *Acacia senegal* tree, and the gum of the sapodilla tree is used to make chewing gum.

Scarecrows

• **Bubble Wrap.** Stuff a scarecrow with Bubble Wrap, the versatile packaging material invented in 1957 by accident when Alfred Fielding and Marc Chavannes, trying to develop a plastic wallpaper with a paper backing, wound up with sheets of bubbles encased in plastic.

• **Clorox** and **L'eggs Sheer Energy Panty Hose.** Use a clean, empty Clorox Bleach jug for the head of a scarecrow by posting the uncapped jug upside-down on a stick and drawing a face on the jug with indelible marker. Pull the waist of a clean, used pair of L'eggs Sheer Energy Panty Hose over the base of the jug and braid the legs for hair.

• **Glad Trash Bags.** Fill small Glad Trash Bags with air, tie them shut, and staple them to tall stakes throughout the garden. The plastic bags, flapping in the breeze, frighten away birds.

• **Glad Trash Bags** and **Dixie Cups.** Cut a Glad Trash Bag into long strips, staple to the lip of a Dixie Cup, and then nail the cup to a tree or a pole in your garden. The plastic strips blowing in the wind will scare birds away.

• **Glad Trash Bags** and **Oral-B Mint Waxed Floss.** Cut a Glad Trash Bag into long strips, string a long piece of Oral-B Mint Waxed Floss between two stakes across the garden, and tie the ends of the strips along the string of dental floss.

• **Oral-B Mint Waxed Floss, Reynolds Wrap,** and **Scotch Magic Tape.** Run a string of Oral-B Mint Waxed Floss between two stakes across your garden just a few inches above a row of plants. Using a pair of scissors, cut a dozen or more strips of Reynolds Wrap one inch wide by five inches long. Tape the strips of aluminum foil along the string of dental floss every few feet. The strips of reflective foil flapping in the breeze will repel birds.

• **Reynolds Wrap** and **Oral-B Mint Waxed Floss.** Cut circles or star shapes from cardboard, wrap the cardboard cutouts in Reynolds Wrap, punch a hole in each shape, and then hang the glittering shapes from fruit trees and berry bushes with a loop of Oral-B Mint Waxed Floss. The sunlight, reflecting from the silvery shapes, will frighten birds away.

• **Slinky.** Stretching a Slinky over your plant rows will scare away deer, raccoons, squirrels, and birds—as will hanging Slinky Juniors from tree branches.

STRANGE FACTS

• *The Scarecrow of Oz*, the ninth book in the Oz series by L. Frank Baum, tells the story of Trot, Cap'n Bill, the Ork, and Button-Bright as they travel to the Land of Oz. The wicked witch Blinkie turns Cap'n Bill into a grasshopper—until the Scarecrow comes to the rescue.

• In the 1939 movie *The Wizard of Oz*, when the Wizard bestows a diploma upon the Scarecrow, the Scarecrow points to his brain and recites: "The sum of the square roots of any two sides of an isosceles triangle is equal to the square root of the remaining side." No such theory exists. The Scarecrow is confusing the Isosceles Triangle Theorem with the Pythagorean Theorem. What he means to say is: "The square of the hypotenuse of a right triangle equals the sum of the squares of the remaining two sides."

- In the 1968 science fiction movie *Planet of the Apes*, starring Charlton Heston and based on the 1963 novel by Pierre Boulle, three American astronauts crash-land on a planet, wander across a desert, and discover scarecrows—before being taken prisoner by talking apes.

- The 1973 movie *Scarecrow* stars Gene Hackman as an ex-con who dreams of opening a car wash in Pittsburgh and Al Pacino as a sailor returning home to the Midwest to see the child born while he was at sea.

- The television adventure series *The Scarecrow and Mrs. King* starred Bruce Boxleitner as Scarecrow—a secret agent who teams up with housewife Amanda King, played by Kate Jackson, to pursue foreign spies.

- The 1988 horror movie *Scarecrows* tells the story of a group of military deserters who, having stolen the Camp Pendleton payroll, fly a pilfered cargo plane to a secluded cornfield inhabited by scarecrows.

Seeding

- **Albers Grits.** Sow small seeds evenly by mixing the seeds with dry Albers Grits to thin them out.

- **Campbell's Tomato Soup.** Protect seedlings in your garden with clean, empty Campbell's Tomato Soup cans. With a can opener, remove the bottoms of the cans. Push a metal cylinder into the soil around each young tomato plant to fend off cutworms, grubs, and other pests. The can will also shelter the sprouting plant from the wind.

- **Carnation NonFat Dry Milk.** Fill a salt shaker with powdered Carnation NonFat Dry Milk and sprinkle over seeds planted in seed-starting cups (see Coca-Cola, Dannon Yogurt, or Dixie Cups below). Cover the powdered milk with a light layer of seed-starting mix. The milk gives the plants extra calcium.

- **Coca-Cola.** Remove the label from a clean, empty two-liter plastic Coca-Cola bottle, drill drainage holes in the bottom, cut the bottle in half with a pair of scissors, and use the bottom half as a planter for seedlings. Or, instead of cutting the bottle in half, lay the bottle on its side, cut a three-inch-wide access flap along the length of the bottle, and drill drainage holes in the other side of the bottle. Fill the bottle halfway with seed-starting mix and plant seeds inside.

- **Con-Tact Paper** and **Oral-B Mint Waxed Floss.** Write the name of the vegetable, herb, or flower and the date of planting on an index card, and cover the card with clear Con-Tact Paper to laminate the card. With a hole puncher, punch a hole in the card, then loop a piece of Oral-B Mint Waxed Floss through the hole. When the seedling is a few inches tall, secure the card to the stem loosely. (For more ways to label seedlings and plants, see page 161.)

- **CoverGirl NailSlicks Classic Red.** Make a convenient ruler to measure the depth for planting seeds by using CoverGirl Nail-Slicks Classic Red Nail Polish to mark off inches along the edge of your garden trowel. You can also use the nail polish to calibrate feet on the handle of a rake, shovel, or hoe.

- **Crayola Chalk.** To make sure seedlings have enough calcium, use a mortar and pestle to grind up a box of Crayola Chalk and then sprinkle the chalk dust (calcium carbonate) over the soil at the beginning of the planting season.

- **Dannon Yogurt** and **Mr. Coffee Filters.** Using a drill with a one-eighth-inch bit, drill several drainage holes in the bottom of a clean, empty Dannon Yogurt cup (or use a hammer and a large nail to poke a hole in the center of the bottom, creating a three-pronged crack radiating out from the center). Line the inside of the cup with a Mr. Coffee Filter, add seed-starting mix, and plant your tomato, pepper, or other seeds. An eight-ounce yogurt cup provides enough room for two or three seedlings of most vegetables. Plant at least three seeds, label the cup with the plant name, and, when plants with delicate roots germinate, thin down to one plant per cup. When the seedling sprouts two full leaves, transplant the seedling with the coffee filter into the earth, where the coffee filter will decompose.

- **Dixie Cups.** To sprout seeds before planting, use a pencil to poke a hole in the center of the bottom of a Dixie Cup. Fill the cup halfway with seed-starting mix. Place the seed inside and cover with more seed-starting mix. Follow directions on the seed packet for proper care, and be sure to label the plant name on the cup with an indelible marker. (For more ways to label seedlings and plants, see page 161.)

• **Domino Sugar.** To see where you're planting small seeds, mix the seeds with Domino Sugar before planting. The white sugar, contrasted against the dark soil, helps you see where you have scattered the seeds and also attracts beneficial microorganisms.

• **Elmer's Glue-All** and **Bounty.** Squeeze out a long line of Elmer's Glue-All along a one-inch-wide strip of Bounty Paper Towel. Place the seeds on the glue (spaced appropriately), let dry, and plant in the garden.

• **Forster Toothpicks.** To sow tiny seeds, fill a small bowl with the seeds, wet the tip of a Forster Toothpick, touch the dampened end to a seed, then touch the seed to moist soil. The damp soil seems to magnetically grab the seed.

• **Frisbee.** To protect newly transplanted seedlings from the wind and sun, push the edge of a clean, old Frisbee into the soil to create a wind- and sun-break.

• **Glad Flexible Straws.** Protect seedlings from cutworms by cutting Glad Flexible Straws into 1.5-inch pieces, slitting each piece lengthwise, and then slipping a section around each stem before transplanting. The straws will prevent cutworms from destroying the plants, and as the plants grow, the cut straws will gently expand to accommodate the stems.

• **Gold Medal Flour** and **Bounty.** Mix enough Gold Medal Flour and water to make a thick paste that can be rolled into balls the size of peas. Insert a seed into each pea-sized ball, space the balls apart at appropriate distances on a one-inch-wide strip of Bounty Paper Towel, and gently press down each pea-sized ball until it sticks to the paper. When the paste dries, plant the strip of paper in the garden.

• **Huggies Baby Wipes.** Empty Huggies Baby Wipes boxes make excellent drainage trays for two small seedling pots.

• **Jell-O** and **Ziploc Storage Bags.** To sow small seeds evenly and easily, mix one package of Jell-O with just enough water to create a thick gel that has the consistency of mustard. Mix small seeds into the gel, pour the mixture into a clean, empty Ziploc Storage Bag, seal securely, cut a small hole in the corner of bag, and then squeeze the bag to squirt a line of goop from the hole into even rows. The Jell-O keeps the seeds moist, the nitrogen in Jell-O enhances plant growth and hastens sprouting, and the sugar feeds the microbes in the soil, producing more nutrients for the plant. You can also squirt a line of the goop onto one-inch-wide strips of Bounty Paper Towel, let dry, then plant the paper strips in the garden.

• **Johnson's Baby Powder.** Sow tiny seeds by pouring them into a clean, empty Johnson's Baby Powder canister, then powder along the garden row.

• **Lipton Tea Bags** and *USA Today.* Accelerate the germination of seeds by mixing two tablespoons of cold, strong brewed Lipton tea into each pound of seed, covering, and setting in the refrigerator for five days. The tannic acid softens the seeds' outer cover. Before sowing, spread the seed to dry for a day or two on pages from *USA Today* on the garage or basement floor.

• **Liquid Paper.** Use Liquid Paper to mark off inches along the edge of your garden trowel to make a convenient ruler to measure the depth for planting seeds. You can also use Liquid Paper to calibrate feet on the handle of a rake, shovel, or hoe.

• **Maxwell House Coffee.** To spread grass seed, punch holes in the bottom of an empty Maxwell House Coffee can with a hammer and a punch, fill with seed, cover with the plastic lid, and shake the can as you walk through your yard.

• **Mr. Coffee Filters.** Soak a Mr. Coffee Filter in water, then line a small planting hole with the coffee filter before adding the plant. The coffee filter slows moisture loss and deters cutworms.

• **Nestea** and *USA Today.* Accelerate the germination of grass seeds by mixing up a quart of unsweetened Nestea instant iced tea according to the directions (without adding sugar or ice). Mix two tablespoons of the tea into each pound of seed, cover, and set in the refrigerator for five days. Before sowing, spread the seed to dry for a day or two on pages from *USA Today* on the garage or basement floor.

• **Oral-B Mint Waxed Floss.** To make sowing and planting in straight rows a breeze, tie one end of a piece of Oral-B Mint Waxed Floss to the top of a pencil, stick the sharpened end in the ground as a stake, and unroll the dental floss across the planting bed. Tie the free end to a second pencil and stake it in the ground. When you're finished sowing or planting, wind the dental floss around one of the pencils so you can reuse your homemade cord and stakes.

• **Oral-B Toothbrush** and **CoverGirl NailSlicks Classic Red.** The handle of a clean, old Oral-B Toothbrush doubles as an excellent dibble to make holes for planting seeds. Use CoverGirl NailSlicks Classic Red nail polish to mark a planting depth on the handle. After planting the seeds, use the toothbrush bristles to sweep soil back over the hole.

• **Reynolds Cut-Rite Wax Paper.** Protect a seedling from cutworms by wrapping the stem loosely with a double-folded four-inch piece of Reynolds Cut-Rite Wax Paper, with two inches of the wax paper in the soil. The wax paper tube will protect the garden plants from cutworms.

• **Reynolds Wrap.** Prevent soilborne diseases by sterilizing your homemade seed-starting mix. Place the seed-starting mix in an oven tray, cover with a piece of Reynolds Wrap, and bake for one hour at 250 degrees Fahrenheit with plenty of ventilation.

• **Reynolds Wrap.** Before planting eggplant, pepper, or tomato seedlings, wrap each stem loosely with a four-inch tube of Reynolds Wrap, giving the seedling room to grow. Plant the seedlings with two inches of the foil stuck in the soil. The foil tubes will protect the garden plants from cutworms.

• **Saran Wrap.** Cover seed flats with Saran Wrap until germination occurs to humidify the seed flats and prevent them from drying out. To avoid fostering disease, do not let too much moisture accumulate.

- **Tabasco Pepper Sauce.** To distribute small seeds more evenly, put them in a clean, empty Tabasco Pepper Sauce bottle and then sprinkle evenly over the soil.

- *USA Today.* Soak a page from *USA Today* in water, then line a planting hole with the damp newspaper before adding the plant. The newsprint slows moisture loss and helps earthworms and microorganisms create nitrogen, potassium, and phosphorus.

STRANGE FACTS

- You can test the potential of seeds by pouring them in a glass of water. The seeds that sink to the bottom are more likely to germinate.

- According to South African tribal legend, at the beginning of all things, the gods gave the animals seeds and plants to cultivate. The hyena, last in line, was given the baobab tree, which the hyena, known for its stupidity, planted upside down—explaining why in the winter, when the branches of trees go bare, the baobab looks like a tree that was uprooted and replanted upside down.

- Jesus never said, "Whatever a man sows, so shall he reap." Saint Paul wrote this famous line in his epistle to the Galatians (6:7).

- In 1876, Brazilian customs officials foolishly allowed English botanist Sir Henry Wickham to take seventy thousand rubber tree seeds from Brazil to England. Wickham insisted the seeds were botanical specimens to be used solely for the royal plant collection at Kew Gardens. Wickham germinated the seedlings at Kew Gardens, then sent them to Ceylon and Malaya, breaking the Brazilian monopoly on raw rubber.

- The 1956 movie *The Bad Seed* stars Patty McCormack as an adorably cute eight-year-old girl who feigns sweetness to conceal the fact that she is actually a cold, calculating, severely disturbed killer.

- The rock band Jethro Tull—best known for the hit songs "Aqualung," "Thick as a Brick," "Locomotive Breath," and "Bungle in the Jungle"—was not named after the group's lead singer (whose name is Ian Anderson) but after the original Jethro Tull, the English horticulturist who invented the seed drill.

• Brazil nuts are actually seeds, not nuts. Brazil nuts do, however, come from Brazil.

• The average coffee tree, grown from seed, bears its first fruit after five to eight years and yields approximately one pound of coffee beans each year.

• The double coconut, which grows only on the Seychelle islands in the Indian Ocean, is the largest seed in the world, weighing up to forty-four pounds.

The Scoop on Albers Grits

In 1895, German immigrant Bernhard Albers, a wholesale grocer, persuaded his four brothers and another partner to go into business with him in Portland, Oregon, using fifteen thousand dollars to form a milling company. By 1899, the five Albers brothers—specializing in cornmeal and grits—bought out their business partner and formed the Albers Bros. Milling Company.

In 1914, the Albers Bros. Milling Company bought the Pacific Cereal Association, acquiring Carnation Wheat and Carnation Oats products. In 1929, Elbridge Amos Stuart, owner of Carnation Milk Products Company (which he founded in 1899 in Kent, Washington), purchased the Albers Bros. Milling Company. In 1984, Nestlé purchased the Carnation Company, acquiring the Albers line of yellow cornmeal, white cornmeal, and grits.

• Grits are made from ground hominy, a food made from hulled Indian corn.

• The box of Albers grits, with its patriotic red and blue colors, pictures a traditional breakfast plate of grits, eggs, and bacon.

• The citizens of St. George, South Carolina, consume more grits than any other town in the world.

• The annual World Grits Festival, held every April in St. George, South Carolina, includes a "Rolling in the Grits" contest in which contestants jump into. a wading pool filled with grits.

• The 1982 movie *Kiss My Grits* stars Bruce Davison, Tony Franciosa, Susan George, and Bruno Kirby.

• In the 1992 cookbook *Gone with the Grits*, author Diane Pfeifer presents 135 vegetarian recipes using grits, including Grits Cherry Cheesecake and Jalapeño Casserole.

Skunks

- **Bounce.** Repel skunks by hanging fresh sheets of Bounce Classic from your fence posts, shrubs, or trees. The fragrance (oleander, a natural repellent) keeps skunks away. Misting the Bounce Classic sheets with water every so often revives the scent.

- **Tabasco Pepper Sauce, McCormick Chili Powder,** and **Ivory Dishwashing Liquid.** Mix three teaspoons Tabasco Pepper Sauce, one teaspoon McCormick Chili Powder, one-half teaspoon Ivory Dishwashing Liquid, and two cups water in a sixteen-ounce trigger-spray bottle. Spray the solution around the perimeter of the yard to repel skunks.

- **Tabasco Pepper Sauce, McCormick Garlic Powder,** and **Wesson Corn Oil.** Mix four tablespoons Tabasco Pepper Sauce, four tablespoons McCormick Garlic Powder, and one-half teaspoon Wesson Corn Oil in one quart water. Fill a trigger-spray bottle with the solution and spray the perimeter of your yard to repel skunks.

SKUNK SMELL

✗ **Arm & Hammer Baking Soda, Hydrogen Peroxide,** and **Dawn.** In a bucket, mix the contents of one small box Arm & Hammer Baking Soda, two cups hydrogen peroxide, one teaspoon Dawn Dishwashing Liquid, and one gallon warm water. Use a scrub brush to wash with this solution.

✗ **Campbell's Tomato Juice.** Empty two one-quart cans of Campbell's Tomato Juice into a bucket, and sponge the juice full-strength all over your body and face and through your hair while sitting in a bathtub with the drain plugged. Fill the bathtub with water and soak in the diluted tomato juice for fifteen minutes, then rinse clean. To deodorize a pet, pour Campbell's Tomato Soup over the animal and rub it in. Sponge it over the pet's face. Rinse and repeat. The acids from the tomatoes neutralize the skunk smell.

✗ **Coca-Cola.** Pour four two-liter bottles of Coke into a bucket, sponge yourself down in the shower, and rinse clean. The acids in the Coca-Cola kill skunk odor.

✗ **Listerine.** Applying Listerine full-strength to the affected areas removes the smell of skunk spray on humans and dogs. (Avoid getting Listerine in eyes or ears.) Then wash with soap and water, and rinse. The antiseptic in Listerine neutralizes the skunk odor.

✗ **Massengill Disposable Douche.** The ingredients in Massengill Disposable Douche neutralize skunk odor. Simply wash yourself or a sprayed animal with this feminine hygiene product, then rinse well.

✗ **Playtex Living Gloves.** If you're washing the smell of skunk from a child or a family pet, be sure to wear Playtex Living Gloves to avoid getting the skunk smell all over yourself.

✗ **ReaLemon.** You'll need several bottles of ReaLemon lemon juice to wash down your body or your pet, but the acids in lemon juice eliminate skunk odor—reportedly better than tomato juice.

STRANGE FACTS

• Famous tongue twister: "The skunk sat on a stump; the skunk thunk the stump stunk, but the stump thunk the skunk stunk."

• The most vile-smelling substances in the world, according to *The Guinness Book of World Records,* are ethyl mercaptan and butyl seleno-mercaptan, "each with a smell reminiscent of a combination of rotting cabbage, garlic, onions, burned toast, and sewer gas."

• Before spraying an enemy, the striped skunk stamps its front feet and hisses or growls.

• A skunk can spray its foul-smelling musk accurately to a distance of up to twelve feet. The odor lingers for several days.

• Skunks eat beetles, caterpillars, crickets, grasshoppers, mice, and rats.

• In German, the word for skunk is *Stinktier.*

Slugs and Snails

• **Budweiser.** Set a plant saucer in a shallow hole in the garden so the lip of the saucer is one-eighth inch above the ground (to prevent beneficial ground beetles from wandering in). Fill the saucer with Budweiser beer. Place a curved terra-cotta roof tile over the saucer to give it shade. Snails and slugs like the taste of beer, crawl in, get drunk, and drown. Apparently the alcohol in the beer destroys their body tissue. Be sure to empty and refill the saucer with fresh beer every two to three days.

• **Coca-Cola.** Fill jar lids with flat Coca-Cola and set in the garden. Slugs and snails, attracted by sweet soda, will slither into the jar lid and be killed by the acids in the Coke.

• **Crayola Chalk.** Slugs will not cross a thick chalk line.

• **Dannon Yogurt.** Rather than setting out a saucer as a trap for snails and slugs, make a trap from a clean, empty Dannon Yogurt container by cutting windows one inch high by two inches wide on each side of the cup, one-half inch below the rim. Bury the prepared yogurt cups in your garden so the windows are one-eighth inch above the ground (to prevent helpful ground beetles from falling in), fill the cups with an inch of liquid bait (see Budweiser on page 247), and replace the lids.

• **Frisbee.** Instead of using a saucer or jar lid to trap snails and slugs, use a clean, old Frisbee filled with Budweiser beer (see page 247).

• **Heinz White Vinegar.** Mix equal parts Heinz White Vinegar and water in a trigger-spray bottle, patrol your garden at night, and spray the solution directly on slugs. The gastropods die almost immediately. Don't make the solution stronger than equal parts vinegar and water, though, or you'll risk damaging plant foliage.

• **Kingsford Charcoal Briquets** and **Ziploc Freezer Bags.** Fill a gallon-size Ziploc Freezer Bag with untreated Kingsford Charcoal Briquets and use a hammer or mallet to smash the charcoal to powder. Sprinkle the charcoal around the border of your garden bed to prevent slugs and snails from crossing into your garden.

• **Miller Genuine Draft, Domino Sugar,** and **Fleischmann's Yeast.** In a clean, empty mayonnaise jar, mix together two cans Miller Genuine Draft Beer (one of the few unpasteurized beers), one tablespoon Domino Sugar, and one teaspoon Fleischmann's Yeast. Set the jar in a warm room (over 70 degrees Fahrenheit) for three days (or until bubbles form in the mixture). Place a plant saucer in a shallow hole in the garden so the lip of the saucer is one-eighth inch above the ground (to prevent beneficial ground beetles from wandering in). Fill the saucer with the enriched beer solution. Place a curved terra-cotta roof tile over the saucer to give it shade. Snails and slugs will be attracted by the sweet aroma of this turbocharged beer, crawl in, get drunk, and drown. Be sure to empty out and refill the saucer with fresh concoction every two or three days.

• **Morton Salt.** Sprinkle Morton Salt lightly around your garden or on the sidewalk close to the grass. When slugs attempt to crawl through the salt, the sodium chloride kills them by reverse osmosis. At night, when nocturnal snails and slugs are active, search their favorite feeding spots with a flashlight and sprinkle Morton Salt on them (or pick them up and drop them into a bucket of salt). The creatures shrivel up and die within five minutes.

• **ReaLemon, Domino Sugar,** and **Smucker's Grape Jelly.** Mix one tablespoon ReaLemon, one tablespoon Domino Sugar, and one tablespoon Smucker's Grape Jelly in a jar lid and set in the garden. Slugs and snails, attracted by the sugar and jelly, will slither in and be killed by the acid lemon juice.

• **3M Sandpaper.** Repel slugs and snails from attacking young plants by cutting a doughnut the size of an old 45 rpm record from a piece of 3M Sandpaper and placing it as a collar around the plant. Snails and slugs avoid crawling over abrasive surfaces.

STRANGE FACTS

• In the 1850s, French immigrant Antione Delmas brought snails to California so he would have an ample supply of *escargot*. The offspring of those original snails destroy millions of dollars' worth of California produce every year.

• The African giant snail, the largest known land gastropod in the world, measures up to 15.5 inches long.

• Snails live from two to twenty years.

• Land snails are hermaphrodites, having both male and female reproductive organs.

• The common garden snail, considered the fastest snail on land, can crawl—using the muscular foot in its body—at a speed of roughly six inches per minute. For a garden snail to travel one mile would require at least seven days, eight hours.

• In the 1967 movie musical *Doctor Doolittle*, starring Rex Harrison and loosely based on the 1920 children's book by Hugh Lofting, Dr. Doolittle travels inside a gigantic sea snail.

The Rise of Fleischmann's Yeast

In 1868, Austro-Hungarian immigrant Charles Fleischmann and his brother Maximillian, determined to improve the bread in America, teamed up with American businessman James Gaff to build a yeast plant in Cincinnati, Ohio. The Fleischmann brothers patented a compressed yeast cake, revolutionizing home and commercial baking in the United States and resulting in superior-tasting bread.

Eager to find a larger audience for America's first commercially produced yeast, the Fleischmanns introduced their yeast at the 1876 Centennial Exposition in Philadelphia. Their "Vienna Bakery" concession stand—offering the ten million visitors fresh Vienna bread, baked on the premises and served with coffee, ices, and chocolate—made Fleischmann's Yeast a household name.

During World War II, Fleischmann Laboratories introduced a revolutionary new product, "Active Dry Yeast"—requiring no refrigeration and activated quickly and easily by adding warm water—so soldiers overseas could enjoy fresh bread.

• In 1890, the Fleischmanns added a research laboratory to their plant in Peekskill, New York. One visitor wrote that the laboratory housed "the sweetest kitchen imaginable, a kitchen with an electric oven in which eight loaves of bread are baked daily. . . . [Only in this way does] the company know . . . exactly what its yeast does day to day."

• The Fleischmanns shipped yeast from their plant in Peekskill, New York, to Canada until 1905, when they opened a facility in Quebec to serve the Canadian market.

• In 1986, Fleischmann's introduced "Quick-Rise Yeast," a highly active, finer grain of dry yeast that raises dough up to fifty percent faster than regular active dry yeast.

• Yeast, a living single-celled microscopic fungus used to make bread rise, is also used to ferment beer and wine.

• In 1994, Fleischmann's introduced Bread Machine Yeast, specially formulated for use in bread machines.

Soil

- **Arm & Hammer Baking Soda.** To test whether soil is too acid, take a sample of the soil, wet it, and add a pinch of Arm & Hammer Baking Soda. If the baking soda fizzes, the soil may be too acid to support most plants and vegetables. Neutralize the acidity of the soil by watering the soil once with a mixture of four tablespoons Arm & Hammer Baking Soda and one quart water.

- **Clorox.** Sift soil by cutting the bottom from an empty, clean Clorox Bleach jug at an angle to make a scoop. Insert a six-inch-diameter piece of one-quarter-inch hardware cloth so that it rests above the uncapped handle hole. Scoop up dirt, sift through the narrow opening, and stones will be caught by the hardware cloth.

- **Gold Medal Flour, French's Mustard,** and **McCormick Ground (Cayenne) Red Pepper.** To repel cats, dissolve two tablespoons Gold Medal Flour, two tablespoons French's Mustard, one tablespoon McCormick Ground Red Pepper, and two cups water in a sixteen-ounce trigger-spray bottle. Shake well and spray around flowerbeds, vegetable gardens, or the perimeter of your yard.

• **Heinz White Vinegar.** Test whether soil is alkaline by taking a sample of the soil and adding a few drops of Heinz White Vinegar. If the vinegar fizzes, the soil is alkaline.

• **Heinz White Vinegar.** To repel cats, fill a trigger-spray bottle with Heinz White Vinegar and spray around the border of your garden and birdbath. The smell of vinegar repulses cats and neutralizes the smell of cat urine used to mark their territory.

• **Kellogg's Frosted Mini-Wheats.** Add leftover crumbs from cereal boxes such as Kellogg's Frosted Mini-Wheats to your garden soil or planter mix. The sugar feeds microorganisms, adding nitrogen to the soil, and the cereal adds potassium and other nutrients.

• **Kingsford Charcoal Briquets** and **Ziploc Freezer Bags.** To neutralize acid and absorb impurities from potting soil, fill a gallon-size Ziploc Freezer Bag with untreated Kingsford Charcoal Briquets and use a hammer or mallet to smash the charcoal briquettes to the size of gravel. Place a one-half-inch layer of gravel at the bottom of the planter, cover with a one-half-inch layer of the crushed charcoal, then fill the planter with more potting soil.

• **Maxwell House Coffee.** If soil is alkaline, digging used coffee grounds into the soil helps reduce the alkalinity. The smell of coffee also repels cats from digging up the plants.

• **Tabasco Pepper Sauce** and **McCormick Ground (Cayenne) Red Pepper.** To prevent a dog from lying on or digging up soil, mix two tablespoons Tabasco Pepper Sauce, two tablespoons McCormick Ground Red Pepper, and two cups water in a sixteen-ounce trigger-spray bottle. Spray the soil with the solution wherever the dog is giving you trouble.

• *USA Today.* Help the earthworms in the soil create nitrogen, potassium, and phosphorus by placing six to eight sheets of *USA Today* on top of the soil and covering with a layer of mulch.

STRANGE FACTS

- Soil is composed of inorganic particles (sand, silt, and clay), organic matter, air, and water. The quality of soil is judged by the proportions of these ingredients and the level of activity by earthworms, fungus, and microorganisms.

- The acidity and alkalinity of soil are measured on the pH scale. The pH runs from 0 (pure acid) to 14 (pure alkali), with the neutral point at 7. Anything below 7 is acid, anything above 7 is alkaline. The numbers on the pH scale increase exponentially. For instance, soil with a pH of 9 is ten times more alkaline than soil with a pH of 8.

- In the 1930s, farmers in the southern United States began planting kudzu, a fast-growing, deep-rooted Asian vine, to prevent soil erosion. While the nitrogen-fixing bacteria that live on kudzu roots help enrich the soil, kudzu can grow up to sixty feet high and spreads so rapidly that it is virtually impossible to control—havoc on the farmland.

- In the late 1960s, billionaire Daniel K. Ludwig bought a parcel of land the size of Connecticut along the Jari River in the Brazilian Amazon basin, determined to mill paper on the site. After having 35,000 workers clear the land and plant it with pine and eucalyptus trees, Ludwig sent enormous barges carrying a giant pulp mill and paper plant—too large to sail through the Panama Canal—from Japan around Africa to the site on the Amazon. After Ludwig spent an estimated one billion dollars on the project, the jungle defeated him. Leaf-cutter ants destroyed crops and supplies, workers contracted malaria and meningitis, and the soil failed to support the pine and eucalyptus trees.

- In an episode of the television comedy series *Taxi*, cab driver John Burns says, "I try to eat only natural things." Dispatcher Louie De Palma replies, "How'd you like a sack of dirt?"

- The bat on the Bacardi Rum label symbolizes the bat guano used to fertilize the soil in which the sugarcane used to make the rum is grown.

Squirrels and Raccoons

- **Campbell's Tomato Soup.** Protect corn from squirrels by removing the bottom of a clean, empty Campbell's Tomato Soup can with a can opener, poking holes around the outside of the can with a hammer and awl, and then placing the can over an ear of corn.

- **Castor Oil.** Repel squirrels by mixing one-half cup castor oil and two gallons water and using the solution to water your vegetable garden. The castor oil enriches the soil while simultaneously repulsing rodents.

- **Crisco All-Vegetable Shortening.** Keep squirrels away from a bird feeder by greasing the pole to the birdhouse with Crisco All-Vegetable Shortening. The squirrels will try to climb up the pole and slide right back down, providing you with hours of free entertainment.

- **Epsom Salt.** To repel raccoons, sprinkle a few tablespoons of Epsom Salt around your garden and garbage cans. Raccoons dislike the taste of salt. Repeat after rain. Epsom Salt is good for your plants and will not harm rodents.

- **Jif Peanut Butter.** Bait a humane box trap, available from your local Animal Control Center, with Jif Peanut Butter to attract squirrels or raccoons. The Animal Control Center will tell you where to release the animals.

- **L'eggs Sheer Energy Panty Hose** and **Oral-B Mint Waxed Floss.** To prevent squirrels or raccoons from destroying growing fruits and vegetables, cut off the feet from a clean, used pair of L'eggs Sheer Energy Panty Hose and slip a foot over an apple, pear, avocado, tomato, eggplant, bunch of grapes, or head of broccoli or cabbage. Seal the open end closed with a piece of Oral-B Mint Waxed Floss. The synthetic fibers keep squirrels and raccoons away, and the flexible hose expands as the fruit or vegetable grows. You can also cut a section from a leg of the panty hose, tie one end closed with dental floss, cover the fruit or vegetable, and then secure the open end shut.

- **McCormick Black Pepper.** To keep squirrels and raccoons away from flowerbeds and vegetable gardens, sprinkle McCormick Black Pepper in your garden. These animals have a keen sense of smell and are repelled by the scent of pepper. After it rains, be sure to re-pepper the garden.

- **McCormick Ground (Cayenne) Red Pepper.** Keep squirrels out of your bird feeder by sprinkling the birdseed with McCormick Ground Red Pepper. The birds cannot taste the pepper, but squirrels can and want nothing to do with it.

- **McCormick Peppermint Oil, Johnson & Johnson Cotton Balls,** and **L'eggs Sheer Energy Panty Hose.** Saturate a few cotton balls with McCormick Peppermint Oil, place inside the foot of a pair of clean, used L'eggs Sheer Energy Panty Hose, and hang from a fence post, tree branch, or bush. The smell of mint repels squirrels and raccoons.

- **Pam Original Cooking Spray.** Coat the pole of a bird feeder with Pam Cooking Spray and watch the squirrels slip and slide but never make it up the pole.

- **Quaker Oats.** Bait a humane box trap, available from your local Animal Control Center, with uncooked Quaker Oats to attract squirrels or raccoons. The Animal Control Center will tell you where to release the animals.

- **Slinky.** To prevent squirrels from climbing up the pole to a bird feeder, secure a Slinky to the bottom of the bird feeder and let it hang down the pole. The bouncing springs will frighten away animal intruders.

- **Tabasco Pepper Sauce, McCormick Chili Powder,** and **Ivory Dishwashing Liquid.** Mix three teaspoons Tabasco Pepper Sauce, one teaspoon McCormick Chili Powder, one-half teaspoon Ivory Dishwashing Liquid, and two cups water in a sixteen-ounce trigger-spray bottle. Spray the solution into the soil around freshly planted bulbs, tulip beds, and young trees to repel squirrels and chipmunks.

- **Tidy Cats.** Repel squirrels and chipmunks from flowerbeds by sprinkling a tablespoon of used Tidy Cats cat box filler (yes, used) on the ground around the base of each flower. (Do not use the cat box filler in vegetable or herb gardens.)

- **USA Today.** To repel raccoons from cornfields, place crumpled-up pages of USA Today between rows of ripening corn. Raccoons hate walking over rustling newspaper.

- **Vaseline Petroleum Jelly.** Coat the pole of a bird feeder with Vaseline Petroleum Jelly to prevent squirrels from being able to climb up the pole.

- **Ziploc Freezer Bag.** Place a portable radio inside a gallon-size Ziploc Freezer Bag, turn the radio on, and seal the bag shut. The noise from a radio, particularly one tuned to a rock 'n' roll station or all-night talk show, repels raccoons—except those intrigued by Howard Stern, Rush Limbaugh, or Dr. Laura Schlessinger.

STRANGE FACTS

- Chipmunks, marmots, prairie dogs, and woodchucks are all members of the squirrel family.

• Squirrels do not live in Australia, Madagascar, or Greenland.

• The smallest squirrel in the world, the African pygmy squirrel, is less than three inches long and has no tail.

• The word *squirrel* originated from the Greek word *skiouros*, meaning "shadow tail."

• The animated television cartoon series *The Bullwinkle Show* costarred Rocket J. Squirrel (nicknamed Rocky), a flying squirrel.

• Flying squirrels, born with a fold of skin stretching from their front leg to their rear leg on each side of their body, can glide up to 150 feet through the air.

• Raccoons, more intelligent than cats, can be easily trained.

• Raccoons are born without black masks of fur around their eyes.

• The Roaring Twenties witnessed the popularity of the raccoon coat.

• In 1954, *Davy Crockett*, a recurring episodic series on *Disneyland* starring Fess Parker as the American frontiersman, popularized his trademark coonskin cap, creating a fad that swept the nation's youth.

• The Beatles' 1968 *White Album* contains the ballad "Rocky Raccoon."

Staking

- **Bubble Wrap** and **Scotch Packaging Tape.** Wrap Bubble Wrap over the tops of stakes and secure in place with Scotch Packaging Tape to avoid painful accidents should anyone trip over the stakes.

- **Forster Toothpicks** and **Scotch Magic Tape.** Straighten bent stems in your garden by making a splint with a Forster Toothpick and Scotch Magic Tape.

- **Glad Flexible Straws.** Fix a bent stem by slitting a Glad Flexible Straw lengthwise and then slipping the straw around the broken stem to create a cast.

- **L'eggs Sheer Energy Panty Hose.** Using a pair of scissors, cut off the toe from the foot of a pair of used, clean L'eggs Sheer Energy Panty Hose, then cut one-inch strips from the leg, creating circular loops of panty hose. Use the loops to gently tie stems, vines, and thin plant trunks to stakes with a figure-eight loop. Or use the entire leg cut from a pair of panty hose to stake a newly planted tree.

- **L'eggs Sheer Energy** and **Oral-B Mint Waxed Floss.** If you're in a pinch, ball up a pair of clean, used L'eggs Sheer Energy Panty Hose over the top of a stake and tie in place with Oral-B Mint Waxed Floss to reduce the risk of serious injury in case anyone trips over the stake.

- **Oral-B Toothbrushes.** Stake up small plants with the handles from old Oral-B Toothbrushes.

- **Q-Tips Cotton Swabs** and **Scotch Magic Tape.** To straighten bent stems in your garden, make a splint with a Q-Tips Cotton Swab and Scotch Magic Tape.

- **Popsicle** and **Scotch Magic Tape.** If you need to mend a bent stem in your garden, cool off by eating an ice-cold Popsicle, then use the Popsicle stick as a splint, held in place with Scotch Magic Tape.

- **Velcro.** Use strips of Velcro to attach the trunks of young trees to stakes.

- **Wilson Tennis Balls.** Cut an X into a clean, old Wilson Tennis Ball and place it over the top of a stake to protect yourself from being stabbed or poked in the eye by accident.

STRANGE FACTS

- Tapping a stake lodged in the ground a few times with a hammer or mallet makes the stake easier to remove.

- The phrase "pull up stakes" means to leave one's job or place of residence, "stakes" means a prize, and "at stake" means at risk.

- The word *stakeout* is slang for police surveillance of a location in the hopes of capturing a criminal in the act.

- The 1987 movie *Stakeout* stars Richard Dreyfuss as a police officer who falls in love with the woman he and his partner, played by Emilio Estevez, are staking out.

• In the children's book *Amelia Bedelia Helps Out*, by Peggy Parish, Miss Emma tells Amelia to stake the beans, so Amelia ties steaks to the plants.

• The word *mistake* originates from the Icelandic word *mistaka*, which literally means "to take in error."

Storing Seeds

- **Avery Laser Labels.** Use an indelible marker to write the name of the type of seeds on a self-sticking Avery address label, and adhere it to the storage container.

- **Carnation NonFat Dry Milk.** Keep seeds dry by mixing them with equal parts powdered Carnation NonFat Dry Milk, which will absorb moisture. Or place the seeds in paper envelopes inside a sealed container with a second envelope filled with powdered milk.

- **Cool Whip.** Use clean, empty Cool Whip canisters to hold loose seeds or to store packets of seeds.

- **Forster Clothes Pins** and **Krazy Glue.** Use Krazy Glue to adhere Forster Clothes Pins to a wooden shelf or wall in your workshop, and then hang seed packets from the clothes pins.

- **Gerber Baby Food.** Fill clean, empty Gerber Baby Food jars with leftover seeds. You can also nail the caps of the food jars under a wooden shelf and screw the jars in place.

• **Gold Medal Flour.** Store seeds in a jar or airtight container, add one-half cup Gold Medal Flour to absorb moisture, and seal tightly.

• **Huggies Baby Wipes.** Use empty Huggies Baby Wipes boxes to hold seed packets.

• **Kingsford's Corn Starch.** Keep seeds dry by mixing them with equal parts Kingsford's Corn Starch, which will absorb any moisture.

• **Kleenex Tissues.** Cut the top off an empty Kleenex Tissues box and store seed packets in the box.

• **Kodak 35mm Film Canister.** Wash empty Kodak 35mm Film canisters with soap and warm water, dry thoroughly, fill with seeds, and label.

• **L'eggs Sheer Energy Panty Hose.** Pour seeds into the foot of a pair of L'eggs Sheer Energy Panty Hose, tie a knot, and hang high indoors to keep the contents dry. The synthetic fibers of the pantyhose also repel rodents and insects.

• **L'eggs Sheer Energy Panty Hose.** Collect seed pods from your garden, place them inside a clean, used leg cut from a pair of L'eggs Sheer Energy Panty Hose, and hang up to dry. When ready, shake the panty hose leg, causing the seeds to fall to the toe of the stocking. Cut off the foot, knot, and store.

• **Maxwell House Coffee.** Maxwell House Coffee cans make perfect seed storage containers.

• **Pringles.** A clean, empty Pringles canister makes an excellent place to store seeds.

• **Reynolds Cut-Rite Wax Paper** and **Scotch Magic Tape.** Make a handy seed packet by folding a piece of Reynolds Cut-Rite Wax Paper in half, folding flaps over the three sides, and taping the flaps in place with Scotch Magic Tape. Label the packet with an indelible marker or seal the original seed packet inside.

• **Ziploc Storage Bags.** Store leftover seeds in Ziploc Storage Bags, label with the type of seed, place in an airtight plastic container, and store in a cool, dry place (such as the back of the refrigerator) until ready for planting.

STRANGE FACTS

• A package of seeds, if stored properly, can remain viable for years. Seeds stored in the refrigerator will remain viable for twice as long as seeds stored at room temperature.

• Instead of throwing rice, which is difficult to clean up, many wedding guests shower the bride and groom with birdseed, which birds and squirrels happily clean up. Throwing rice or birdseed at a wedding symbolizes fertility.

• In the biblical story of Onan (Genesis 38:1–10), Judah marries off his eldest son, Er, to a woman named Tamar. Unfortunately, Er "was wicked in the sight of the Lord; and the Lord slew him." Judah orders his second son, Onan, to marry Tamar, in accordance with the custom of levirate marriage. "And Onan knew that the seed would not be his," the Bible tells us, "and it came to pass, when he went in unto his brother's wife, that he spilled it on the ground, lest he should give seed to his brother." Contrary to popular belief, God slays Onan for refusing to perpetuate his dead brother's name—not for spilling his seed.

• American pioneer John Chapman, best remembered as Johnny Appleseed, planted huge numbers of apple trees as he traveled alone from western Pennsylvania through Ohio, Indiana, and Illinois, from 1797 until his death in 1845.

• In an episode of *Gilligan's Island*, the Skipper says, "Everything grows from seeds."

"Not everything," replies Gilligan.

"Yes, Gilligan, everything," insists the Skipper. "Orange trees grow from orange seeds. Apple trees grow from apple seeds. And watermelons grow from watermelon seeds."

"Yeah," says Gilligan, "but birds don't grow from birdseed."

• As a boy, Steven Spielberg kept parakeets in his bedroom, flying free. Recalled his mother, Leah, in *Time* magazine: "There would be birds flying around and birdseed all over the floor. I'd just reach in to get the dirty clothes."

• The word *seedy* means "shabby."

Tomatoes

• **Campbell's Tomato Soup.** Protect young tomato plants in your garden with clean, empty Campbell's Tomato Soup cans. With a can opener, remove the bottoms of the soup cans. Push a metal cylinder into the soil around each young tomato plant to fend off cutworms, grubs, and other pests. The can will also shelter the sprouting plant from the wind.

• **Carnation NonFat Dry Milk.** Prevent blight, blossom-end rot, and other common tomato diseases by sprinkling a handful of Carnation NonFat Dry Milk in the planting holes before setting in tomato transplants. If desired, add Epsom Salt and a shovelful of compost (see Epsom Salt on page 265). After planting, sprinkle two tablespoons powdered milk into the soil, then gently mix into the soil. Repeat every few weeks. Carnation NonFat Dry Milk adds calcium to the soil.

• **Clorox.** To water a tomato plant more efficiently, cut the bottom off a clean, empty Clorox Bleach jug and bury the uncapped top, neck down, next to the tomato plant. Then water the plant by filling up the plastic bottle with water. The water goes to the roots where needed. You can also drill small holes (or make pinpricks) around an entire jug, bury the jug right-side up next to a plant, fill the jug with water, and let the water slowly seep out of the holes into the soil.

• **Clorox.** Make solar-powered radiant heaters by filling several clean, empty Clorox Bleach jugs with water, sealing the caps tightly, and placing them around tomato plants to protect them from the cold. During the day, the sun heats up the water in the jugs. At night, the heated water radiates warmth for the tomato plants nearby. To make the jugs even more effective, spray-paint them flat black to absorb more heat. When you no longer need the solar-powered radiant heaters, use the water on your plants.

• **Crayola Chalk.** To make sure tomato plants have enough calcium, use a mortar and pestle to grind up a box of Crayola Chalk and then sprinkle the chalk dust (calcium carbonate) over the soil at the beginning of the planting season.

• **Coca-Cola.** Cut a two-inch-diameter hole in the side of a clean, empty two-liter Coca-Cola bottle, near the bottom. Drill a one-sixteenth-inch hole in the cap (one-eighth-inch for clay soil). Plant the capped bottle upside down in the soil near tomato plants (six inches deep and roughly one foot away from the base of the plants). Fill the bottle with water every four days by placing a hose in the hole you cut in the base. For greater saturation, drill roughly a dozen holes in the top rounded part of the bottle before burying it.

• **Dixie Cups.** Protect baby tomato plants by removing the bottoms of Dixie Cups and pushing the cups into the soil to encircle young plants.

• **Domino Sugar.** To grow sweeter, juicier tomatoes, add a teaspoon of Domino Sugar to the watering can when the tomatoes begin to show color, minimizing the amount of water you give to the plants.

• **Epsom Salt.** Tomatoes prefer soil with a neutral pH. To plant, dig a hole one foot wide and put in a layer of compost mixed with one teaspoon Epsom Salt and one-half cup bonemeal.

• **Glad Trash Bags.** Produce an early crop of tomatoes by slicing open the sides of black Glad Trash Bags to make long sheets and placing the black plastic on vegetable beds as mulch. Secure the plastic in place with stones. Cut slits into the plastic to accommodate your tomato transplants. The radiant heat created by the plastic warms the soil an additional 3 degrees Fahrenheit. You can roll the plastic sheets up at the end of the season and use them again next year. Be certain to water beneath the impermeable plastic sheet with a drip line or soaker hose. Then put row covers over the tomato plants (see Hula Hoop below) for three to four weeks.

• **Glad Trash Bags.** Staple small Glad Trash Bags to tomato stakes. The plastic bags, flapping in the breeze, frighten deer away from your garden.

• **Goodyear Tires.** To protect tomato plants in your garden, lay Goodyear Tires on the ground and plant tomato seedlings inside them. The tires will shelter the sprouting plants from the wind, and the dark rubber will absorb heat from the sun and warm the soil.

• **Hula Hoop, Bubble Wrap,** and **Scotch Packaging Tape.** Building row covers can protect tomato plants from the cold. Make hoop supports by cutting Hula Hoops in half and inserting the legs firmly into the soil. Cover with a canopy made from sheets of Bubble Wrap and secure in place with Scotch Packaging Tape, making sure the sheets of Bubble Wrap are high enough not to touch the plants. You can also secure the Bubble Wrap by staking the ends to the ground with wire. At the end of the season, roll up the Bubble Wrap to be used again the following year. (Be sure to monitor the temperatures inside this minigreenhouse to make certain you do not burn out your plants, or substitute sheer curtains for the Bubble Wrap.)

• **Hydrogen Peroxide.** To kill anthracnose (a disease evidenced by little sunken black spots on tomatoes), fill a sixteen-ounce trigger-spray bottle with one ounce hydrogen peroxide and two cups water, and mist the plants once a week with the solution.

• **Hydrogen Peroxide.** Prevent late blight on tomato plants by filling a trigger-spray bottle with hydrogen peroxide and misting the plants every evening from late August until early September.

• **Jell-O.** To give tomato plants additional nitrogen, mix an envelope of powdered Jell-O into one cup boiling water, stir until the gelatin powder dissolves, mix with three cups cold water, then pour around the bases of the plants. The gelatin helps the plants retain water, the nitrogen in Jell-O enhances plant growth and hastens sprouting, and the sugar feeds the microbes in the soil, producing more nutrients for the plants.

• **L'eggs Sheer Energy Panty Hose.** To stake tomato plants, use a pair of scissors to cut off the toe from the foot of a pair of used, clean L'eggs Sheer Energy Panty Hose, then cut one-inch strips from the leg, creating circular loops of panty hose. Use the loops to gently tie stems, vines, and thin plant trunks to stakes with a figure-eight loop.

• **L'eggs Sheer Energy Panty Hose** and **Oral-B Mint Waxed Floss.** To prevent birds, rodents, raccoons, or squirrels from destroying young tomatoes, cut off the feet from clean, used pairs of L'eggs Sheer Energy Panty Hose, slip a foot over each tomato, and seal the open end closed with a piece of Oral-B Mint Waxed Floss. The synthetic fibers keep birds away, and the flexible hose expands as the tomato grows. You can also cut a section from a leg of the panty hose, tie one end closed with dental floss, cover a tomato, and then secure the open end shut.

• **Maxwell House Coffee.** To protect baby tomato plants, remove the top and bottom from Maxwell House Coffee cans, place a can over each plant, and step on the can to set firmly in the soil. Remove cans when plants are a few weeks old.

• **Nestea.** Mix up a quart of unsweetened Nestea instant iced tea according to the directions (without adding sugar or ice) and fertilize tomato plants with the solution. Or simply sprinkle the powdered mix directly on the soil. As the tea decomposes, the nutrients work their way into the soil.

• **Pampers.** Place an opened Pamper, plastic-side down, in the bottom of a large planter, cover with four inches of soil, put the tomato plant in position, and fill the planter with soil. The superabsorbent polymer flakes inside the Pamper will retain water, cutting your watering time in half. Water moderately to avoid the possibility of overwatering the tomato plant.

- **Reynolds Wrap.** Before planting a tomato seedling, wrap the stem loosely with a four-inch tube of Reynolds Wrap, giving the seedling room to grow. Plant the seedling with two inches of the foil in the soil. The foil tube will protect the tomato plants from cutworms.

- **Reynolds Wrap.** Place sheets of Reynolds Wrap on the ground between rows of tomato plants and secure in place with stones. The light reflected by the foil repels aphids and the radiant heat can hasten the ripening of tomatoes by up to two weeks. Check the tomato plants daily to make sure the aluminum foil is not reflecting too much light back onto the plant, burning it.

- **20 Mule Team Borax.** Before planting tomato plants in the early spring, add one teaspoon 20 Mule Team Borax into the planting hole and mix with the soil. The borax hastens blossoming and brings on an early tomato crop.

- *USA Today.* If an impending frost forces you to pick tomatoes while they're still green, ripen them by wrapping each one in a page of *USA Today* and letting sit for a few days until ripe.

- **Vaseline, Ziploc Storage Bags,** and **Maxwell House Coffee.** Paint the outside and bottom of a clean, empty Maxwell House Coffee can yellow. Pound a six-foot wooden stake into the ground alongside your tomato plants (or as a stake for one of the tomato plants). Attach the yellow coffee can upside down to the top of the stake (using a hammer and nail, or an electric drill with a Phillips head screwdriver bit and a drywall screw). Cover the can with a gallon-size Ziploc Storage Bag and coat the plastic bag with Vaseline Petroleum Jelly. Whiteflies, attracted to the color yellow, will get stuck in the Vaseline on the Ziploc bag, which can then be replaced as needed. Place one trap every two feet.

STRANGE FACTS

- Contrary to popular belief, the tomato is a fruit, not a vegetable.

- Until the nineteenth century, Americans purportedly considered tomatoes to be poisonous. Legend holds that, in 1820, a wealthy eccentric named Robert Gibbon Johnson, determined to prove the tomato to be a harmless, edible fruit, stood before a crowd at the courthouse in Salem, New Jersey, and ate a basketful of tomatoes.

• In the lyrics to the 1937 hit song "Let's Call the Whole Thing Off," Ira Gershwin enunciates different pronunciations for the word *tomato*. His brother George Gershwin wrote the music.

• In the nineteenth century, tomatoes—then an exotic Mexican fruit—were called "love apples."

• In the 1978 campy cult movie *Attack of the Killer Tomatoes*, a special government task force pursues murderous tomatoes. The cast includes actor Jack Riley, who played Mr. Carlson on *The Bob Newhart Show*.

• In 1981, to save money on government-subsidized school lunches, the United States Department of Agriculture announced its plan to classify ketchup as a vegetable and sunflower seeds as meat. Public ridicule prompted the Reagan administration to withdraw the plan.

• The tomato plant is one of the few plants that can be replanted much deeper in the soil, burying the stem. If you do this, the plant will grow new roots along the buried stem.

• The leaves of tomato plants are toxic if eaten.

• The word *tomato* is slang for an attractive woman or girl.

• In 1985, G. Graham of Edmond, Oklahoma, grew the largest recorded tomato plant in history, measuring 53.5 feet tall. The following year, Graham grew the world's largest tomato, weighing seven pounds, twelve ounces.

• Tomatoes grow on both bushes and vines.

• The 1991 movie *Fried Green Tomatoes*, adapted from the novel *Fried Green Tomatoes at the Whistle Stop Café*, by Fannie Flagg, stars Kathy Bates, Mary Stuart Masterson, Mary-Louise Parker, Jessica Tandy, and Cicely Tyson.

• In 1995, Domino's Pizza used more than two million cases of pizza sauce, requiring more than 170 million pounds of tomatoes.

• Varieties of heirloom tomatoes with intriguing names include 'Abraham Lincoln', 'Arkansas Traveler', 'German Johnson', and 'Mortgage Lifter' (also known as 'Radiator Charlie').

• Every August, the town of Buñol, Spain, hosts "La Tomatina," the world's largest tomato fight, in which nearly twenty thousand people hurl some 150,000 fresh tomatoes at each other within an hour.

TOMATO SAUCE STAINS

✗ **Arm & Hammer Baking Soda.** Are your Tupperware and Rubbermaid containers stained red from tomato sauce? Use Arm & Hammer Baking Soda as you would any cleansing powder to scrub the stains from the containers.

✗ **Clorox.** To clean tomato sauce stains from inside plasticware containers, fill the containers with one part Clorox Bleach to two parts water, let sit for ten minutes, then rinse clean.

✗ **Efferdent.** To clean tomato sauce stains from plasticware containers, fill the containers with very hot water, drop in two Efferdent tablets, and let sit overnight. Then wash as usual.

✗ **Pam Original Cooking Spray.** Prevent tomato sauce from staining your Tupperware or Rubbermaid containers by simply spraying the insides of the containers with Pam Cooking Spray before filling with any tomato-based sauces.

✗ **Purell.** A squirt of Purell Instant Hand Sanitizer on the inside of your Rubbermaid or Tupperware container when washing helps get the plasticware squeaky clean.

✗ **ReaLemon.** Tired of that cabinet filled with red-stained Tupperware and Rubbermaid containers? Rub the discolored plastic storage items with ReaLemon lemon juice and let them sit in the sun for a day to gently bleach the plastic back to its original color.

Tools

CLEANING

- **Aqua Net Hair Spray.** Protect the wooden handles of gardening tools by spraying the wood with a thin coat of Aqua Net Hair Spray. The hair spray acts like shellac, preserving the wood and protecting it from the elements.

- **Clean Shower.** To prolong the life of sharp tools, such as pruning shears, hatchets, and saws, spray Clean Shower on the blades after each use.

- **Clorox.** Disinfect your pruning tools after each use with a mixture of three-quarters cup Clorox Bleach in one gallon water. Let soak for an hour, then rinse and dry.

- **Colgate Toothpaste.** Shine up your garden tools with a squirt of Colgate Regular Flavor Toothpaste. Rub with a soft cloth, then rinse thoroughly.

- **Crisco All-Vegetable Shortening.** Preserve the wooden handles of gardening tools by coating them with a dab of Crisco All-

Vegetable Shortening. Rub the shortening into the wood, then buff with a soft, clean cloth.

• **Cutex Nail Polish Remover.** To clean scissors, soak a cotton ball in Cutex Nail Polish Remover and carefully clean the scissor blades.

• **Listerine.** To avoid spreading fungal and bacterial diseases, sterilize your pruning tools with Listerine after each use. Mix one cup Listerine per gallon of water in a bucket and soak the pruning shears in the solution for one hour, then rinse clean and dry.

• **Oral-B Toothbrushes.** Clean caked-on dirt from crevices of your tools with a clean, old Oral-B Toothbrush.

• **Purell.** Disinfect pruning tools by coating the blades with Purell Instant Hand Sanitizer. The ethyl alcohol in Purell kills bacteria and fungi.

• **Reynolds Wrap.** Crumple up a piece of Reynolds Wrap to scrub tools clean.

• **Scrubbing Bubbles.** Spray Scrubbing Bubbles on filthy tools, let sit for a few minutes, then rinse clean with a hose and dry.

• **Smirnoff Vodka.** Sterilize your pruning tools with a mixture of two cups Smirnoff Vodka per gallon of water after each use to avoid spreading fungal diseases. Soak the pruning shears in the solution for one hour, then rinse clean and dry.

LUBRICATION

• **Castor Oil.** Lubricate gardening tools with a few drops of castor oil instead of petroleum.

• **ChapStick.** Rubbing ChapStick lip balm over the pivot joints of gardening tools provides ample lubrication to keep them working smoothly.

• **Crisco All-Vegetable Shortening.** Use a dab of Crisco All-Vegetable Shortening to lubricate the pivot joint of gardening tools, such as pruners.

• **Pam Original Cooking Spray.** A quick spritz of Pam Cooking Spray lubricates gardening tools easily and effortlessly.

• **Star Olive Oil.** A drop of Star Olive Oil on moving parts of pliers, hedge clippers, and pruning shears keeps them well lubricated and working smoothly.

• **Vaseline Petroleum Jelly.** Lubricate the pivot area of your pruning shears and other gardening tools with Vaseline Petroleum Jelly.

• **WD-40.** Oil the pivot joint of your hedge clippers, pruning shears, pliers, and scissors with a short blast of WD-40, the water displacement formula developed after forty attempts.

• **Wesson Corn Oil.** Lubricate gardening tools with a few drops of the corn oil named after company founder Dr. David Wesson, the plant chemist who, in 1899, developed the technology to create the world's first edible vegetable oil.

MAKING

• **Clorox.** To make a watering can, use an electric drill with a one-eighth-inch bit to carefully drill holes in the bottom of a clean, empty Clorox Bleach jug. Simply fill the jug with water to use.

• **Clorox.** Create a handy fertilizer scoop by capping an empty, clean Clorox Bleach jug and cutting it diagonally across the bottom.

• **Clorox.** Make a small hoe for weeding between plants by capping a clean, empty Clorox Bleach jug and cutting the jug in half diagonally, creating a triangular piece that includes the handle and leaving a curved point at the end.

• **Clorox.** Make weights to secure plastic or aluminum covers in place by filling clean, empty Clorox Bleach jugs with water and replacing the caps securely. The water-filled jugs double as solar-powered radiant heaters. During the day, the sun heats up the water in the jugs. At night, the heated water radiates warmth for the tender seedlings nearby. To make the jugs even more effective, spray-paint them flat black to absorb more heat.

- **CoverGirl NailSlicks Classic Red.** Make a convenient ruler to measure the depth for planting seeds and bulbs by using Cover-Girl NailSlicks Classic Red nail polish to mark off inches along the edge of your garden trowel. You can also use the nail polish to calibrate feet on the handle of a rake, shovel, or hoe.

- **L'eggs Sheer Energy Panty Hose.** To make a fruit picker, use a pair of pliers to cut apart a wire clothes hanger. Form a hoop approximately six inches in diameter and attach to the end of a ten-foot-long wooden pole. Cut off an entire leg from a pair of used, clean L'eggs Sheer Energy Panty Hose, stretch the open end of the leg around the hoop, and sew it in place. Use the net basket to pick fruits from high branches.

- **Liquid Paper.** Use Liquid Paper to mark off inches along the edge of your garden trowel to make a convenient ruler to measure the depth for planting bulbs. You can also use Liquid Paper to calibrate feet on the handle of a rake, shovel, or hoe.

- **Maxwell House Coffee** and **Bubble Wrap.** To make a fruit picker, use a pair of tin snips to carefully cut a V shape (approximately one inch tall) into the top rim of a clean, used Maxwell House Coffee can. With a pair of pliers, carefully bend the pointed corners slightly inward so that when you're picking fruit with the can, the bent sides will hold the fruit in the can. Drill two one-quarter-inch holes in the opposite side of the can and drill similar holes in the end of a six-foot-long piece of pine (two inches by three-quarters inch). Wire the can to the wooden pole. Cut two or three pieces of Bubble Wrap to place at the bottom of the can as a cushion for the picked fruit.

- **Maxwell House Coffee.** To spread granular fertilizer, punch holes in the bottom of an empty Maxwell House Coffee can with a hammer and a punch, fill with fertilizer, cover with the plastic lid, and shake the can as you walk through your garden.

- **Oral-B Mint Waxed Floss.** To make sowing and planting in straight rows a breeze, tie one end of a piece of Oral-B Mint Waxed Floss to the top of a pencil, stick the sharpened end in the ground as a stake, and unroll the dental floss across the plant bed. Tie the free end to a second pencil and stake it in the ground. When you're finished sowing or planting, wind the dental floss around one of the pencils so you can reuse your homemade cord and stakes.

- **Oral-B Toothbrush** and **CoverGirl NailSlicks Classic Red.** The handle of a clean, old Oral-B Toothbrush doubles as an excellent dibble to make holes for planting seeds. Use CoverGirl NailSlicks Classic Red nail polish to mark a planting depth on the handle. After planting the seeds, use the toothbrush bristles to sweep soil back over the hole.

- **Tide.** To make a heavy-duty scoop for fertilizer, cut off the top of a liquid Tide bottle just above the handle.

- **Windex.** Use a clean, empty Windex bottle as a mister for plants. Clean the bottle with dishwashing liquid and water to remove traces of any undesirable chemicals.

RUST

- **Alberto VO5 Conditioning Hairdressing.** To prevent tools from rusting, give your tools a thin coat of Alberto VO5 Conditioning Hairdressing. Use a soft cloth to wipe off the excess, leaving behind a very thin, virtually invisible protective coating. VO5's protectants actually prevent tarnish and rust.

- **Arm & Hammer Baking Soda.** To clean rust from tools, mix a thick paste of Arm & Hammer Baking Soda with water, apply to the tool with a damp sponge, rub, rinse, and dry.

- **Canada Dry Club Soda.** Loosen rusty tools by soaking them in Canada Dry Club Soda.

- **ChapStick.** Prevent tools from rusting by giving them a light coat of ChapStick—in any flavor.

- **Clean Shower.** To remove rust from tools, spray with Clean Shower and let dry, then rinse clean and allow to dry again.

- **Coca-Cola.** Soak a rusted tool in carbonated Coca-Cola overnight, then rinse clean. The carbonated soda loosens the rust.

- **Crayola Chalk.** Prevent tools from rusting by placing a piece of Crayola Chalk in your toolbox to absorb moisture.

- **Heinz White Vinegar.** To remove rust from gardening tools, soak the rusted implements in undiluted Heinz White Vinegar overnight.

- **Kingsford Charcoal Briquets.** Prevent tools from rusting by placing an untreated Kingsford Charcoal Briquet in your toolbox to absorb moisture.

- **Kool-Aid.** Soaking tools in Kool-Aid and then scrubbing well cleans rust.

- **Morton Salt** and **ReaLemon.** To clean rust from household tools, make a paste using two tablespoons Morton Salt and one tablespoon ReaLemon lemon juice. Apply to the rusted tool with a dry cloth and rub clean.

- **Pam Original Cooking Spray.** To prevent gardening tools from rusting, spray the clean tools with a light coat of Pam Cooking Spray. If tool parts are rusted together, a quick spritz of Pam Cooking Spray helps break them free.

- **Turtle Wax.** Prevent tools from rusting by giving them a light coat of Turtle Wax.

- **Vaseline Petroleum Jelly.** Applying a generous coat of Vaseline Petroleum Jelly over tools prevents them from rusting.

STORAGE

- **Scotch Packaging Tape.** Fold a piece of Scotch Packaging Tape over the edge of any small tool, punch a hole in the tape, and hang on a peg in your workshop.

- *USA Today.* After cleaning and lubricating your garden tools at the end of the season, wrap them in sheets of newspaper and store.

TOTING AND USING

- **Bubble Wrap** and **Scotch Packaging Tape.** Avoid blisters and make rakes, shovels, and hoes easier to handle by wrapping the handles with Bubble Wrap secured in place with Scotch Packaging Tape.

- **Clorox.** Cut off the top of a clean, empty Clorox Bleach jug above the handle to make a handy tool carrier.

- **Dr. Scholl's Moleskin.** Avoid blisters and make rakes, shovels, and hoes easier to handle by wrapping the handles with Dr. Scholl's Moleskin.

- **Tide.** Make a tool bucket to tote trowels and small spades by cutting off the top of an empty, clean liquid Tide bottle just above the handle.

- **Wilson Tennis Balls.** To help physically challenged people hold gardening tools, cut small slits in opposite sides of a Wilson Tennis Ball. Insert the handle of a small gardening tool through the tennis ball so a person with Parkinson's disease, arthritis, or any impairment that causes crippled or shaky hands can grip the ball and be able to use the tool.

STRANGE FACTS

- Comedian Tim Allen based his hit television comedy series *Home Improvement* on a character that loves tools and hosts a television show called *Tool Time.*

- A "tool," aside from being a mechanical implement, is a person manipulated by another for his own purposes.

- Actor Peter O'Toole—star of the movies *Lawrence of Arabia, Lord Jim, Man of La Mancha,* and *My Favorite Year*— attended a Catholic school where the nuns beat him to "correct" his left-handedness.

- The tool used to measure blood pressure is called a sphygmomanometer.

- In German, a hoe is called a *Hacke,* a rake is called a *Harke,* and a shovel is called a *Schaufel.*

The Hots for Kool-Aid

Around 1918 in Hastings, Nebraska, twenty-five-year-old Edwin Perkins—having concocted flavoring extracts and perfumes, published a weekly newspaper, and served as postmaster—set up a mail-order business called Perkins Products Co. to sell his concoctions through magazine advertisements.

One of Perkins's more popular products was a concentrated drink mix called Fruit Smack, available in six flavors at an economical price. Unfortunately, shipping the four-ounce glass bottles of syrup was costly and the bottles frequently broke in the mail. In 1927, Perkins devised a method to dehydrate Fruit Smack so the resulting powder could be packaged in paper envelopes. He then designed and printed envelopes with the product's new name: Kool Ade (which would later become Kool-Aid).

The dramatic drop in postage costs enabled Perkins to wholesale Kool-Aid for ten cents a packet to stores. In 1929, he distributed Kool-Aid (available in strawberry, cherry, lemon-lime, grape, orange, and raspberry) through food brokers to grocery stores nationwide.

By 1931, the strong demand for Kool-Aid prompted Perkins to stop making his other products so he could devote all his attention to Kool-Aid. He moved the entire Kool-Aid operation to Chicago to streamline distribution, be closer to supplies, and prepare for further expansion. After World War II, Perkins expanded the Kool-Aid factory, and by 1950, three hundred employees produced nearly a million packets of Kool-Aid every day.

In 1953, Perkins sold Kool-Aid to General Foods. Within a year, General Foods introduced a new advertising campaign for the drink mix, featuring the Smiling Face Pitcher, which has become an American icon. In 1989, General Foods merged with Kraft.

• During the Depression, Kool-Aid inventor Edwin Perkins cut the price of a packet of Kool-Aid in half, to just five cents.

• Kool-Aid can be used to dye hair temporarily. Simply mix the contents from a packet of any flavor Kool-Aid with a little water to make a thick paste and apply to your hair. The coloring is nontoxic and washes out after a few shampoos.

• In 1955, General Foods introduced Kool-Aid in root beer and lemonade flavors.

• In 1964, General Foods developed presweetened Kool-Aid, which was redeveloped in 1970.

• Kool-Aid is the official soft drink of the state of Nebraska.

• Kool-Aid can be used to clean a toilet bowl. Empty a packet of any flavor Kool-Aid into the toilet, scrub with a toilet brush, and flush clean.

Wasps

- **Aunt Jemima Original Syrup.** Coating a few small pieces of cardboard with Aunt Jemima Original Syrup and placing them around the perimeter of the yard will attract wasps. The stinging insects will get stuck in the gooey syrup.

- **Bounce.** To repel wasps while you're working in the garden, tie a sheet of Bounce Classic through one of your belt loops or the plastic flap in the back of your baseball cap. Oleander, the fragrance in Bounce Classic, repels insects.

- **Budweiser** and **Oral-B Mint Waxed Floss.** Pop open a can of Budweiser beer, pour out one-quarter of the beer (or drink it if you're so inclined), and tie a loop of Oral-B Mint Waxed Floss through the convenient hole in the flip-top tab. Hang the open beer can from a fence post or tree branch near where wasps are giving you trouble. Wasps love beer. They fly into the can, drink the beer, get drunk, and drown.

- **Con-Tact Paper** and **Domino Sugar.** Sprinkle the sticky side of a sheet of Con-Tact Paper with Domino Sugar. Hang the sweetened Con-Tact Paper wherever you wish to trap wasps.

• **Country Time Lemonade.** Drill several one-half-inch holes in the plastic lid of a clean, empty jar. Mix four teaspoons Country Time Lemonade powdered drink mix and two cups water in the jar and place it where wasps gather. The stinging insects will climb into the jar and drown in the acid drink.

• **Domino Sugar** and **ReaLemon.** Drill several one-half-inch holes in the lid of a clean, empty jar. Mix five tablespoons Domino Sugar, three tablespoons ReaLemon lemon juice, and two cups water in the jar, and place it outside where wasps gather. The bees and wasps will fly into the jar and drown in the acid lemon juice.

WASP STINGS

✗ **Adolph's Meat Tenderizer.** Make a paste from Adolph's Original Unseasoned Tenderizer and water, and apply to wasp stings, making sure you have removed the stinger. The enzymes in meat tenderizer break down the proteins in wasp venom.

✗ **Arm & Hammer Baking Soda** and **Band-Aid Bandages.** Make a paste from Arm & Hammer Baking Soda and water, apply to the sting, and cover with a Band-Aid Bandage. The baking soda simultaneously draws out the venom and neutralizes the sting.

✗ **Bayer Aspirin.** Wet the skin and rub a tablet of Bayer Aspirin—named after company founder Friedrich Bayer—over the bite (unless, of course, you are allergic to aspirin). Salicin, the active ingredient in aspirin, helps control inflammation.

✗ **Domino Sugar.** Make a paste from a teaspoon of Domino Sugar and water, and rub the sticky mixture over the bite for a few minutes. The sugar neutralizes the poison from the sting.

✗ **Green Giant Sweet Peas** and **Bounty.** Applying an ice pack to a wasp sting constricts the blood vessels, slowing the venom, relieving the swelling, and easing the pain. Use a plastic bag of frozen Green Giant Sweet Peas as an ice pack. The sack of peas conforms to the shape of your body. If the bag of peas feels too cold, place a Bounty Paper Towel between your skin and the bag.

✗ **Heinz White Vinegar.** Saturate a cotton ball with Heinz White Vinegar and apply to the wasp sting. The acetic acid neutralizes the venom, relieving the stinging pain.

✗ **Lipton Tea Bags.** Place a dampened Lipton Tea Bag over the sting and hold it in place for ten minutes. The tannic acid in the tea relieves the stinging sensation and also draws the stinger to the surface of the skin, making it easier to remove.

✗ **Listerine.** Dabbing Listerine on wasp stings relieves the pain instantly. The antiseptic—named in honor of nineteenth-century British surgeon Sir Joseph Lister—kills the proteins in the venom and disinfects the sting.

✗ **MasterCard.** Remove the stinger and venom sac from the skin by scraping the edge of a MasterCard against the skin in the opposite direction that the stinger entered.

✗ **Orajel.** Applying a dab of Orajel—a topical pain reliever for toothache pain—to a wasp sting numbs the pain immediately.

✗ **Pepto-Bismol.** This pink-colored mixture of pepsin and bismuth salicylate, originally marketed as "Bismosal: Mixture Cholera Infantum," soothes itching when slathered on a wasp sting.

✗ **Popsicle.** Scrape the stinger out with the exposed end of the Popsicle stick, then apply the icy Popsicle to the sting to relieve the pain.

✗ **Preparation H.** Applying a liberal coat of the hemorrhoid cream Preparation H to the sting helps remove the stinger (by reducing swelling) and provides immediate relief from the stinging pain.

✗ **Ziploc Storage Bag** and **Bounty.** Applying a Ziploc Storage Bag filled with ice to a wasp sting constricts the blood vessels, slowing the venom, relieving the swelling, and easing the pain. If the bag of ice feels too cold, place a sheet of Bounty Paper Towel between your skin and the bag.

• **Ivory Dishwashing Liquid.** Add one teaspoon Ivory Dishwashing Liquid to a sixteen-ounce trigger-spray bottle filled with water, shake well, and spray the wasps. The soap dries up the insects, causing them to die instantly.

• **L'eggs Sheer Energy Panty Hose** and **Oral-B Mint Waxed Floss.** To prevent wasps from destroying fruit on trees, cut off the feet from a clean, used pair of L'eggs Sheer Energy Panty Hose, slip a foot over the fruit, and seal the open end closed with a piece of Oral-B Mint Waxed Floss. The synthetic fibers keep wasps away, and the flexible hose expands as the fruit grows. You can also cut a section from the leg of the panty hose, tie one end closed with dental floss, cover the fruit, and then secure the open end shut.

• **Mountain Dew** and **Ivory Dishwashing Liquid.** Add two teaspoons Ivory Dishwashing Liquid to an open can of Mountain Dew and place the can near wasps. The sugary soda attracts the insects and the Ivory Dishwashing Liquid breaks the surface tension of the soda, inhibiting the insects from being able to crawl back out of the liquid, where they drown.

• **Smirnoff Vodka.** Fill a sixteen-ounce trigger-spray bottle with Smirnoff Vodka and spray the wasps. The alcohol in vodka kills wasps instantly, and you can celebrate, if so inclined, with the leftover vodka.

STRANGE FACTS

• Wasps can be beneficial to your garden, preying on aphids, beetle grubs, caterpillars, gypsy moths, maggots, mealybugs, and the larvae of ants.

• Wasps are a large family of insects that includes hornets and yellow jackets.

• Most beneficial wasps (brachonids, chalcids, encarsias, and trichogrammas) are less than one-quarter inch long. Ichneu-monid wasps, which are also beneficial, grow up to two inches long, but can be as small as one-sixteenth inch long.

• Beneficial wasps lay their eggs on the eggs or larvae of an insect host. When the eggs hatch, the developing wasps spin cocoons on the host.

• In 1709, satirist Jonathan Swift, author of *Gulliver's Travels*, wrote: "Laws are like cobwebs, which may catch small flies, but let wasps and hornets break through."

• Fear of wasps is called *spheksophobia*.

• In the 1960 cult horror film *Wasp Woman*, directed by Roger Corman, a cosmetics executive turns into a monstrous wasp.

Watering

• **Campbell's Tomato Soup.** Make a simple rain gauge by setting a clean, empty Campbell's Tomato Soup can outside. An inch of water in the can means an inch of rainfall.

• **Canada Dry Club Soda.** Feed flat Canada Dry Club Soda to your houseplants or outdoor plants. The minerals in club soda are beneficial to plants.

• **Clorox.** To water a deep-rooted tomato plant more efficiently, cut the bottom off a clean, empty, uncapped Clorox Bleach jug and bury, neck down, next to the plant. Then water the plant by filling the jug with water. The water goes to the roots where needed. You can also drill small holes (or make pinpricks) around an entire jug, bury it right-side up next to a plant, fill the jug with water, and let the water slowly seep out of the holes into the soil.

• **Clorox.** To make a watering can, use an electric drill with a one-eighth-inch bit to carefully drill holes in the bottom of a clean, empty Clorox Bleach jug. Simply fill the jug with water to use.

- **Coca-Cola.** Cut a two-inch-diameter hole in the side of a clean, empty two-liter Coca-Cola bottle, near the bottom. Drill a one-sixteenth-inch hole in the cap (one-eighth-inch for clay soil). Plant the capped bottle upside down in the soil near tomato or melon plants (six inches deep and roughly one foot away from the base of the plant). Fill the bottle with water every four days by placing a hose in the hole you cut in the base. For greater saturation, drill roughly a dozen holes in the top rounded part of the bottle before burying it.

- **Depends.** Planter leaking water? Set the pot inside a pair of Depends, creating a diaper for the plant. Conceal the Depends diaper by placing the pot inside a second, larger pot.

- **Dixie Cup.** Make a simple rain gauge by setting a clean, empty paper Dixie Cup outside. An inch of water in the cup denotes an inch of rainfall.

- **French's Mustard.** To water delicate seedlings, clean a French's Mustard squeeze bottle in hot soapy water, then fill the bottle with tepid water, screw the cap on securely, and squeeze the water around seedlings.

- **Gatorade.** Watering plants with Gatorade adds potassium to the soil, and the sugar feeds microorganisms, adding nitrogen.

- **Huggies Pull-Ups.** If your planter is leaking water, set the pot inside a pair of Huggies Pull-Ups, creating an absorbent diaper for the plant. Place the pot inside a second, larger pot to conceal the Pull-Up.

- **Jell-O.** Work a few teaspoons of powdered Jell-O into the soil of houseplants to absorb water and prevent it from leaking out of the bottom of the pot. The absorbent gelatin also reduces how often you need to water the plants. The nitrogen in Jell-O enhances plant growth and hastens sprouting, and the sugar feeds the microbes in the soil, producing more nutrients for the plant.

- **Johnson's Baby Powder.** Fill a clean, empty Johnson's Baby Powder canister with water and use as a convenient watering can for small plants.

- **L'eggs Sheer Energy Panty Hose.** If you collect rainwater from rain gutter downspouts, cut off a foot from a pair of used, clean L'eggs Sheer Energy Panty Hose, disconnect an accessible section of the pipe, place the panty hose foot over one of the sections of pipe, and reattach. The piece of panty hose will work as a filter, sifting debris from the water. Clean the panty hose filter frequently to avoid clogging.

- **Lipton Tea.** Invigorate houseplants and ferns by watering them once a week with a weak, tepid brewed Lipton tea. The tea attracts acid-producing bacteria and fills the soil with nutrients.

- **Maxwell House Coffee.** With a hammer and nail, punch a few holes in the bottom of a clean, empty five-pound Maxwell House Coffee can. Place a can by each plant in your garden and fill with water, creating a slow drip system to give the soil a deep soaking.

- **Nestea.** Mix up a quart of unsweetened Nestea instant iced tea according to the directions (without adding sugar or ice) and water houseplants and ferns with the nutrient solution.

- **Pampers.** Using a pair of scissors, carefully cut open a Pampers disposable diaper, and pot a plant by alternating potting soil with the superabsorbent polymer flakes from the diaper. The polymer flakes absorb three hundred times their weight in water, reducing how often you need to water your potted plants. The gelatinous polymer also stores nutrients, slowly feeding the plants.

- **Pampers.** Place an opened Pampers plastic-side down in the bottom of a large planter, cover with four inches of soil, put the tomato plant in position, and fill the planter with soil. The superabsorbent polymer flakes inside the Pampers will retain water, cutting your watering time in half. Water moderately to avoid the possibility of overwatering the tomato plant.

- **Saran Quick Covers.** To prevent water from dripping all over the floor while watering hanging plants, place a Saran Quick Cover around the bottom of the hanging planter before watering. The plastic cap catches the drips. Wait one hour before removing and save the Quick Cover to use the next time you water your plants.

• *USA Today.* When watering houseplants with a mister, hold a section of *USA Today* behind the plant to avoid getting water on furniture or walls.

• **Windex.** Use a clean, empty Windex bottle as a mister for plants. Clean the bottle with dishwashing liquid and water to remove traces of any chemicals.

STRANGE FACTS

• Watering plants at night encourages foliar diseases. Watering plants in the early morning prevents moisture from evaporating rapidly and enables the plants to dry by nightfall.

• Watering plants, trees, and lawns for thirty minutes twice a week is better than watering for ten minutes every day. The more deeply a plant is watered, the deeper the water penetrates the soil, encouraging roots to grow deeper and ultimately allowing the plant to survive on less water. (Young plants, however, have shallow roots and should be watered lightly and frequently.)

• Convinced that the sun died every night and needed human blood to give it strength to rise the next morning, the Aztecs sacrificed 15,000 men a year to the sun god, Huitzilopochtli. The Aztec Empire, ruling Mexico during the fifteenth and early sixteenth century, frequently started wars with other states to capture prisoners to sacrifice.

• In 1945, Grand Rapids, Michigan, and Newburgh, New York, became the first cities in the United States to add fluoride to their water.

• Begun in 1960, construction of the Aswân High Dam on the Nile River south of Aswân necessitated the relocation of ninety thousand people and a massive ancient Egyptian monument at

Abu Simbel—at a combined cost of 1.5 billion dollars and fifteen years of work. Lake Nasser, created by the dam, spreads out so far that massive amounts of water evaporate, raising the concentration of salt in the Nile River. Consequently, water from the Nile River can no longer be used to irrigate some crops, and sardines from the Mediterranean Sea no longer enter the mouth of the Nile. The low-water level of Lake Nasser powers only four of the ten turbines at the dam and irrigates only half the land anticipated.

• In an episode of the television comedy *Gilligan's Island*, Mary Ann, after planting seeds, says, "When in doubt, use the farmer's formula: one part sunshine, two parts water, three parts prayer."

• In 1980, Texaco began drilling for oil from a new rig in the middle of Lake Peigneur in Louisiana. The water immediately drained from the 1,300-acre lake, sucking eight tugboats, nine barges, five houses, a mobile home, and two oil rigs into the abandoned salt mine beneath the lake.

• Mexico City is sinking at the rate of six to eight inches a year because the city is built on top of a natural underground water source that is being drained by wells for the fifteen million residents of the city.

• The average American uses seventy gallons of water each day.

Weeds

• **Clorox.** Make a small hoe for weeding between plants by capping a clean, empty Clorox Bleach jug and cutting the jug in half diagonally, creating a triangular piece that includes the handle, leaving a curved point at the end.

• **Clorox.** Secure plastic or aluminum weed covers in place by filling clean, empty Clorox Bleach jugs with water, replacing the caps securely, and using the jugs as weights. The water-filled jugs double as solar-powered radiant heaters. During the day, the sun heats up the water in the jugs. At night, the heated water radiates warmth for the tender seedlings nearby. To make the jugs even more effective, spray-paint them flat black to absorb more heat. When you no longer need the weights or solar-powered radiant heaters, use the water on your plants.

• **Coca-Cola.** To shield healthy plants from organic weed killers, cut off the bottom of a clean, used two-liter Coca-Cola bottle and cover the weeds with the top half of the bottle. Insert the nozzle of a trigger-spray bottle filled with organic herbicide into the neck of the Coca-Cola bottle and spray.

• **Dustbuster.** Prevent dandelion seeds from blowing all over your garden and lawn by using a Dustbuster to vacuum the seed heads. Your neighbors may think you've lost your mind, but they'll be weeding while you're enjoying your weed-free garden.

• **Glad Trash Bags.** Slice open the sides of black Glad Trash Bags to make long sheets and place the black plastic over the weeds, securing with stones so no light can reach the plants. After a week or two, the weeds should be dead.

• **Heinz White Vinegar.** To kill weeds in the garden or between the cracks in the sidewalk and driveway, pour Heinz White Vinegar directly on them.

• **Morton Salt.** Pouring Morton Salt on weeds on a dry, sunny day kills the plants. Avoid getting salt on any plants you want to thrive.

• **Smirnoff Vodka.** Mix three tablespoons Smirnoff Vodka and two cups water in a sixteen-ounce trigger-spray bottle. Spray weeds well, without getting the alcohol solution on other plants. The vodka dehydrates the weeds.

• **20 Mule Team Borax.** To kill Creeping Charlie on your lawn, mix exactly five teaspoons 20 Mule Team Borax and one quart water in a pump spray bottle. Spray the solution evenly over the trouble spots—the amount above should cover a twenty-five-square-foot area of lawn. (The Borax may cause the grass to yellow temporarily.)

• *USA Today.* Thoroughly wet a section of *USA Today* so the pages cling together, place the soggy newspaper mat over weeds, and anchor in place with rocks or soil so no light can reach the weeds. After a week, the weeds should be dead and you can remove the newspaper. If you're using this technique in a garden or flowerbed, water the plants well before mulching with newspaper.

STRANGE FACTS

• In the final couplet of *Sonnet 94*, published in 1609, William Shakespeare wrote:

> For sweetest things turn sourest by their deeds;
> Lilies that fester smell far worse than weeds.

• Home gardeners spend more than 200 million dollars a year on chemical herbicides to kill weeds and unwanted plants. Chemical herbicides pollute groundwater, degrade soil, and are often carcinogenic.

• The simplest way to prevent an abundance of weeds is to pull weeds before they set seed.

• Queen Anne's lace, goldenrod, tansy, common sorrel, wild daisy, stinging nettle, and lamb's-quarters are all desirable weeds that attract beneficial insects to your garden.

• Many weeds—including chickweed, dandelion, and lamb's-quarters—are edible and can be mixed into salads.

• Weeds can help you determine whether your garden soil is acid or akaline. Weeds like lady's thumb and docks grow in strongly acid soils, while weeds like sagebrush and woody asters grow in alkaline soils.

• The giant hogweed, the largest weed in the world, grows up to twelve feet tall with leaves three feet long.

• The purple nutsedge, a land weed native to India, is the most damaging weed in the world, attacking fifty-two different types of crops in ninety-two countries. It grows up to thirty-nine inches tall, and its seeds can germinate at 95 degrees Fahrenheit and remain viable in temperatures down to minus 68 degrees Fahrenheit.

• Rubbing the leaf of the common weed plantain between your fingers and then pressing the extracted juice on a bee sting relieves the pain.

• The melaleuca tree, a native of Australia introduced to Florida in 1900, is actually a weed.

• In 1944, English economist William Henry Beveridge wrote, "Ignorance is an evil weed."

• The word *weed* is slang for marijuana.

• The 1987 movie *Weeds* stars Nick Nolte as a prisoner sentenced to life without parole in San Quentin who, by writing a play, wins his freedom.

Whiteflies

- **Dustbuster** and **Listerine**. Place a cotton ball moistened with Listerine inside the nozzle of the Dustbuster before inserting the bag, then use the Dustbuster to suck whiteflies off leaves and out of the air. (Hold the Dustbuster lightly over the plant with one hand and hold the leaves with the other hand to prevent them from being sucked into the Dustbuster and ripped.) The antiseptic on the cotton ball will help kill the whiteflies inside the Dustbuster. When you're finished, empty the pests into a bucket of soapy water.

- **Listerine** and **Ivory Dishwashing Liquid**. Repel whiteflies from plants by mixing one-half teaspoon Listerine (regular flavor), one-half teaspoon Ivory Dishwashing Liquid, and two cups water in a sixteen-ounce trigger-spray bottle. Use once every two weeks as an insecticide on fruit and vegetable gardens. (Be sure to test the solution on a few leaves of the plant and watch for a day to make sure the formula does not burn the leaves.)

• **McCormick Garlic Powder** and **Ivory Dishwashing Liquid.** Mix three tablespoons McCormick Garlic Powder, one-half teaspoon Ivory Dishwashing Liquid, and one quart water in a blender to create a concentrate. Pour two ounces of the concentrate into a sixteen-ounce trigger-spray bottle, fill the rest of the bottle with water, shake well, and spray plants to repel whiteflies. (Choose the plants you intend to spray with garlic carefully, since garlic also repels beneficial insects.)

• **Murphy Oil Soap.** To kill pesky whiteflies on houseplants, mix equal parts Murphy Oil Soap and water in a trigger-spray bottle and mist the affected plants.

• **Scotch Packaging Tape** and **Oral-B Mint Waxed Floss.** Take a yellow piece of cardboard (like a bright yellow file folder) and cover it with clear Scotch Packaging Tape facing sticky-side out. Punch a hole in the top of the cardboard and hang it with a loop of Oral-B Mint Waxed Floss over the infested plant. Whiteflies are attracted to the color yellow, and when they fly up from the plant, they will get stuck on the adhesive.

• **Smirnoff Vodka** and **Q-Tips Cotton Swabs.** To remove whiteflies from plants, dab the little critters with a Q-Tips Cotton Swab dipped in Smirnoff Vodka. Or mix equal parts Smirnoff Vodka and water in a sixteen-ounce trigger-spray bottle and spray on plant leaves in the cool of the day. Do not use alcohol on delicate plants like African violets. (Before treating the entire plant, test this alcohol formula on one of the plant's leaves and wait one day to make certain it doesn't burn the leaf.)

• **Tabasco Pepper Sauce** and **Wesson Corn Oil.** To repel whiteflies, add two teaspoons Tabasco Pepper Sauce and one-half teaspoon Wesson Corn Oil in a sixteen-ounce trigger-spray bottle. Fill the rest of the bottle with warm water and shake well. Spray on plants.

• **Vaseline, Ziploc Storage Bags,** and **Maxwell House Coffee.** To get whiteflies off tomato plants, paint the outside and bottom of a clean, empty Maxwell House Coffee can yellow. Pound a six-foot wooden stake into the ground alongside your tomato plants. Attach the yellow coffee can upside down to the top of the stake (using a hammer and nail, or an electric drill with a Phillips head screwdriver bit and a drywall screw). Cover the can with a gallon-size Ziploc Storage Bag and coat the bag with Vaseline Petroleum Jelly. The whiteflies, attracted to the color yellow, will get stuck in the Vaseline on the Ziploc bag, which can then be replaced as needed. Place one trap every two feet throughout your tomato rows.

STRANGE FACTS

- Beelzebub, prince of the devils in the New Testament and second in command to Satan in John Milton's epic poem *Paradise Lost*, is Hebrew for "Lord of the Flies"—the inspiration for William Golding's 1954 novel of the same name.

- Adult whiteflies are roughly one-sixteenth inch long and look like miniature moths with white wings.

- If you shake a branch of a plant infested with whiteflies, the pests will swarm, creating what looks like a cloud of white smoke.

- In the 1958 movie *The Fly*, David Hedison stars as a scientist who accidentally turns himself into a giant fly. The 1986 remake stars Jeff Goldblum.

- Whiteflies excrete a sticky honeydew that tends to attract black mold to plant leaves.

- In 1991, millions of whiteflies attacked fields in California's Imperial Valley near the Mexico border, destroying 95 percent of the fall melon crop. Farmers dubbed the destructive poinsettia strain of the sweet-potato whitefly the "Superbug."

Worms

- **Domino Sugar.** To prevent microscopic and parasitic nematode worms from piercing the roots of plants and causing root knots, apply five pounds of Domino Sugar for every 250 square feet of garden. Microorganisms feeding on the sugar will increase the organic matter in the soil, making an inhospitable environment for the nematodes.

- **Goodyear Tires** and *USA Today.* To raise worms, fill the inside of the rim of five or six old Goodyear Tires with shredded pages of *USA Today.* Stack the tires on top of each other on the ground and fill with layers of shredded newspaper, kitchen scraps, and a few red wiggler starter worms. Add indoor and outdoor organic matter to this worm-powered compost bin. The rubber tires insulate the worms from harsh winter weather, and as the rubber heats up, the worms make their way higher inside the tires.

- **Grandma's Molasses.** To prevent microscopic and parasitic ne-matode worms from piercing the roots of plants and causing root knots, fill a hose-attached sprayer with one jar of Grandma's Molasses and spray on up to one thousand square feet of lawn. Microorganisms and insects feeding on the molasses will increase the organic matter in the soil, making an inhospitable environment for the nematodes.

• **Maxwell House Coffee.** Breed worms by adding used Maxwell House Coffee grounds to your worm bed.

• *USA Today.* Give earthworms a food they love by placing six to eight sheets of *USA Today* on the soil and covering with a layer of mulch.

STRANGE FACTS

• Earthworms excrete three essential plant nutrients: nitrogen, potassium, and phosphorus.

• In 1864, a bootlace worm washed ashore at St. Andrews, Fife, Great Britain, measuring 180 feet in length.

• Contrary to popular belief, an earthworm sliced in half cannot regenerate.

• Scientists have named and identified more than three thousand species of earthworm.

• Each square foot of the top several inches of the average garden contains roughly fifty earthworms.

• The 217,800 earthworms living in an acre of garden digest between seven tons of soil and one thousand tons of soil, depending on the species, climate, and soil conditions.

• The nightcrawler, the most common species of earthworm in North America, grows up to twelve inches long.

• Insects Inter, a fast-food chain in Thailand, specializes in cooked bugs, selling fried worms with chili sauce.

• Nightcrawlers have been known to tunnel six feet deep.

- The earthworm has five hearts and no eyes.

- Actor Cary Grant's birth name was Archibald Leach.

- In the 1959 horror movie *Attack of the Giant Leeches*, starring Yvette Vickers (who also starred in the 1958 cult horror movie *Attack of the 50-Foot Woman*), giant leeches infest a town in the Florida Everglades.

- In the 1988 comedy movie *A Fish Called Wanda*, Monty Python veteran John Cleese plays an English barrister named Archibald Leach.

- The fear of being infested with worms is called *helminthophobia*.

- The earthworm has both male and female reproductive organs but requires contact with another earthworm to reproduce.

Acknowledgments

At Rodale, I am grateful to Margot Schupf, for championing my cause and making this book a labor of love, and to my editor, Christine Bucks, for her patience and fortitude. I am also deeply indebted to Tara Long, Dan Andreason, Jason Schneider, Keith Biery, Nancy Rutman, Jodi Schaffer, Nanette Bendyna, Ellen Phillips, Tami Booth, Stephanie Tade, Katrina Cwitkowitz, Janine Slaughter, Laura Mory, and Linda Rutenbar. Endless thanks to the astounding publicity talents of Mary Lengle, Heidi Krupp, Jennifer Heeseler, and Kim-from-LA.

My heartfelt thanks also go out to the thousands of people who have visited my Web site and taken the time to send me e-mail sharing their ingenious tips for the brand-name products we all know and love.

A very special thanks to my agent, Jeremy Solomon; my manager, Barb North; my Web-site partner, Michael Teitelbaum; Dustbuster inventor Carroll Gantz, for sharing his recollections; and Ellyn Small and Stacey Bender at Bender-Hammerling.

Above all, all my love to Debbie, Ashley, and Julia.

Sources

BOOKS AND PERIODICALS

• *Africa on a Shoestring* by Geoff Crowher (Victoria, Australia: Lonely Planet, 1986)

• *All-New Hints from Heloise* by Heloise (New York: Perigee, 1989)

• *America's Stupidest Business Decisions* by Bill Adler (New York: Quill, 1997)

• *Another Use For* by Vicki Lansky (Deephaven, Minnesota: Book Peddlers, 1991)

• *Ask Anne & Nan* by Anne Adams and Nancy Walker (Brattleboro, Vermont: Whetstone, 1989)

• *The Bag Book* by Vicki Lansky (Deephaven, Minnesota: Book Peddlers, 2000)

• *Baking Soda Bonanza* by Peter A. Ciullo (New York: Harper-Perennial, 1995)

• *The Beatles: An Oral History* by David Pritchard and Alan Lysaght (New York: Hyperion, 1998)

• *The Beatles Forever* by Nicholas Schaffner (New York: McGraw-Hill, 1977)

• *The Blunder Book* by M. Hirsh Goldberg (New York: Quill, 1984)

• *The Book of Lists* by David Wallechinsky, Irving Wallace, and Amy Wallace (New York: William Morrow, 1977)

• *The Book of Lists 2* by Irving Wallace, David Wallechinsky, Amy Wallace, and Sylvia Wallace (New York: William Morrow, 1980)

- *The Book of 1,001 Home Health Remedies* by the editors of *Natural Healing Newsletter* (Peachtree City, Georgia: FC&A, 1993)

- *Can You Trust a Tomato in January?* by Vince Staten (New York: Simon & Schuster, 1993)

- *China: A Travel Survival Kit* by Alan Samagalski and Michael Buckley (Victoria, Australia: Lonely Planet, 1984)

- *The Complete Works of William Shakespeare* (London: Abbey Library, 1974)

- *A Dash of Mustard* by Katy Holder and Jane Newdick (London: Chartwell Books, 1995)

- *The Dictionary of Misinformation* by Tom Burnam (New York: Thomas Y. Crowell, 1975)

- *Dictionary of Trade Name Origins* by Adrian Room (London: Routledge & Kegan Paul, 1982)

- *The Doctors Book of Food Remedies* by Selene Yeager and the editors of *Prevention* Health Books (Emmaus, Pennsylvania: Rodale, 1998)

- *The Doctors Book of Home Remedies* by editors of *Prevention* Magazine (Emmaus, Pennsylvania: Rodale, 1990)

- *The Doctors Book of Home Remedies II* by Sid Kirchheimer and the editors of *Prevention* Magazine (Emmaus, Pennsylvania: Rodale, 1993)

- *Encyclopedia of Pop Culture* by Jane & Michael Stern (New York: HarperCollins, 1992)

- *Familiar Quotations, Fifteenth Edition* by John Bartlett, edited by Emily Morison Beck (New York: Little, Brown, 1980)

- *Famous American Trademarks* by Arnold B. Barach (Washington, D.C.: Public Affairs Press, 1971)

- *The Film Encyclopedia* by Ephraim Katz (New York: Perigee, 1979)

- *Great Gardening Formulas* edited by Joan Benjamin and Deborah L. Martin (Emmaus, Pennsylvania: Rodale, 1998)

- *The Guinness Book of World Records* (New York: Bantam, 1998)

- *Heinerman's Encyclopedia of Healing Herbs & Spices* by John Heinerman (West Nyack, New York: Parker Publishing, 1996)

- *Hints from Heloise* by Heloise (New York: Arbor House, 1980)

- *The Holy Bible New International Version* (Grand Rapids, Michigan: Zondervan, 1989)

- *The Holy Scriptures* (Philadelphia: The Jewish Publication Society of America, 1955)

- *Home Remedies from the Country Doctor* by Jay Heinrichs, Dorothy Behlen Heinrichs, and the editors of *Yankee* Magazine (Emmaus, Pennsylvania: Rodale, 1999)

- *Home Remedies: What Works* by the editors of *Prevention* Health Books (Emmaus, Pennsylvania: Rodale, 1998)

- *Hoover's Company Profile Database* (Austin, Texas: The Reference Press, 1996)

- *Hoover's Guide to Private Companies 1994–1995* (Austin, Texas: The Reference Press, 1995)

- *Household Hints & Formulas* by Erik Bruun (New York: Black Dog and Leventhal, 1994)

- *Household Hints & Handy Tips* by *Reader's Digest* (Pleasantville, New York: Reader's Digest Association, 1988)

- *Household Hints for Upstairs, Downstairs, and All around the House* by Carol Reese (New York: Henry Holt and Co., 1982)

- *How the Cadillac Got Its Fins* by Jack Mingo (New York: HarperCollins, 1994)

- *Kitchen Medicines* by Ben Charles Harris (Barre, Massachusetts: Barre, 1968)

- *The Kruger National Park* by Leo Braack (Cape Town, South Africa: Struik, 1983)

- *Lennon Remembers* by Jann Wenner (New York: Pocket Books, 1971)

- *Make It Yourself* by Dolores Riccio and Joan Bingham (Radnor, Pennsylvania: Chilton, 1978)

- *Mary Ellen's Best of Helpful Hints* by Mary Ellen Pinkham (New York: Warner/B. Lansky, 1979)

- *Mary Ellen's Greatest Hints* by Mary Ellen Pinkham (New York: Fawcett Crest, 1990)

- *Medical Blunders* by R. M. Youngston (New York: New York University Press, 1996)

- *Mythology* by Edith Hamilton (New York: Little, Brown, 1940)

- *National Geographic World* (Washington, D.C.: National Geographic Society, December 2000)

- *1001 Hints & Tips for Your Garden* by the editors of *Reader's Digest* (Pleasantville, New York: Reader's Digest, 1996)

- *1001 Ingenious Gardening Ideas* edited by Deborah L. Martin (Emmaus, Pennsylvania: Rodale, 1998)

- *Oops!* by Paul Kirchner (Los Angeles: General Publishing Books, 1996)

- *The Origins of Everyday Things* by the editors of *Reader's Digest* (London: Reader's Digest, 1999)

- *The Oxford Companion to English Literature, Fourth Edition* edited by Sir Paul Harvey (Oxford: Claredon Press, 1973)

- *The Oxford Dictionary of Modern Quotations* by Tony Augarde (Oxford: Oxford University Press, 1991)

- *Panati's Extraordinary Origins of Everyday Things* by Charles Panati (New York: HarperCollins, 1987)

- *Practical Problem Solver* by *Reader's Digest* (Pleasantville, New York: Reader's Digest, 1991)

- *The Random House Dictionary of the English Language, Unabridged Edition* (New York: Random House: 1969)

- *Reader's Digest Book of Facts* (Pleasantville, New York: Reader's Digest, 1987)

- *The Resourceful Gardener's Guide* edited by Christine Bucks and Fern Marshall Bradley (Emmaus, Pennsylvania: Rodale, 2001)

- *Ripley's Believe It or Not! Encyclopedia of the Bizarre* by Julie Mooney and the editors of *Ripley's Believe It or Not!* (New York: Black Dog & Leventhal, 2002)

- *Rodale's Book of Hints, Tips & Everyday Wisdom* by Carol Hupping, Cheryl Winters Tetreau, and Roger B. Yepsen, Jr. (Emmaus, Pennsylvania: Rodale, 1985)

- *Scientific Blunders* by R. M. Youngston (New York: Carroll & Graf, 1998)

- *A Separate Reality* by Carlos Castaneda (New York: Simon and Schuster, 1971)

- *Shout! The Beatles in Their Generation* by Philip Norman (New York: Warner, 1981)

- *So Who the Heck Was Oscar Meyer?* by Doug Gelbert (New York: Barricade Books, 1996)

- *The Starr Evidence* edited by Phil Kuntz (New York: Pocket Books, 1998)

- *Strange Stories, Amazing Facts* (Pleasantville, New York: Reader's Digest, 1976)

- *Sunset Western Garden Book* by the editors of Sunset Books and *Sunset* Magazine (Menlo Park, California: Sunset, 1995)

- *Symbols of America* by Hal Morgan (New York: Viking, 1986)

- *Time Almanac Reference Edition 1994* (Washington, D.C.: Compact Publishing, 1994)

- *The 20th Century* by David Wallechinsky (New York: Little, Brown, 1995)

- *Van Gogh* by Pierre Cabanne (London: Thames and Hudson, 1963)

- *Why Did They Name It . . . ?* by Hannah Campbell (New York: Fleet, 1964)

- *The* Woman's Day *Help Book* by Geraldine Rhoads and Edna Paradis (New York: Viking, 1988)

- *The World Almanac and Book of Facts 1993* (Matwah, New Jersey: World Almanac Books, 1993)

- *The World Almanac and Book of Facts 1998* (Matwah, New Jersey: World Almanac Books, 1998)

- *The World Almanac and Book of Facts 2000* (Matwah, New Jersey: World Almanac Books, 2000)

- *The World Book Encyclopedia* (Chicago: World Book, 1985)

Trademark Information

"Adolph's" is a registered trademark of Lipton Inc.

"Albers" is a registered trademark of Nestlé.

"Alberto VO5" is a registered trademark of Alberto-Culver USA Inc.

"Alka-Seltzer" is a registered trademark of Miles Inc.

"Aqua Net" is a registered trademark of Faberge USA Inc.

"Arm & Hammer" is a registered trademark of the Church & Dwight Co. Inc.

"Armor All" is a registered trademark of the Armor All Products Corp.

"Aunt Jemima" is a registered trademark of the Quaker Oats Co.

"Avery" is a registered trademark of Avery Dennison Corp.

"Balmex" is a registered trademark of Macsil Inc.

"Ban" is a registered trademark of Chattem Inc.

"Band-Aid" is a registered trademark of Johnson & Johnson.

"Barbasol" is a registered trademark of Pfizer Inc.

"Barnum's Animals" is a registered trademark of Nabisco.

"Bayer" is a registered trademark of the Bayer Corp.

"BenGay" is a registered trademark of Pfizer Inc.

"Blue Bonnet" is a registered trademark of ConAgra Brands Inc.

"Bounce" is a registered trademark of Procter & Gamble.

"Bounty" is a registered trademark of Procter & Gamble.

"Bubble Wrap" is a registered trademark of the Sealed Air Corp.

"Budweiser" is a registered trademark of Anheuser-Busch Inc.

"Campbell's" is a registered trademark of the Campbell Soup Co.

"Canada Dry" is a registered trademark of Cadbury Beverages Inc.

"Carnation" is a registered trademark of the Nestlé Food Co.

"Cascade" is a registered trademark of Procter & Gamble.

"ChapStick" is a registered trademark of the A. H. Robbins Co.

"Charmin" is a registered trademark of Procter & Gamble.

"Cheerios" is a registered trademark of General Mills Inc.

"Cheez Whiz" is a registered trademark of Kraft Foods.

"Clairol" and "Herbal Essences" are registered trademarks of Clairol.

"Clean Shower" is a registered trademark of Clean Shower, L.P.

"Clorox" is a registered trademark of the Clorox Co.

"Coca-Cola" and "Coke" are registered trademarks of the Coca-Cola Co.

"Colgate" is a registered trademark of Colgate-Palmolive.

"Comet" is a registered trademark of Procter & Gamble.

"Con-Tact" is a registered trademark of Rubbermaid Inc.

"Conair" and "Pro Style" are registered trademarks of the Conair Corp.

"Cool Whip" is a registered trademark of Kraft Foods.

"Coppertone" is a registered trademark of Schering-Plough HealthCare Products Inc.

"Country Time" and "Country Time Lemonade" are registered trademarks of Dr Pepper/Seven Up Inc.

"CoverGirl" and "NailSlicks" are registered trademarks of the Noxell Corp.

"Cracker Jack" is a registered trademark of Frito-Lay.

"Crayola" is a registered trademark of Binney & Smith Inc.

"Cream of Wheat" is a registered trademark of Nabisco.

"Crisco" is a registered trademark of Procter & Gamble.

"Cutex" is a registered trademark of MedTech.

"Dannon" is a registered trademark of the Dannon Co.

"DAP" is a registered trademark of DAP Inc.

"Dawn" is a registered trademark of Procter & Gamble.

"Depends" is a registered trademark of Kimberly-Clark World-wide Inc.

"Dial" is a registered trademark of the Dial Corp.

"Dixie" is a registered trademark of the James River Corp.

"Domino" is a registered trademark of the Domino Sugar Corp.

"Downy" is a registered trademark of Procter & Gamble.

"Dr. Bronner's" is a registered trademark of All-One-God-Faith Inc.

"Dr. Scholl's" is a registered trademark of Schering-Plough HealthCare Products Inc.

"Dustbuster" is a registered trademark of Black & Decker.

"Easy-Off" is a registered trademark of Reckitt Benckiser Inc.

"Efferdent" is a registered trademark of Warner-Lambert.

"Elmer's Glue-All" and Elmer the Bull are registered trademarks of Borden.

"Endust" is a registered trademark of the Sara Lee Corp.

"Fleischmann's" and "Active Dry Yeast" are registered trademarks of Specialty Brands.

"Formula 409" is a registered trademark of The Clorox Co.

"Forster" is a registered trademark of Diamond Brands Inc.

"French's" is a registered trademark of Reckitt Benckiser Inc.

"Frisbee" is a registered trademark of Mattel Inc.

"Gatorade" is a registered trademark of the Gatorade Co.

"Gerber" is a registered trademark of the Gerber Products Co.

"Geritol" is a registered trademark of Beecham Inc.

"Glad" is a registered trademark of the First Brands Corp.

"Gojo" is a registered trademark of Gojo Industries Inc.

"Gold Medal" is a registered trademark of General Mills Inc.

"Goodyear" is a registered trademark of Goodyear Inc.

"Grandma's" is a registered trademark of Mott's USA.

"Green Giant" is a registered trademark of the Pillsbury Co.

"Gunk" is a registered trademark of the Radiator Specialty Co.

"Hartz" is a registered trademark of the Hartz Mountain Co.

"Heinz" is a registered trademark of the H.J. Heinz Co.

"Huggies" and "Pull-Ups" are registered trademarks of the Kimberly-Clark Corp.

"Hula Hoop" is a registered trademark of Wham-O Inc.

"Irish Spring" is a registered trademark of Colgate-Palmolive.

"Ivory" is a registered trademark of Procter & Gamble.

"Jell-O" is a registered trademark of Kraft Foods.

"Jet-Dry" is a registered trademark of Reckitt Benckiser Inc.

"Jif" is a registered trademark of Procter & Gamble.

"Johnson's" and "Johnson & Johnson" are registered trademarks of Johnson & Johnson.

"Joy" is a registered trademark of Procter & Gamble.

"Kaopectate" is a registered trademark of the Pharmacia Corp.

"Karo" is a registered trademark of CPC International Inc.

"Kellogg's" and "Mini-Wheats" are registered trademarks of the Kellogg Co.

"Kingsford" is a registered trademark of the Kingsford Products Co.

"Kingsford's" is a registered trademark of Bestfoods.

"Kiwi" is a registered trademark of the Sara Lee Corp.

"Kleenex" is a registered trademark of the Kimberly-Clark Corp.

"Kodak" is a registered trademark of the Eastman Kodak Co.

"Kool-Aid" is a registered trademark of Kraft Foods.

"Krazy" is a registered trademark of Borden Inc.

"L'eggs" and "Sheer Energy" are registered trademarks of the Sara Lee Corp.

"Lestoil" is a registered trademark of The Clorox Co.

"Lewis Labs" is a registered trademark of Lewis Labs.

"Lipton," "The 'Brisk' Tea," and "Flo-Thru" are registered trademarks of the Thomas J. Lipton Co.

"Liquid Paper" is a registered trademark of the Liquid Paper Corp.

"Listerine" is a registered trademark of Warner-Lambert.

"Lubriderm" is a registered trademark of Warner-Lambert.

"Lysol" is a registered trademark of Reckitt Benckiser Inc.

"Massengill" is a registered trademark of SmithKlein Beecham.

"MasterCard" is a registered trademark of MasterCard International Inc.

"Maxwell House" and "Good to the Last Drop" are registered trademarks of the Maxwell House Coffee Co.

"Maybelline" is a registered trademark of Maybelline.

"McCormick" is a registered trademark of McCormick & Co. Inc.

"Miller" and "Genuine Draft" are registered trademarks of the Miller Brewing Co.

"Minute Rice" is a registered trademark of Kraft Foods.

"Miracle Whip" is a registered trademark of Kraft Foods.

"Mop and Glo" is a registered trademark of Reckitt Benckiser Inc.

"Morton" and the Morton Umbrella Girl are registered trademarks of Morton International Inc.

"Mott's" is a registered trademark of Mott's Inc.

"Mountain Dew" is a registered trademark of PepsiCo Inc.

"Mr. Clean" is a registered trademark of Procter & Gamble.

"Mr. Coffee" is a registered trademark of Mr. Coffee Inc.

"Mrs. Stewart's" is a registered trademark of Luther Ford & Co.

"Murphy" is a registered trademark of the Colgate-Palmolive Co.

"Nestea" and "Nestlé" are registered trademarks of Nestlé.

"Noxzema" is a registered trademark of Procter & Gamble.

"Ocean Spray" is a registered trademark of Ocean Spray Cranberries Inc.

"Orajel" is a registered trademark of Del Laboratories Inc.

"Oral-B" is a registered trademark of Oral-B Laboratories.

"Orville Redenbacher's" and "Gourmet" are registered trademarks of Hunt-Wesson Inc.

"Pam" is a registered trademark of American Home Foods.

"Pampers" is a registered trademark of Procter & Gamble.

"Pepto-Bismol" is a registered trademark of Procter & Gamble.

"Phillip's" is a registered trademark of the Bayer Corp.

"Pine-Sol" is a registered trademark of the Clorox Co.

"Play-Doh" is a registered trademark of Hasbro Inc.

"Playtex," "Living," and "Made Strong to Last Long" are registered trademarks of Playtex Products Inc.

"Pledge" is a registered trademark of S. C. Johnson & Son Inc.

"Popsicle" is a registered trademark of Good Humor-Breyers Ice Cream.

"Post-it" is a registered trademark of 3M.

"Preparation H" is a registered trademark of Whitehall-Robbins.

"Pringles" and "Potato Crisps" are registered trademarks of Procter & Gamble.

"Purell" is a registered trademark of Gojo Industries Inc.

"Q-Tips" is a registered trademark of the Chesebrough-Pond's USA Co.

"Quaker Oats" is a registered trademark of the Quaker Oats Co.

"ReaLemon" is a registered trademark of Borden.

"Reddi-wip" is a registered trademark of ConAgra Brands Inc.

"Reynolds," "Reynolds Wrap," and "Cut-Rite" are registered trademarks of Reynolds Metals.

"Rit" is a registered trademark of BestFoods.

"S.O.S" is a registered trademark of the Clorox Co.

"Saran Wrap" and "Quick Covers" are registered trademarks of S. C. Johnson & Son Inc. in the United States and Canada.

"Scotch," "Scotch-Brite," and "Scotchgard" are registered trademarks of 3M.

"Scrubbing Bubbles" is a registered trademark of S. C. Johnson & Son Inc.

"Secret" is a registered trademark of Procter & Gamble.

"7-Up" is a registered trademark of Dr Pepper/Seven Up Inc.

"Simple Green" is a registered trademark of Sunshine Makers Inc.

"Skin-So-Soft" is a registered trademark of Avon Products.

"Slinky" is a registered trademark of James Industries.

"Smirnoff" is a registered trademark of United Vintners & Distributors.

"Smucker's" is a registered trademark of the J. M. Smucker Co.

"Spam" is a registered trademark of the Hormel Foods Corp.

"Spray 'n Wash" is a registered trademark of Reckitt Benckiser Inc.

"Star" is a registered trademark of Star Fine Foods.

"Stayfree" is a registered trademark of McNeil-PPC Inc.

"SueBee" is a registered trademark of Sioux Honey Association.

"Sun-Maid" is a registered trademark of Sun-Maid Growers of California.

"Tabasco" is a registered trademark of the McIlhenny Co.

"Tampax" is a registered trademark of Tambrands Inc.

"Tang" is a registered trademark of Kraft Foods.

"3M" is a registered trademark of 3M.

"Tide" is a registered trademark of Procter & Gamble.

"Tidy Cats" is a registered trademark of the Ralston Purina Co.

"Tupperware" is a registered trademark of Tupperware World-wide.

"Turtle Wax" is a registered trademark of Turtle Wax Inc.

"20 Mule Team" and "Borax" are registered trademarks of United States Borax & Chemical Corp.

"Uncle Ben's" and "Converted" are registered trademarks of Uncle Ben's Inc.

"*USA Today*" is a registered trademark of Gannett News Service.

"Vaseline" is a registered trademark of the Chesebrough-Pond's USA.

"Velcro" is a registered trademark of Velcro Industries.

"Vicks" and "VapoRub" are registered trademarks of Procter & Gamble.

"WD-40" is a registered trademark of the WD-40 Co.

"Wesson" is a registered trademark of Hunt-Wesson Inc.

"Wilson" is a registered trademark of the Wilson Sporting Goods Co.

"Windex" is a registered trademark of S. C. Johnson & Son Inc.

"Wonder" is a registered trademark of the Interstate Brands Corp.

"Wrigley's" and "Wrigley's Spearmint" are registered trademarks of the Wm. Wrigley Jr. Co.

"Ziploc" is a registered trademark of S. C. Johnson & Son Inc.

Index

Underscored page references indicate boxed text.

planters in winter, 210, 211
tomatoes, 266
as strawberry collar, 22
Budweiser beer
for controlling insects, 247,
279
as fertilizer, 11, 79, 168
for growing moss, 185
as insect repellent, 16
Bulbs, 33–35

C

Cabbage, 36–38
Campbell's Tomato Juice,
for cleaning skunk odors,
245
Campbell's Tomato Soup
for cleaning garlic from hands,
106
for controlling insects, 1, 64
Campbell's Tomato Soup cans
for protecting
corn, 26, 51, 254
pepper plants, 197
potatoes, 204
seedlings, 237
tomatoes, 264
as rain gauge, 284
Canada Dry Club Soda
for cleaning rust, 275
as fertilizer, 142, 210, 284
Carnation NonFat Dry Milk
for cleaning houseplants, 143
for controlling
aphids, 7
diseases, 70
for cooking corn, 51
for growing moss, 185
as paint, 193–94
for preventing
blight, 264
blossom-end rot, 174, 197,
264
for seed-starting, 109, 237
for storing seeds, 261
for treating poison ivy, 202

Cascade dishwashing powder
for cleaning
clothing, 44
patio furniture, 194
vases, 57
for controlling
diseases, 70–71, 210
fungus, 96
for treating poison ivy, 202
Castor oil
for controlling
moles, 120
rodents, 225
squirrels, 254
as fertilizer, 143, 210
for lubricating tools, 272
Cat litter. See Tidy Cats cat box filler
Cats, 39–41
Chalk. See Crayola Chalk
ChapStick
for cleaning shoes, 46
for lubricating tools, 272
for preventing rust, 275
Charmin Bath Tissue rolls
as bird feeders, 29
as seed-starting pots, 112
Cheerios, for feeding birds, 26
Cheez Whiz, for cleaning clothing,
44
Chili powder. See McCormick Chili
Powder
Cinnamon. See McCormick Ground
Cinnamon
Clairol Herbal Essences Shampoo,
for cleaning
clothing, 44
hands, 128
Clean Shower
for cleaning
patio furniture, 178, 194
rust, 275
for prolonging life of tools, 271
Clorox Bleach
for cleaning
garbage cans, 100
outdoor surfaces, 178

French's Mustard
    for controlling cats, 39, 84, 251
    for watering seedlings, 285
Frisbees
    as birdbaths, 27
    for germinating, 111
    for protecting seedlings, 239
    as slug and snail trap, 248
Fruits, washing, 94
Fruit trees, 90–94
Fungus, 95–99

G

Garbage cans, 100–102
Gardenias, 103–4
Garlic, 105–7, 106–7. *See also*
    McCormick Garlic Powder
Gatorade, as fertilizer, 80, 229, 285
Gatorade bottles
    for making
        flower vase, 56
        hot caps, 140
    for protecting plants from
        rabbits, 222
    for storing birdseed, 27
Gerber Baby Food, for controlling
    insects, 150
Gerber Baby Food jars
    as gnat traps, 118, 150
    for storing
        garlic, 105
        seeds, 261
Geritol
    for controlling diseases, 71
    as fertilizer, 80, 143, 211
Germinating, 109–115
Glad Flexible Straws
    for arranging flowers, 56
    for controlling
        cutworms, 64–65, 149–50, 239
        gophers and moles, 121
    for making plant labels, 161,
        162
    for propagating cuttings, 62
    for staking, 258
    for stemming strawberries, 22

Glad Trash Bags
    as boots, 42
    for cleaning barbecues, 14
    for controlling
        birds, 22, 27
        Colorado potato beetles, 204–5
        deer, 67, 266
        diseases, 71, 83
        fungus, 96
        moles, 120–21
        weeds, 175
    for germinating, 111
    as greenhouse for seedlings, 18,
        51–52
    for killing
        poison ivy, 200
        weeds, 290
    for making scarecrows, 234–35
    as mulch, 189, 266
    for protecting
        barbecues, 15
        eggplants, 76
        planters in winter, 211
    as raincoat, 44
    for storing potting soil, 211
Gloves, 116–17. *See also* Playtex
    Living Gloves
Gnats, 118–19
Gold Medal Flour
    for controlling
        cats, 39, 84, 251
        insects, 2, 36, 150
    for seeding, 239
    for storing seeds, 262
Goodyear Tires
    as compost bin, 48
    for planting and protecting
        eggplants, 76
        herbs, 134
        peppers, 197–98
        potatoes, 205
        strawberries, 22
        tomatoes, 266
    for storing hoses, 137
    for vermicomposting, 296
Gophers, 120–22

Grandma's Molasses
for controlling
diseases, 71, 90
fungus, 96
insects, 2, 150, 296–97
rabbits, 222
as fertilizer, 80
history of, 98
Grapes, 123–27
Green Giant Sweet Peas, for
treating
mosquito bites, 183
wasp stings, 280
Grits. See Albers Grits
Gunk Brake Cleaner, for cleaning
clothing, 45

H

Hair dryers. See Conair Pro Style
1600 Hair Dryer
Hair spray. See Aqua Net Hair
Spray
Hand cleaners, 106, 128–30
Hartz Parakeet Seed, for feeding
birds, 27, 29
Harvesting, 132–33
Hats, 43
Heinz Apple Cider Vinegar
for cleaning bird poop, 30
for controlling
coddling moths, 90, 150
diseases, 90
gnats, 118
Japanese beetles, 158
as fertilizer, 143, 211
as insect repellent, 16
Heinz Ketchup, for barbecuing, 15
Heinz White Vinegar
for cleaning
clothing, 45
fruits and vegetables, 94
garlic from hands, 106
patio furniture, 178, 194
planters, 211
rust, 276
vases, 57

for controlling
ants, 2
cats, 40, 252
diseases, 71–72, 205
Japanese beetles, 158
mealybugs, 143, 150
slugs and snails, 248
as fertilizer, 11–12, 22–23, 103
for killing
grass, 168
weeds, 290
for prolonging cut flowers, 56
for protecting
birdbaths, 27
flowers, 84
for testing soil, 252
for treating
mosquito bites, 183
poison ivy, 202
wasp stings, 281
Herbs, 134–36
Honey. See SueBee Honey
Hoses, 137–38
Hot caps, 139–41
Houseplants, 142–47
Huggies Baby Wipes, for cleaning
hands, 107, 129
shoes, 46
Huggies Baby Wipes containers
as drainage trays, 212, 239
as seed-starting pots, 111
for storing seeds, 262
Huggies Pull-Ups, for retaining
water in planters, 144, 212,
285
Hula Hoops
for controlling diseases, 36–37,
72, 76–77, 150–51, 205
history of, 78
for protecting
melons, 175
tomatoes, 266
for ripening strawberries, 23
for shading lettuce, 171
Hydrogen Peroxide
for cleaning skunk odors, 245

for controlling
   diseases, 72, 111, 266
   fungus, 61, 96
   for prolonging cut flowers,
      56

I

Insects, 148–57. *See also specific
   insects*
Irish Spring Soap, for controlling
   deer, 52, 68
Ivory Dishwashing Liquid
   for cleaning hands, 130
   for controlling
      aphids, 8, 9, 153
      cats and dogs, 40
      Colorado potato beetles,
         205
      cucumber beetles, 151
      diseases, 72, 74, 177, 228
      flea beetles, 153
      fungus, 98
      grasshoppers, 153
      Japanese beetles, 158–59
      mealybugs, 155
      moles, 120
      mosquitoes, 180
      moths, 151
      rabbits, 172, 223
      rodents, 92, 226–27
      skunks, 244
      spider mites, 19, 153
      squirrels and raccoons, 256
      stink bugs, 19
      wasps, 282
      whiteflies, 293, 294
   for fertilizing lawns, 79, 168
   for identifying cutworms, 65,
      168
   for protecting
      bulbs, 34
      cabbage, 37
      flowers, 85
      houseplants, 144, 151
Ivory Soap, for treating mosquito
   bites, 183

J

Japanese beetles, 158–60
Jell-O gelatin
   for controlling
      diseases, 72
      fungus, 96
   as fertilizer, 80, 267
   for germinating, 111
   for retaining water in planters,
      144, 212, 285
   for sowing seeds, 240
Jet-Dry
   for cleaning garlic from hands,
      107
   history of, 108
Jif Peanut Butter
   for baiting traps, 255
   for cleaning
      garlic from hands, 107
      sap, 216, 232
   for controlling deer, 68
   for feeding birds, 27
   for lubricating lawn mower,
      164
Johnson & Johnson Cotton Balls
   for controlling
      ants, 4
      deer, 68
      squirrels and raccoons, 255
   for prolonging cut flowers, 56
   for prolonging plastic gloves,
      116
Johnson's Baby Oil
   for cleaning
      hands, 129
      sap, 216, 232
   for controlling Japanese beetles,
      158
   as insect repellent, 118
   for protecting corn, 52, 151
Johnson's Baby Powder
   for controlling ants, 2
   for putting on gloves, 116
   for sowing seeds, 240
Johnson's Baby Powder container,
   as watering can, 285

325

K

Kaopectate, for controlling grasshoppers, 151

Karo Corn Syrup
for cleaning clothing, 45
for growing moss, 185

Kellogg's Frosted Mini-Wheats, as fertilizer, 80, 252

Kellogg's Raisin Bran, for feeding birds, 27

Kingsford Charcoal Briquets
for controlling slugs and snails, 248
for neutralizing soil, 252
for preventing rust, 276
for prolonging cut flowers, 56

Kingsford's Corn Starch
for cleaning clothing, 45
for putting on gloves, 116
for storing seeds, 262
for treating poison ivy, 203

Kiwi Shoe Polish, for staining patio furniture, 194

Kleenex Tissues boxes, for storing seeds, 262

Knee pads, 43–44

Kodak 35mm Film, for planning flower gardens, 84

Kodak 35mm Film canisters
for germinating, 111
for storing seeds, 262

Kool-Aid
for cleaning rust, 276
history of, 278

Krazy Glue
for mending hoses, 137
for storing seeds, 261

L

Labels, 161–63

Lawn mowers, 164–66

Lawns, 167–70

L'eggs Sheer Energy Panty Hose
for cleaning
patio furniture, 195
shoes, 46

for controlling
birds, 23, 27–28
deer, 52, 68
insects, 2–3, 150
squirrels and raccoons, 255
for filtering rainwater, 286
as insect repellent, 118–19
for making
compost tea, 80
filter for lawn mower, 164–65
fruit-picking basket, 90–91, 132, 274
knee pads, 23, 43
scarecrows, 234
as outdoor soap holder, 129
for padding plant stakes, 259
for protecting
broccoli, 151–52, 226, 255
cabbage, 36, 37, 151–52, 226, 255
eggplants, 77, 151–52, 226, 255
fruit, 91, 124–25, 151–52, 226, 255, 282
pepper plants, 198
pumpkins, 220
tomatoes, 151–52, 226, 255, 267
vegetables, 37, 198, 220, 226, 255
for retaining soil in planters, 144, 212
for securing bags in garbage cans, 100
for staking, 258
for storing
bulbs, 33
garlic, 105
onions, 191
seeds, 262
for straining fertilizers, 80
for treating poison ivy, 203
for tying
bean vines, 19
corn plants, 52
flowers, 12, 84, 103
grapevines, 123–24
houseplants, 144

potted plants, 212
rosebushes, 229
tomato plants, 267
Lemon Joy, for controlling
mosquitoes, 180
Lemon juice. *See* ReaLemon
Lestoil, for cleaning clothing, <u>45</u>
Lettuce, 171–73
Lewis Labs Brewer's Yeast Flakes,
for fertilizing roses, 229
Lip balm. *See* ChapStick
Lipton Tea Bags
for composting, 49
for fertilizing
beds and planters, 81, 84, 189
flowering plants, 12, 103–4
houseplants, 144, 145, 286
potted plants, 212
roses, 229
for germinating, 111–12, 168,
240
for repairing brown spots on
lawns, 168
for retaining water in planters,
212
for treating
mosquito bites, <u>183</u>
wasp stings, <u>281</u>
Liquid Paper, for marking trowels,
33–34, 240, 274
Listerine
for cleaning
skunk odors, <u>245</u>
tools, 272
for controlling
diseases, 12, 73, 216
fungus, 97
insects, 91, 149, 152, 293
as fertilizer, 79
as insect repellent, 180
for prolonging cut flowers, 57
for protecting bulbs, 34
for treating
mosquito bites, <u>183</u>
poison ivy, <u>203</u>
wasp stings, <u>281</u>

Lubriderm
for cleaning shoes, <u>46</u>
for putting on gloves, 117
Lysol, for controlling diseases, 73,
216

M

Massengill Disposable Douche, for
cleaning skunk odors, <u>245</u>
MasterCard, for treating wasp
stings, <u>281</u>
Maxwell House Coffee
for barbecuing, 15
for cleaning garlic from hands,
<u>107</u>
for composting, 49
for controlling
cats, 40
insects, 3, 294–95, 297
moles, 121
for fertilizing
flowering plants, 12, 84, 104
houseplants, 81, 145
lawns, 168
potted plants, 212–13
roses, 230
for germinating, 134
for neutralizing soil, 252
for protecting trees from lawn
mower, 165
for ripening melons, 175
for sowing seeds, 240
Maxwell House Coffee cans
for controlling whiteflies, 268,
294–95
for making fruit picker, 91,
132–33, 274
for protecting tomato plants,
267
as seed or fertilizer spreader,
168, 274
for storing seeds, 262
for watering, 286
Maybelline Crystal Clear Nail
Polish, for securing screws
in lawn mower, 165

Oral-B Toothbrush *(cont.)*
  as dibble, 241, 275
  for making plant labels, 162
  for staking, 259
Orville Redenbacher's Gourmet
    Popping Corn, for feeding
    birds, 28

P

Pam Original Cooking Spray
  for cleaning
    barbecues, 14
    hands, 130
    patio furniture, 195
    sap, 233
    tomato sauce stains, 270
  for controlling
    birds, 28
    mosquitoes, 181
  for lubricating tools, 217, 273
  for preventing
    grass buildup on lawn mowers,
      165
    rust, 276
  for protecting bird feeders, 255
Pampers diapers
  for arranging flowers, 58
  for germinating, 112
  for retaining water in planters,
    145, 213, 267, 286
Paper towels. *See* Bounty Paper
    Towels
Patio furniture, 193–96
Peanut butter. *See* Jif Peanut Butter
Peas, frozen. *See* Green Giant
    Sweet Peas
Peppermint oil. *See* McCormick
    Peppermint Oil
Peppers, 197–99
Pepto-Bismol, for treating wasp
    stings, 281
Phillip's Milk of Magnesia, for
    treating mosquito bites, 184
Pine-Sol
  for cleaning clothing, 45
  for controlling diseases, 73

Plastic wrap. *See* Saran Wrap
Play-Doh
  for cleaning hands, 130
  history of, 131
Playtex Living Gloves. *See also*
    Gloves
  for baiting traps, 121
  for cleaning skunk odors, 245
  fingertip-less, 117
  for handling
    chile peppers, 198
    poison ivy, 200–201
  for handpicking insects, 151, 153,
    159
Pledge furniture polish
  history of, 196
  for preserving patio furniture,
    195
Poison ivy, 200–203, 202–3
Popsicles, for treating mosquito
    bites, 184
Popsicle sticks
  for germinating, 113
  as plant labels, 162
  for staking, 259
  for treating wasp stings, 281
Post-it Notes, as plant labels, 162
Potatoes, 204–8
Potpourri, 86–87
Potted plants, 209–14
Preparation H, for treating
  mosquito bites, 184
  poison ivy, 203
  wasp stings, 281
Pringles cans, for storing seeds,
    262
Pruning, 215–19
Pumpkins, 220–21
Purell
  for cleaning
    tomato sauce stains, 270
    tools, 272
  for controlling
    diseases, 73, 217
    fungus, 97
  history of, 218

Q

Q-Tips Cotton Swabs
    for controlling
        aphids and mealybugs, 150,
            153, 206
        cabbageworms, 153
        whiteflies, 153, 294
    for hand-pollinating, 91
    for protecting
        cabbage, 37
        houseplants, 143, 146
    for staking, 259
    for treating mosquito bites, 182
Quaker Oats
    for baiting traps, 255–56
    for feeding birds, 28
    for treating poison ivy, 203

R

Rabbits, 222–24
Raccoons, 254–57
ReaLemon
    for cleaning
        hands, 24, 107, 130
        rust, 276
        skunk odors, 245
        tomato sauce stains, 270
    for controlling insects, 8, 249, 280
    for treating poison ivy, 203
Reddi-wip
    for fertilizing pumpkins, 220
    for growing moss, 186
Reynolds Cut-Rite Wax Paper
    for controlling cutworms, 65, 241
    for drying flowers, 86–87
    for storing seeds, 262
Reynolds Wrap
    for cleaning
        barbecues, 14
        bird poop, 30
        tools, 272
    for controlling
        birds, 28
        deer, 68
        diseases, 73, 241
        fungus, 97

gophers and moles, 121
        insects, 8, 65, 153
        rabbits, 223
        rodents, 226
    for forcing bulbs, 34
    for germinating, 112
    for growing sod, 169
    for hastening rose bloom, 230
    for increasing light for
        houseplants, 145
    for keeping planters moist, 145
    for making
        radiant heat, 268
        scarecrows, 235
    as mulch, 189
    for planting seedlings, 198
    for prolonging life of onions, 191
    for propagating cuttings, 61
    for protecting
        beans, 19
        berries, 23, 24
        corn, 52–53
        eggplants, 77
        fruit trees, 91–92
        peppers, 198
        seedlings, 241
        tomatoes, 268
    for retaining water in planters,
        213
Rice. See Minute Rice; Uncle Ben's
        Converted Brand Rice
Rit Dye, for staining patio furniture,
        195
Rodents, 225–27
Roses, 228–31

S

Sap, 232–33
Saran Quick Covers, for preventing
        drips from hanging plants,
        146, 213, 286–87
Saran Wrap
    for germinating, 109, 113, 134, 241
    for propagating cuttings, 61–62
    for revitalizing houseplants, 146
    for storing cabbage, 37

Smucker's Grape Jelly, for controlling
  slugs and snails, 249
Soft drinks. *See* Canada Dry Club
  Soda; Coca-Cola; 7-Up
Soil, 251–53
S.O.S Steel Wool Soap Pads
  for cleaning shoes, <u>46</u>
  as fertilizer, 13, 85
Spam, for cleaning
  patio furniture, 195
  shoes, <u>46</u>
Spray 'n Wash, for cleaning shoes, <u>46</u>
Squirrels, 254–57
Staking, 258–60
Star Olive Oil
  for cleaning
    hands, 130
    houseplants, 146
  for controlling
    diseases, 74
    fungus, 97
    insects, 8, 181
  for fertilizing ferns or palms, 81,
    146, 213
  for lubricating tools, 273
  for preserving herbs, 135
Stayfree Maxi Pads
  as knee pads, 44
  for protecting hatbands, 43
Straws. *See* Glad Flexible Straws
SueBee Honey
  for controlling flies and gnats,
    119, 153
  for feeding birds, 29
Sugar. *See* Domino Sugar
Sun-Maid Raisins, for feeding birds,
  29
Syrup. *See* Aunt Jemima Original
  Syrup; Karo Corn Syrup

T
Tabasco Pepper Sauce
  for composting, 49
  for controlling
    cats and dogs, 40, 252
    diseases, 74

    fungus, 98
    insects, 8, 153, 154, 159, 294
    rabbits, 172, 223
    rodents, 92, 226–27
    skunks, 244
    squirrels and raccoons, 256
  for protecting
    beans, 19
    bulbs, 34
    flowers, 85
    grapes, 126
    roses, 230
Tabasco Pepper Sauce bottle, for
  sowing seeds, 242
Tampax Tampons, for cleaning
  shoes, <u>46</u>
Tang, for controlling aphids, 9
Tea. *See* Lipton Tea Bags; Nestea
3M Sandpaper, for controlling slugs
  and snails, 249
Tide laundry detergent
  for cleaning patio furniture, 178,
    195
  as fertilizer, 81
Tide laundry detergent bottle, for
  making
    scoop, 275
    tool carrier, 277
Tidy Cats cat box filler
  for barbecuing, 16
  for controlling
    gophers and moles, 121, 227
    squirrels and raccoons, 256
  for deodorizing garbage cans, 101
Tomatoes, 264–70
Tomato sauce stains, <u>270</u>
Tools, 271–77
Toothpicks. *See* Forster Toothpicks
Tupperware
  for drying flowers, <u>87</u>
  history of, <u>89</u>
  for storing bareroot perennials,
    85
Turtle Wax
  for cleaning shoes, <u>46</u>
  for polishing patio furniture, 195

About the Author

JOEY GREEN—author of *Polish Your Furniture with Panty Hose, Paint Your House with Powdered Milk, Wash Your Hair with Whipped Cream*, and *Clean Your Clothes with Cheez Wiz*—got Jay Leno to shave with Jif peanut butter on *The Tonight Show*, Rosie

O'Donnell to mousse her hair with Jell-O on *The Rosie O'Donnell Show*, and Katie Couric to drop her diamond engagement ring in a glass of Efferdent on *Today*. He gave Meredith Vieira a facial with Elmer's Glue-All on *The View*, conditioned Conan O'Brien's hair with Miller High Life beer on *Late Night with Conan O'Brien*, and rubbed French's Mustard on Wayne Brady's chest on *The Wayne Brady Show*. He has been seen polishing furniture with Spam on *Dateline NBC*, cleaning a toilet with Coca-Cola in *The New York Times*, and washing his hair with Reddi-wip in *People*.

Green, a former contributing editor to *National Lampoon* and a former advertising copywriter at J. Walter Thompson, is the author of more than twenty-five books, including *The Zen of Oz: Ten Spiritual Lessons from Over the Rainbow, You Know You've Reached Middle Age If . . .*, and *The Mad Scientist Handbook*. A native of Miami, Florida, and a graduate of Cornell University, he wrote television commercials for Burger King and Walt Disney World and won a Clio Award for a print ad he created for Eastman Kodak. He backpacked around the world for two years on his honeymoon and lives in Los Angeles with his wife, Debbie, and their two daughters, Ashley and Julia.